COLORADO'S
BEST

COLORADO'S
BEST

THE ESSENTIAL GUIDE TO FAVORITE PLACES

BRUCE CAUGHEY AND
DOUG WHITEHEAD

FULCRUM PUBLISHING
Golden, Colorado

Library of Congress Cataloging-in-Publication Data

Caughey, Bruce, 1960–
    Colorado's best : the essential guide to favorite places / Bruce
        Caughey and Doug Whitehead.
        p. cm.
    Includes index.
    ISBN 1-55591-435-7 (pbk.)
    1. Colorado—Guidebooks. I. Whitehead, Doug. II. Title
    F774.3 .C39 2000
    917.8804'33—dc21   00-021366

Printed in Canada
0 9 8 7 6 5 4 3 2 1

Editorial: Daniel Forrest-Bank, Michelle Asakawa
Design and composition: Rudy Ramos
Cover art: Mathew McFarren
Back cover photo: Mountain bikers enjoy cross-country thrills at
Winter Park Resort. Photo by Rod Walker for Winter Park Resort.
Map: Marge Mueller, Gray Mouse Graphics
Author photos (p. 219): Eyes on Photography

Fulcrum Publishing
16100 Table Mountain Parkway, Suite 300
Golden, Colorado 80403
(800) 992-2908 • (303) 277-1623
www.fulcrum-books.com

To our daughters
Julia and Shannon Caughey
and Mara and Emma Whitehead
for the joy and laughter they share each day

———————

Contents

Acknowledgments xv
Introduction xvii
Colorado State map xx

THE FRONT RANGE 1

Cultural & Historical

Best College Campus—University of Colorado at Boulder 4
Best Collection of Tourist Traps—Colorado Springs 5
Best Photography Gallery—Camera Obscura (Denver) 6
Best Place to Watch Money Being Made—U.S. Mint (Denver) 7
Best Local Art Gallery—The Foothills Art Center (Golden) 8
Best Weather Watching—National Center for Atmospheric
    Research (Boulder) 9
Best Dino Evidence—Dinosaur Ridge (west of Denver) 10
Best Place to Be a Kid—Tiny Town (west of Denver) 10
Best Bookstore—Tattered Cover (Denver) 11
Best Medieval Fantasy—Renaissance Festival (Larkspur) 11
Best Cultural Festival—Greek Festival (Denver) 13
Best Culture in Suburbia—Arvada Center for the Performing Arts 13
Best College Sports Scene—University of Denver Hockey 14
Best Place to See Junk Transformed—Swetsville Zoo
    (near Fort Collins) 14
Best Hardware Store—McGuckins (Boulder) 15
Best Place to See the Ocean in Colorado—Ocean Journey (Denver) 15
Best Place to Be Dazzled by Butterflies—Butterfly Pavilion and
    Insect Center (Westminster) 17

Outdoor Activities & Events

Best Outdoor Music Venue—Red Rocks Amphitheater (near Denver) . . .18
Best Walking Mall—Pearl Street Mall (Boulder) 18
Best People Watching—Washington Park (Denver) 19
Best Amusement Park—Six Flags/Elitch Gardens (Denver) 20
Best Biking and In-Line Skating—Denver Greenway Trails 21
Best "Primitive" State Park—Roxborough 22
Best Park for a Picnic—Chautauqua Park (Boulder) 23
Best Urban Oasis—Jefferson County Open Space 24
Best Backyard Camping—Golden Gate Canyon State Park 24

Best Moderate Mountain Biking—Horsetooth Mountain Park
and Lory State Park (Fort Collins) 25
Best Soaking After a Hike—Eldorado Artesian Springs (near Boulder) . . .26
Best Trailhead—Colorado Trail/Waterton Canyon (Denver) 27
Best Fun Times at a Reservoir—Lake Pueblo State Park 27
Best Rock Climbing Close to the City—Eldorado Canyon
(near Boulder). 28
Best Foot Race—Bolder Boulder 29
Best Statewide Event—Colorado State Fair (Pueblo) 30
Best Offbeat Outdoor Festival—Kinetic Conveyance Challenge
(Boulder). 30
Best Scenery at a Golf Course—Arrowhead Golf Club (near Denver) 31
Best Scottish-Style Links—Riverdale Dunes (Brighton) 32
Best Disk Golf Course—Edora Park (Fort Collins) 32
Best Zoo—Cheyenne Mountain Zoo (Colorado Springs) 33
Best Polar Bear Habitat—Denver Zoo 34

Where to Eat, Drink & Stay
Best Brew Town—Fort Collins 35
Best Colorado Chiles—Pueblo Chiles 36
Best Free Tour—Celestial Seasonings Tour of Tea (Boulder) 36
Best Chicago Cuisine in Colorado—Mustard's Last Stand
(Denver and Boulder) 37
Best Beans with Breakfast—Lucile's (Boulder) 38
Best Nightlife District—LoDo (Denver) 38
Best Exotic Teahouse—Boulder Dushanbe Tea House 40
Best Pool Hall—Wynkoop Brewing Company (Denver) 41
Best Fried Chicken—Castle Café (Castle Rock) 42
Best Mexican Food—La Cueva (Denver) 42
Best Bed-and-Breakfast—Abriendo Inn (Pueblo) 43
Best Refurbished Inn—Cliff House (Manitou Springs) 44
Best Historic Hotel—Brown Palace (Denver) .44
Best Exclusive Night's Stay—The Broadmoor (Colorado Springs) 45

NORTHWEST 47
Cultural & Historical
Best Local Arts Scene—Aspen Music Festival and School 50
Best Place to Experience Colorado as It Once Was—North Park 51
Best Canyon Passageway—Glenwood Canyon Trail 52
Best Ghost Town—Ashcroft 53

Outdoor Activities & Events
Best Fly-Fishing—Fryingpan River 54
Best Mountain Golf Course—Steamboat Sheraton
(Steamboat Springs) 55

Best Land o' Lakes—Grand Mesa 55
Best In-Town Rafting—Yampa River (Steamboat Springs) 56
Best Place to See Moose—Colorado State Forest 57
Best Historic Mountain Bike (Jeep) Route—Marble, Crystal and
  Lead King Basin 59
Best Rock Arches—Rattlesnake Canyon (west of Grand Junction) 60
Best Hot Springs—Strawberry Park Hot Springs (Steamboat Springs) . . .60
Best Dog-Lovers' Spectacle—Meeker Classic Sheepdog
  Championship Trials 61
Best Multiday Raft Trip—Dinosaur National Monument 62
Best Dogsledding—Krablooniks (Snowmass) 63
Best Hut System—10th Mountain Division Hut System 64
Best Ski Town—Aspen 65
Best Bowl Skiing and Boarding—Vail 66
Best Family Ski Area—Sunlight Mountain Resort
  (near Glenwood Springs) 67
Best Tree Skiing—Steamboat Springs 67

Where to Eat, Drink & Stay
Best Wholesome Breakfast and Lunch—Daily Bread Café
  (Glenwood Springs) 68
Best Brunch—Redstone Inn 68
Best Unusual Dining Experience—Pine Creek Cookhouse (Ashcroft) . . .69
Best Elbows-Rubbing with Rich and Famous—Aspen 70
Best Wine Tasting—Palisade 71
Best Cinnamon Roll—Winona's (Steamboat Springs) 72
Best Historic Hotel—Hotel Jerome (Aspen) 72
Best Rustic Lodge—Trappers Lake Lodge (east of Meeker) 73
Best Chain Hotel—Hyatt Regency (Beaver Creek) 74
Best Dude Ranch—Latigo Ranch (North Park) .75

NORTH-CENTRAL 77
Cultural & Historical
Best Operatic Experience—Central City Opera .80
Best Place to Celebrate a Dead Hero—Buffalo Bill Museum and
  Grave (near Golden) 81
Best Way into the Mountains Without Driving—The Ski Train
  from Denver to Winter Park 81
Best Short Railroad Trip—Georgetown Loop Railroad 82

Outdoor Activities & Events
Best Sailing—Lake Dillon (Dillon) 83
Best Public Golf Course—Pole Creek (near Fraser) 84
Best Destination to Bag Four Fourteeners—Mounts Democrat,
  Cameron, Lincoln and Bross 85

Best Mountain Biking System—Winter Park and Fraser 86
Best Place to Make Your Relatives Gasp—Mount Evans Road 87
Best Wildlife Viewing—Rocky Mountain National Park 88
Best Place to Pretend It's the Sixties—Rocky Grass Festival (Lyons) 89
Best Wild River—Poudre River 90
Best Program for Disabled—National Sports Center for the Disabled
    (Winter Park) 91
Best Sledding—Winter Park and Fraser 92
Best Outdoor Ice-Skating—Evergreen Lake .93
Best Bump Skiing—Mary Jane (Winter Park) .93
Best Expert Runs at a Small Ski Area—Berthoud Pass 94
Best Late-Season Snow—Arapahoe Basin 95
Best Collection of Ski Areas—Summit County 95

Where to Eat, Drink & Stay
Best Hot Dog Stand—Coney Island (Aspen Park) 97
Best Intimate Dining—Alpine Café (Breckenridge) 97
Best Home-Cooked Meals—The Happy Cooker (Georgetown) 98
Best View from a Porch Swing—Grand Lake Lodge 99
Best Transformation of a Hot Springs—Hot Sulphur Springs Resort . . .100
Best Romantic Bed-and-Breakfast—RiverSong (Estes Park) 101
Best View from a Lodge—Lodge at Breckenridge 102
Best Plush Dude Ranch—C-Lazy-U (near Granby) 103

EASTERN PLAINS 105
Cultural & Historical
Best Equinox Phenomenon—Picture Canyon (near Springfield) 108
Best View of Life on the Santa Fe Trail—Bent's Old Fort National
    Historic Site (near La Junta) 109
Best Little-Known Historic Site—Boggsville (Las Animas) 110
Best Indian Museum—Koshare Indian Museum (La Junta) 110
Best Reminder of Labor Struggles—Ludlow Memorial Monument
    (north of Trinidad) 111
Best Plains History—Centennial Village (Greeley) 112
Best Evidence of Dinosaurs—Picket Wire Canyonlands
    (south of La Junta) 113
Best Roadside Stop for Kids—Kit Carson County Carousel
    (Burlington) 114
Darkest Moment in Colorado History—Sand Creek Massacre
    Memorial 114
Best Victorian Opulence—Bloom Mansion (Trinidad) 115
Best Railroad Museum—Limon Heritage Museum and Railroad Park . . .116
Best Oddball Attraction—Genoa Tower and Museum 117
Best Outdoor Art—City of Loveland 118

Outdoor Activities & Events
Best Prairie—Pawnee National Grassland (northeast of Greeley) 119
Best Prairie Links—Hugo Golf Club 119
Best State Park and Putt—Lathrop State Park (Walsenburg) 120
Best Way to Get "In the Mood"—Glenn Miller Festival
(Fort Morgan) 121

Where to Eat, Drink & Stay
Best Dinner and a Show—Brush Livestock Exchange/
Drover's Restaurant 122
Best Chicken-Fried Steak—Fireside Junction Restaurant (Limon) 123
Best Colorado Melons—Rocky Ford Cantaloupe 124
Best Restaurant for Unusual Local Cuisine—Bruce's (Severance) 125
Best Memorable Night's Stay—Elk Echo Ranch Bed-and-Breakfast 125
Best Rest in the Old West—Chicosa Canyon Bed-and-Breakfast
(north of Trinidad) 126
Best Bed-and-Breakfast—Sod Buster Inn Bed-and-Breakfast
(Greeley) 127

SOUTH-CENTRAL 129
Cultural & Historical
Best Religious Shrine—Stations of the Cross (San Luis) 132
Best Spiritual Convergence—Crestone 133
Best Ongoing Construction Project—Bishop Castle
(north of San Isabel) 134
Best Scenic Byway—Highway of Legends
(southwest of Walsenburg) 136
Best Collection of Scenic Drives—Cañon City Area 136
Best Old West Town—South Park City (Fairplay) 138
Best Historic Mining District—Route of the Silver Kings (Leadville) . . .139
Best Steam Engine Train Ride—Cumbres & Toltec Scenic Railroad
(Antonito to Chama, New Mexico) 139
Best Reestablished Train Route—Royal Gorge Route (Cañon City) 140
Best Weavings—Eppie Archuleta's Studio (Capulin) 141
Best Monument to a Sports Hero—Jack Dempsey Museum
(Manassa) 142
Best Historical Crossroads—Fort Garland 143

Outdoor Activities & Events
Best Rafting—Arkansas River 143
Best Single-Track Biking—Monarch Crest Trail 145
Best Rock Climbing—Shelf Road Recreation Area (near Cañon City) . .145
Best Animal Sanctuary—Mission:Wolf (near Gardner) 146
Best Bird-Watching—Monte Vista National Wildlife Refuge 147

Best Fossilized Bugs—Florissant Fossil Beds 147
Best Wheelchair Wilderness Experience—Wilderness on Wheels
   (Pike National Forest) 148
Best Desert in the Mountains—Great Sand Dunes National
   Monument (near Alamosa) 149
Best Out-of-Place Animals—Colorado Alligator Farm
   (north of Alamosa) 151
Best Hot Springs—Mount Princeton Hot Springs (Nathrop) 151
Best Music Festival—Jazz in the Sangres (Westcliffe) 152
Best Snowcat Skiing—Monarch Ski and Snowboard Area 153
Best Nordic Skiing—Fairplay Nordic Center .153

Where to Eat, Drink & Stay
Best Southwestern Fare—Emma's Hacienda (San Luis) 154
Best Steakhouse—True Grits (Alamosa) 155
Best Dining in the Boondocks—Antero Grill (north of Salida) 155
Best Cheap Burgers and Malts—The Owl Cigar Store (Cañon City) . . .156
Best Cheap Eats—Cripple Creek Casinos 157
Best Drive-In Without a Car—Movie Manor (Monte Vista) 158
Best Small-Town Bed-and-Breakfast—El Convento (San Luis) 159
Best Historic Hotel—Imperial Hotel (Cripple Creek) 159

SOUTHWEST 161

Cultural & Historical
Best Walk Among the Ancients—Ute Mountain Tribal Park
   (Towaoc) 164
Best Anasazi Tour—Trail of the Ancients (Durango–Cortez vicinity) . .165
Best Mountain Drive—San Juan Skyway (Ouray, Durango, Telluride) . .167
Best Ride on the Rails—Durango & Silverton Narrow Gauge Railroad . .168
Best Boat Ride—Black Canyon Boat Tours (west of Gunnison) 169
Best Mine Tour—Old Hundred Mine (near Silverton) 170
Best Ghost Town—Animas Forks (north of Silverton) 170
Best Stagecoach Ride—Mancos Valley Stage Line 172
Best Indian Museum—Ute Indian Museum (Montrose) 173
Best Navajo Weavings—Toh–Atin Gallery (Durango) 174

Outdoor Activities & Events
Best White-Water Adventure—Upper Animas River (Silverton) 175
Best Single-Track Mountain Biking—Gunnison National Forest 175
Best Four-Wheel-Drive Adventure—Alpine Loop Scenic Byway
   (Lake City, Ouray, Silverton) 176
Best White-Knuckle Drive—Black Bear Pass (Telluride) 178
Best Natural Wonder—Wheeler Geologic Area
   (near Creede) 178
Best Canyon—Black Canyon of the Gunnison National Park 179

Best Float Fishing—Gunnison Gorge 180
Best Scenic Reservoir—Taylor Park Reservoir
   (northeast of Gunnison) 181
Best Accessible State Park—Ridgway State Park (south of Montrose) . .181
Best Time to See Wildflowers—Crested Butte Wildflower Festival 183
Best Scenic Links—The Cliffs Golf Course at Sheraton Tamarron
   Resort (Durango) 183
Best Collection of Festivals—Telluride 184
Best Agricultural Festival—Olathe Sweet Corn Festival 185
Best Out-of-the-Way Culture—Creede Repertory Theater 186
Best Celebration of Ute Culture—Council Tree Pow Wow and
   Cultural Festival (Delta) 187
Best Fall-Colors Drive—Kebler Pass (Crested Butte) 187
Best Hot Springs—Pagosa Hot Springs 188
Best Ice Climbing—Ouray Ice Park 189
Best Powder Skiing—Wolf Creek Ski Area 190
Best Steep and Deep Skiing—Telluride 191

Where to Eat, Drink & Stay
Best Small-Town Dining—Crested Butte 191
Best Country Dining—Glenn Eyrie Restaurant (Montrose) 193
Best Pizza—Farquart's (Durango) 193
Best Steakhouse—Ole Miner's Steakhouse (east of Pagosa Springs) 194
Best Historic Hotel—Strater Hotel (Durango) .194
Best Bed-and-Breakfast—Blue Lake Ranch (near Hesperus) 196
Best Small-Town Lodgings—Ouray County 197

Alphabetical Listing of Places & Activities 199
Index 207
About the Authors 219

Acknowledgments

Locals in small towns and big cities across the state remain the true "experts" who helped write this book with their easygoing sharing of insights and directions to their favorite places.

The Colorado Historical Society has been an invaluable resource over the years, especially Stan Oliner, Peg Ekstrand and Eric Paddock. Thanks to Dianne Howie, Marlene Blessing and Marykay Cicio of Fulcrum Publishing for their unbridled enthusiasm for this project from the beginning. The expert editorial support of Daniel Forrest-Bank and Michelle Asakawa helped the book greatly. Thanks to the dedicated professionals, too numerous to mention by name, of the National Park Service, U.S. Forest Service, Bureau of Land Management, Colorado State Parks and various museums, open space districts and other custodians of Colorado's heritage for happily sharing their knowledge. We would also like to recognize the many ski area and chamber of commerce folks who contributed their valuable assistance and advice.

Thanks for research assistance and good suggestions from Mark Stevens and Roy Burley. Loads of appreciation to Linda and Les Limon, Claudia Carboni and Susan Spackman for excellent ideas on covering their hometowns. A very important thank-you goes to Dean Winstanley, who supported this project with his understanding and good humor.

ESPECIALLY FROM BRUCE:
Special thanks to Ken and Judith Caughey, who instilled a curiosity in Colorado from early on and opened countless doors with their steady guiding hands. In a year of major changes, they served as anchors of patience, understanding and love. And, Mom, thanks for scouring for meaningful historical quotes! Thanks also to

Rick O'Connell and my friends and colleagues in Douglas County for accommo-
dating and encouraging my dual careers and time with my two daughters.

ESPECIALLY FROM DOUG:

Much of my contribututution to this book comes from my years producing, shooting,
writing and editing for News 4's *Colorado Getaways*. Thanks to all the talented
reporters, photographers and editors who helped to expand my knowledge of the
state, especially retired reporter Leo McGuire for setting a high standard of travel
writing for me to follow.

Special thanks to my wife, Barb, for being a wonderful travel and life
companion. Because of her enthusiastic help in carving out time for me to write
in the midst of our busy lives with two young daughters, this project became a
far more pleasant undertaking than I might have imagined. Finally, thanks to my
father, Orrick, for bringing me out to Colorado in 1971, driving me over Monarch
Pass and dropping me off in Gunnison into an unknown and exciting Colorado
future. God rest his soul.

Introduction

*My days and nights, as I travel here—what an exhilaration—not the air alone, and the
sense of vastness, but every local sight and feature. Everywhere something characteristic . . .*
                                                    —Walt Whitman, from *Aerial Effects*

This book of "bests" doesn't promise to be everything to everyone. However, we
did put together a book where absolutely anyone can find something valuable and
interesting to do in Colorado. So, although we may not cover your hobby adequately,
you'll be able to enjoy some incredible Colorado places that we highlight within
these pages. Our mission has been to surprise and delight you with our choices.
To do so we headed out on the road during the past year to gain firsthand insights
and perspectives. From our first massive brainstormed list we have winnowed,
deleted, added and changed our favorites, sometimes debating their merits long
into the night.

   To be sure, the following chapters are full of bias and opinions, and our
research method could hardly be considered scientifically valid. With some apolo-
gies, we have left out certain niches of activity and included others based solely on
our interests. But even if you can't find the
state's best snowmobile trails or duck-hunting
blinds, you will learn that this book comes
from our hearts, and our passion and love for
this state should be easy to detect. It comes
from a true desire to share hidden gems and
out-of-the-way places without skipping over
some of the obvious, still compelling choices.
So whether you are heading up the I-70 corridor for some great skiing or pulling off the
road for the best burrito in the San Luis
Valley, we've got something for you. We did
intentionally leave out a few hidden gems
(for example, Bruce's favorite fishing hole),
but mostly, we give you the complete scoop.

The abundance of wildlife is what makes
Colorado special, like these Mountain
Goats in the Mt. Evans Range. *Photo by
Bruce Caughey.*

Here we are: two guys who have spent the past decade exploring, researching, writing, photographing and sharing our firsthand knowledge of the state in books and on television. We decided to put our heads together and choose our favorites. Although our guide is not comprehensive, it does highlight places and activities that we're sure you will just love. We hope you'll enjoy this book and have some great experiences traveling the back roads and blue highways of our wonderful state.

PRACTICAL CONSIDERATIONS

Colorado's Best covers a range of year-round activities and has been organized with the reader in mind. With the state broken into logical regions—The Front Range, Northwest, North-Central, Eastern Plains, South-Central, Southwest—you'll be able to get a sense of where to look on the map to plan your itinerary. So flip through the book, check out the write-ups and find where your interests lie.

In addition to regional breakouts, we have grouped the "bests" into three categories to match with your interests within each region: (1) Cultural and Historical; (2) Outdoor Activities and Events; and (3) Where to Eat, Drink and Stay. In the back, a cross-reference guide and an index can help you determine if we have covered your favorite places or perhaps help you track down a place when you already know the name.

Because we love traveling with our kids, you'll find plenty of family-friendly outings within these pages. We have highlighted the best things to do with kids with a symbol (☺) and hope you will head out to enjoy the activities and places sure to create lasting memories with your children. In addition to places to go with the kids, when you want to get out of town for romance or other quiet adult times, we provide ideas.

COLORADO HIGHLIGHTS

In addition to the main body of entries, we want to reference some of the best of the best. Because of geographic disparity, many of our choices cross boundary lines. For example, few places on the planet boast more great peaks to climb: In Colorado, fifty-four of them top out at over fourteen thousand feet (affectionately known as "fourteeners"). We also have a fondness for climbing the more isolated ridges of thirteen-thousand-foot peaks and find great joy in early-season hiking in the lower elevations. Another "best" feature has to be the 471-mile Colorado Trail. Stretching from Denver to Durango, this amazing route encompasses a diversity of scenery, landscape, history and culture; it can be taken in its entirety or in chunks over time.

The high peaks of the Sawatch Range tower above the Arkansas River Valley.
Photo by Doug Whitehead.

Colorado has so much to offer. The task of picking "Colorado's best" challenges
even those of us who have, perhaps, traveled and studied the state more than the
average tourist. Colorado never ceases to amaze anglers, art lovers, climbers and
runners, history buffs, wildlife watchers, festivalgoers, river rats, skiers, mountain
bikers, hikers and motorists, buyers of fresh produce and diners of fine cuisine, hot
springs soakers, train riders, beer drinkers and wine connoisseurs, those who like
to rough it and those who like to be pampered, fun seekers, truth seekers, sojourners,
risk takers and adventurers of all kinds. It's easy to run out of adjectives to describe
the state's majestic and varied scenery, and its history—including the days of the
Gold Rush, the Santa Fe Trail, Mexican and Spanish Territory, Ute ancestral lands
and the Anasazi, and the woolly mammoth and the dinosaurs. Colorado's sheer
variety is astonishing in its breadth and impact.

Pick the "best"? For skiing, snowboarding, museums, galleries, nightlife, history,
people, music festivals, culture, hut trips, stage rides, fishing, golf and numerous
other activities, you'll find our favorites. We hope you'll do everything in your
power to head out in all seasons to enjoy this great state.

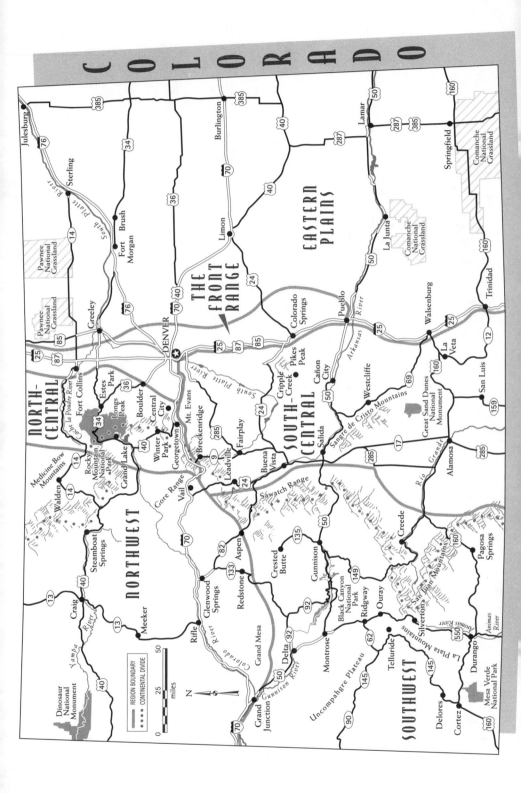

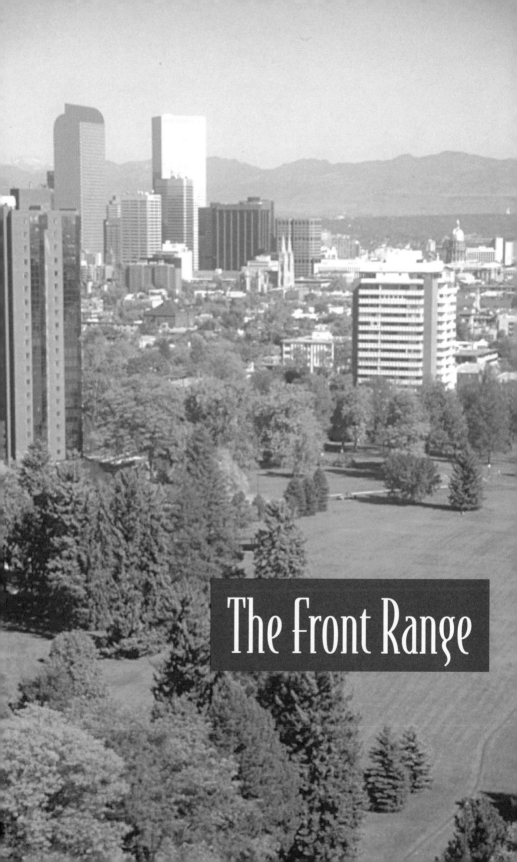

The Front Range

Previous page: A view of the Denver skyline from just east of Cheesman Park. *Photo by Bruce Caughey.*

The Front Range

From the very beginning, the confluence of Cherry Creek with the South Platte River acted like a magnet in drawing the immigrants to it. Despite the lack of trees and the somewhat barren aspects of the infant town [Denver], it was a welcome sight to the traveler, weary from the long and tiring stage ride across the plains. Miners deserting the high hills during the winter months found it equally attractive. Every year the place grew more civilized.

—Carl Ubbelohde, Maxine Benson and
Duane A. Smith, from *A Colorado History*

Connecting from south to north, a string of cities—Pueblo, Colorado Springs, Denver, Boulder, Fort Collins—began popping up along the Front Range of the Rocky Mountains in the mid-1800s. These vibrant places started as centers of commerce, shuttling and refining the ore mined from the mountains as well as supporting the agricultural and ranching economies of the eastern plains.

Today, with sustained growth and change driven by the economic engine of Metro Denver, and a more than desirable quality of life, the urban edges seem to be getting less defined all the time. It used to seem like a stretch of imagination to think of a great Front Range city, but now it's just a matter of time. After a century of boom-and-bust economic swings, it seems like this linear concentration of civilization, nestled against the Rockies, has finally come into its own, thanks in large measure to the wellspring of talented individuals who have decided to live, learn, work and play here.

When organizing this book into regions, it became clear to us that this logical grouping of urban, suburban and rural areas known as the Front Range may in fact be the most identifiable resource in the Rocky Mountain West. With dramatic mountain views from many street corners, it's easy to see the appeal and the balance of life that keeps attracting newcomers.

Our mission to uncover the very best attributes of the Front Range by nature causes us to turn away from the hassles that have come with growth and change. It's not that we are unaware of them, but problems and concerns get enough ink and airtime already. Our effort has been to delve into what "best" attributes can be found along the Front Range. We came across incredible places, including historical markers of the past, romantic retreats and great things to do with the kids.

We have skipped some of the obvious attractions, such as the Natural History Museum (and IMAX Theater), Denver Art Museum and Colorado History Museum. This doesn't mean you should consider skipping these wonderful resources; it just means we wanted to uncover some less obvious places and so have included the small towns to the north and south of Metro Denver. Instead of getting caught in a rut, perhaps you'll get a charge out of something new and unexpected. Whether you are coming to this area for a short vacation or have already put down roots, these fifty-plus "bests" from all along the Front Range should be on your shortlist of things to see and do.

Cultural & Historical

BEST COLLEGE CAMPUS
University of Colorado at Boulder

The stately six-hundred-acre CU Boulder campus with its attractive sandstone and red tile-roofed buildings, massive trees and long walkways captures a welcome backdrop to higher learning. In the shadow of the dramatic uplift of the Flatirons, the campus emanates beauty and a strong architectural connection to its surroundings. To the uninitiated, students seem aimless as they wander to and from classes and hang out at the outdoor fountains at the University Memorial Center (UMC) courtyard. The UMC draws people inside for lunch at the Alferd Packer Grille, to buy a CU mug at the University Bookstore, or down the hall for video games and bowling.

At times it feels like CU has not yet shed the party school image it reveled in during the excessive 1960s and 1970s. In fact, much has changed, but for the most part students still maintain an easygoing atmosphere that has existed in Boulder for decades. Despite obvious pressures to the contrary, Boulder manages to stay apart from and unhurried by nearby Denver. As one prominent resident puts it, "Boulder is fifteen square miles of land surrounded by reality."

To get a feel for the campus, wander past Old Main, the university's first stately building, which was already under construction when Colorado became a state in 1876. "It loomed before us gaunt and alone in the pitiless

Graceful Macky Auditorium sits at the northern edge of the stately University of Colorado–Boulder campus. *Photo by Bruce Caughey.*

clear light—no tree nor shrub nor any human habitation was in sight," wrote Jane Sewall, daughter of CU's first president, in 1877. In the intervening years, the campus has come a long way, and Old Main still stands as a spruced-up reminder of the days of yore. The initial freshman class of twelve students has grown to more than twenty-five thousand students today. To learn about the storied history of the university, tour the inside of Old Main and visit the CU Heritage Center (Tues. through Fri., 10 A.M. to 4 P.M.). The University of Colorado Museum, Norlin Library and Folsom Field (home of the CU Buffaloes Big 12 football team) are other good stops while on campus. To get to the campus, drive north on I-25 from Denver to the Boulder Turnpike (Hwy. 36) and continue twenty-seven miles northwest. Follow the signs to the campus. **(303) 492-1411.**

☺ BEST COLLECTION OF TOURIST TRAPS
Colorado Springs

You can see it all in this modern city nestled at the base of 14,110-foot Pikes Peak: from Anasazi ruins moved 350 miles from their home (Manitou Springs Cliff Dwellings) to Madame Tussaud's wax figurines of presidents and pop culture icons (Hall of Presidents). On Hwy. 115, it's tough to miss the RV-sized beetle that announces a massive collection of bugs at the May Natural History Museum. And that's just scratching the surface!

With its paved underground walkways and a humongous, aboveground gift shop, Cave of the Winds still packs 'em in with impressive crowd management; they claim you can't miss their laser light show on the nearby canyon walls. Colorado Springs has become the Colorado capital of cheesy, albeit sometimes very worthwhile, attractions. Its slightly tarnished distinction continues to be vigorously promoted by the city's elite, who have always welcomed tourists to pull off the highway to enjoy a numbing quantity of attractions.

We're not here to cast dispersions. For example, it's understandable that Santa's North Pole is, without a doubt, a young child's favorite detour. The lights, music, elves and kiddy rides all complement Santa Claus's (real beard) newfound home at the foot of Pikes Peak. And the World Figure Skating Hall of Fame is just the ticket for some visitors. So, too, the Flying W Ranch, which has served up chuckwagon dinners and cowboy music since the 1950s.

The nerve of some local entrepreneurs can be stunning. For example, the "Grandest Mile of Scenery in Colorado" at Seven Falls is pretty nice but, to us, hardly worth the steep admission price. More than a quarter-million visitors pay up annually to see a so-called natural waterfall and canyon illuminated by a thousand multicolored lights and "enhanced" by piped-in music. You can skip the entrance fee and still get a good view of the falls by heading up North Cheyenne Canyon and hiking up the mellow, mile-long Mt. Cutler trail to the falls. Remember, free National Forests comprise one fifth of Colorado's land, not to even mention National Parks, State Parks, Bureau of Land Management land and Wilderness Areas. Alas, it's so much sweeter to find your very own waterfalls and canyons!

BEST PHOTOGRAPHY GALLERY
Camera Obscura (Denver)

Most people wouldn't recognize the names: Kertesz, Cunningham, Bourke–White, Man Ray. For years, these and a host of other masters of photography have had their works exhibited in a small brick building on the corner of **Thirteenth and Bannock Sts.** in Denver. Known internationally for its unceasing support and presentation of the world's finest black-and-white and color photography, Camera Obscura Gallery remains obscure and underappreciated in its own backyard. The man behind this photographic tour de force is the venerable Hal Gould.

There is hardly a photographer Gould doesn't know personally whose work appears in his gallery. Every two months, a new show opens with a reception, many times attended by the artist. A fine photographer in his own right, Gould displays a wealth of knowledge that comes from decades of intimate involvement in the field. At eighty years old, he knows he could make a better living in stronger photography markets like Santa Fe or New York. Gould chooses to stay in Colorado, gracing the region with unparalleled access to the world's greatest photographers. Camera Obscura is considered one of the top galleries in the country for photographers to exhibit their work.

Climb the narrow stairway to the second floor to hunt through an extensive collection of photo books by or about virtuosos of the medium. Expert framing services are available. Closed Mondays. (303) 623-4059.

☺ BEST PLACE TO WATCH MONEY BEING MADE
U.S. Mint (Denver)

Located in a Florentine-looking fortress surrounded by a telltale spiked iron fence and machine gun turrets, the U.S. Mint remains the only place to watch actual money being made in Colorado—legally. The Mint has been called "a billion-dollar institution with a one-cent complex," thanks to its affinity for producing trainloads of shiny new pennies. Employees have used coining machines to stamp out ten billion coins annually in a central-Denver location, just west of the City and County Building.

The production of legal tender in Colorado started in 1860 when two partners in the Clarke–Gruber Company began minting four denominations of gold coins, thanks to a loophole in the law that didn't specify minting as a government function. In 1864, a year before the laws changed, Clarke–Gruber managed to sell out to Uncle Sam, thus creating the Denver branch of the U.S. Mint. Over the years, billions of dollars of gold have been stored at this major repository, with surprisingly few criminal incidents.

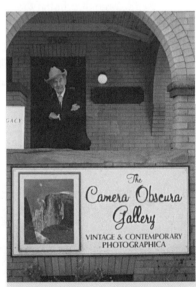

Of course, there was the time in 1920 when Orville Harrington, a Colorado School of Mines graduate, absconded with $80,000 of gold ingots, deftly slipping them into his vest pocket over a period of months before finally being caught. In December 1922, bandits surprised guards in front of the Mint and managed to

Hal Gould has been welcoming people to his Camera Obscura Gallery for decades. *Photo by Doug Whitehead.*

steal $200,000 of brand-new five-dollar bills being moved there for safekeeping. A Federal Reserve guard was killed in the ensuing gun battle, and four weeks later one of the bandits showed up dead—bullet-riddled and frozen—on the front seat of the getaway car inside a Capitol Hill garage. Some $80,000 was later recovered in St. Louis, but no arrests were ever made.

Today's excitement comes from a guided tour through the heavily guarded building. Visitors line up during weekdays around the perimeter for free first-come, first-served tours. During the twenty-minute tour you'll get a sense of the volume of coinage created here, as well as the history, technology and artistry involved in making money. Every coin made here gets stamped with a small "D" on the front side just below the date. Interesting gift shop. No photography allowed. **320 W. Colfax Ave.; (303) 405-4761.**

BEST LOCAL ART GALLERY
The Foothills Art Center (Golden)

The arts are alive and well in Denver. From the exquisite collections of the Denver Art Museum to the annual, ever-popular Cherry Creek Arts Festival held July 4 weekend, amateurs and aficionados alike flock to the metro-area arts scene. Contributing to that vibrancy in a spirited way, The Foothills Art Center thrives in a quiet Golden neighborhood.

Housed in a historic church built in 1872, the unique exhibit space itself is a work of art. In the original sanctuary, Director Carol Dickinson mounts stunning

shows with a "nature" theme, set amidst stained glass and a vaulted ceiling, enhancing the ambiance inspired by the subject and quality of works hung on its walls. For example, the 1997 "Canyon Walls" exhibit was a perfect match, with grand depictions of canyons displayed in the cavernous confines of this temple of art. Smaller areas in the gallery allow related art to be shown in conjunction with the main show. Since

Housed in a historic church, The Foothills Art Center gallery building creates unique spaces for viewing artwork. *Photo by Doug Whitehead.*

1968, The Foothills Art Center has brought nationally recognized art jurors to judge its annual exhibitions. The Rocky Mountain National Watermedia Show, North American Sculpture Exhibition, Colorado Clay Exhibition and Colorado Art Open all attract local and national artists. Hoping to engage a broad audience, Foothills puts much thought into presenting art that relates to universal experience. It also is committed to placing Colorado artists in national perspective, including local talent with nationally known masters of a particular genre.

The Foothills Art Center is located at **Fifteenth St. and Washington Ave.** in Golden. Open seven days a week. No admission charge. **(303) 279-3922.**

☺ BEST WEATHER WATCHING
National Center for Atmospheric Research (Boulder)

Few places rival the National Center for Atmospheric Research (NCAR) for its picture-perfect setting in the foothills above Boulder. In a striking facility designed by I. M. Pei to resemble cliff dwellings built by Colorado's ancient residents, visitors learn about weather research and then go out into the weather for a hike on open-space trails. NCAR's Mesa Lab welcomes visitors for free self-guided tours or with some advance notice will arrange customized tours for groups of adults or children. Sponsored in part by the National Science Foundation, the lab serves as a place for visitors to appreciate scientific research that impacts our everyday lives.

Technical research includes efforts to determine the dynamics and impacts of everything from global warming to wind shear. Scientists delve into mathematical models of sea surface temperature impacts on weather to atmospheric changes due to the use of chlorofluorocarbons. With the help of Cray supercomputers, a range of computer simulations analyze various climatic components that interact to create our weather. Although some of the multisyllable words you will encounter at NCAR may intimidate you at first, the interactive displays and helpful staff manage to make sense of the complex research.

And when you get tired of it all, head outside for some hiking or a picnic in the adjacent Boulder County Open Space. Many trail options, including a wheel-chair-accessible trail, leave right from NCAR's back door. Keep your eyes peeled for deer along the pretty drive up to the lab and take some time to enjoy the top-of-the-world views back east over the plains. **1850 Table Mesa Dr.**; **(303) 497-1000**; www.ncar.ucar.edu.

☺ BEST DINO EVIDENCE
Dinosaur Ridge (west of Denver)

To the untrained eye, it's just another hill in a state full of mountains. But look a little closer and you'll see that the ridge known locally as the Hogback is really an ancient landscape tilted on its side. Look closer still and discover dinosaur tracks from huge beasts that roamed the area eons ago. The first stegosaurus bones ever discovered were found right here along Dinosaur Ridge.

Once a month from May through October the road over the Hogback to Morrison is closed to car traffic. Volunteers from the Friends of Dinosaur Ridge, including retired geologists and paleontologists, station themselves at various points along the way, each filling in for visitors a different piece of the geologic puzzle revealed in the exposed layers. From mysterious orbs in the rock thought to be footprints of an apatosaur to small imprints made from the tiny shells of ancient crustaceans, a picture of life along the edge of a onetime sea emerges. This was a popular throughway for theropods and their brethren.

If the theory holds true that today's birds are yesterday's dinosaurs, then maybe it makes sense why this landform has now become known as a highway for hawks. Any day during the months of March and April, you can make the fifteen-minute hike up to the top of the ridge to join researchers on the Hawk Watch Project, counting thousands of hawks, eagles, falcons and other raptors as they ride the air currents on their northward migration. The connection between dinosaurs and birds notwithstanding, this spine along the foothills continues to attract nature's travelers to this particular spot on earth.

The Dinosaur Ridge Visitors Center is located on the east side of the Hogback, where Alameda Ave. crosses C-470. **(303) 697-DINO.**

☺ BEST PLACE TO BE A KID
Tiny Town (west of Denver)

To be perfectly honest, this "best" pick ended as a coin toss between the ever-popular Children's Museum in Denver and Tiny Town. We decided to give the nod to Tiny Town after a summer expedition with a few members of the under-four-foot-tall set. They loved every moment of peering inside the miniature fire station, homes, churches, stores and, of course, taking the dwarf railway (with actual-size conductor) around the village. The day was topped off by sharing a picnic on a shaded grassy area at the twenty-acre facility. The best part? Watching kids imagine themselves as giants, bending over to peer inside windows at the realistic-looking furnishings and miniature figures of people. Open daily from Memorial Day to Labor Day. Small fee. Located south of Denver off Hwy. 285 and Turkey Creek Rd. **6249 S. Turkey Creek Rd.**; **(303) 697-6829.**

☺ BEST BOOKSTORE
Tattered Cover (Denver)

With four levels packed with all manner of publications, the Tattered Cover in Cherry Creek remains Colorado's favorite book-buying destination. Add a funky café and a gourmet restaurant atop its more than 150,000 titles, and an extensive newsstand, and this store becomes a magnet for book lovers. People go out of their way to shop here—not only due to the breadth and depth of the books available but because of the well-versed sales staff. They excel at helping you find that hard-to-name volume you heard about from a friend but cannot quite remember.

Despite the name, this store does not sell used or tattered books. Customers are, however, encouraged to plop down on a comfortable overstuffed chair or couch and leaf through books while bathed in soft lamplight. Nobody's going to hurry you—and if you get hungry you can retreat to the first-floor café, or upstairs to the fancier confines of the Fourth Story restaurant and bar.

Book aficionados appreciate the large number of signings and readings the store offers. Everybody from local authors to megastars claim status as a result of a Tattered Cover appearance. When owner Joyce Meskis opened her first bookstore just two blocks away from the Cherry Creek location some twenty-five years ago, she found the neighborhood receptive, but her dreams soon outgrew her space. After several expansions, Meskis enlisted employees and even some of her loyal customers to haul boxes of books into her current Cherry Creek location at **2955 E. First Ave.**; **(303) 322-7727**; **www.tatteredcover.com.** Check out the lower downtown sister store at **1628 Sixteenth St., (303) 436-1070**; though a bit smaller, it offers a similar book-buying ambiance.

☺ BEST MEDIEVAL FANTASY
Renaissance Festival (Larkspur)

Blink twice, rub your eyes and realize that you have traveled four hundred years backward to the days of King Henry VIII and Queen Anne Boleyn. In a village setting in the woods near Larkspur, a costumed cast of hundreds engages guests in a Renaissance fantasy complete with jousters, jugglers and jigglers (the ladies' dress of the day features ample cleavage). More than two hundred village artisans create original crafts and, though many art forms are not authentic to the times, nothing is mass produced. Of course, along with all the music and merrymaking comes a wealth of hearty food (roasted turkey legs and corn on the cob are perennial favorites), sweets and drink.

This sometimes bizarre, always unpredictable festival has been running during summer weekends since the mid-1970s. You can participate in the scene just by walking around and not being shy. The leather goblets, flowered head wreaths, gargoyles, jewelry and clothing seem perfectly appropriate at the festival, but you might want to consider how they'll look back home. Various scheduled shows include the pageantry of knights in a jousting match before the king and queen, and the amazing antics of a hypnotist. Don't miss the coarse hilarity of Puke and Snot. "This is the version of Robin Hood your parents rent when you're off at camp!" they said while bounding around the stage in tights and making audience members blush between guffaws. The Endangered Cat Show, Tortuga Twins and sword swallowing by Thom Sellectomy continue to delight crowds.

Kids will likely see and hear stuff outside their parents' normal bounds, but they absolutely love the magic of this place. In addition to the memorable highlight of combat jousting, they can enter the Children's Realm and ride a camel, pet a potbellied pig or climb into the dragon swing; all this happens in the midst of a living museum.

Located in Larkspur, off I-25 between Denver and Colorado Springs, the festival takes place during eight summer weekends from mid-June through early August. Admission is charged; bring cash (or credit cards) for what's in store inside. Free for kids under five. **(303) 688-6010;** www.coloradorenaissance.com.

The king and queen greet the audience before the jousting match at the annual Renaissance Festival in Larkspur. *Photo by Bruce Caughey.*

☺ BEST CULTURAL FESTIVAL
Greek Festival (Denver)

The rapid-fire strains of oddly tuned string instruments bring an upbeat tempo to Denver's annual Greek Festival in late June. Novices learn how to folk dance to the music, but when the experts show up in traditional costumes, most newcomers back away from the spotlight and join the circle. Male Greek dancers delight festivalgoers with leaping, high-energy moves, and the more subtle steps of female dancers bring a quiet beauty to the forefront. This festival appeals greatly to all the senses—the most memorable being the smells and tastes of traditional food, which can be purchased at the many stands. Not much compares with the scent of grilling *souvlaki* as you wander around the Greek marketplace. The squid, too, tastes wonderful when prepared by people who have eaten this delicacy for generations. And don't even think about skipping a slice of *baklava*, a honey-laden pastry, or a custard dish called *galaktobouriko*. Vendors sell authentic crafts, clothing and jewelry as you get lost in the feel of a traditional Greek village. The festival takes place adjacent to the unique gold dome of the Greek Orthodox Cathedral of the Assumption. If you have time, take a tour inside to see the impressive collection of Byzantine icons. The festival has been going strong since the mid-1960s, and we predict it will continue to be a draw for generations to come. Small admission fee. **4610 E. Alameda Ave.**; **(303) 388-9314.**

☺ BEST CULTURE IN SUBURBIA
Arvada Center for the Performing Arts

The depth of culture in suburbia has always been shallower than in urban settings, college towns and artisan communities. Thankfully, the movers and shakers in Old Town Arvada felt they could avoid cultural dearth by putting together this center. On a large plot of land in northwest Metro Denver, they built a large center with a five-hundred-seat indoor theater, twelve-hundred-seat outdoor amphitheater, art display areas and dance areas. The complex, with its large grassy slope, now features a terrific new playground, replete with a colorful serpent that twists its way along a high-tech, padded flooring. Little ones climb, hang, explore and enjoy every part from the tip of its scaled tail to the dragon's massive head, with its toothful grin, flared nostrils and large, arched eyeballs.

Check the listings to see what's happening here. You can enjoy everything from professionally produced plays and musical or dance events to a variety of classes and a very popular winter crafts show. Located at **6901 Wadsworth Ave., Arvada.** Listen to a recording on classes, concerts and plays at **(303) 431-3080.**

BEST COLLEGE SPORTS SCENE
University of Denver Hockey

This category presented one of the most difficult choices in the entire book. In a not-too-scientific methodology, having rooted out our alumni bias and natural sports preferences, we came up with the most dynamic sports legacy in the entire state—University of Denver (DU) hockey. Sure, we thought about college football, including the once-dominant CU Buffaloes, the emergent CSU Rams and even the Air Force Academy Falcons with their lightning-bolt helmets and pristine foothills location north of Colorado Springs. But truly nothing compares to the energy and longtime traditions of the DU Pioneers, among the country's top NCAA Division I hockey teams. Even its arch-rival, Colorado College, cannot quite compete with the energy, enthusiasm and traditions that come with the Pioneers.

You can forget about the bench-clearing brawls that make pro hockey seem at times a parody of what the sport intended. Sit up close in the new 6,200-seat Magness Ice Arena, part of the copper-skinned Daniel L. Ritchie Center (just west of University Blvd. and I-25) and you'll benefit twice: (1) you won't run up the limit on your gold card; and (2) you'll get an up-close view of muscle, grit and finesse on ice. The rowdy student section and band ensemble help energize the entire arena. With no red line, the pace of this game can reach frantic pitches as the puck slides frantically back and forth across the ice. At just $6 to $18 per ticket, the DU Pioneers provide a value guarantee on your entertainment dollar. The season runs from October to mid-March. Call **(303) 871-2336** for tickets and information.

☺ BEST PLACE TO SEE JUNK TRANSFORMED
Swetsville Zoo (near Fort Collins)

Bill Swet, a soft-spoken man in faded blue overalls, rules over an imaginary kingdom of fanciful dinosaurs, bizarre creatures and imaginary friends. Swet decided to do something with all the rubbish that collects outside of farmhouses and slowly rusts away. He transformed what must have been a mountain of accumulated throwaway gears, flywheels, scrap metal and defunct machinery into more than seventy offbeat sculptures. Some playful, some sinister, these sculptures make every adult visitor wonder: "What could possibly motivate someone to do this?" The kids, however, couldn't care less. They will go nuts over this place, enjoying all of the strange sculptures that lie in wait along the winding grassy pathway. Bring a lunch and hang out for a while.

Besides all of the sculptures, Swet operates a miniature steam railway that plies a .75-mile route beside the Poudre River. It's all free, but Swet says donations are accepted. Be sure to check out the welded metal turrets that dwarf the front entrance to Swet's small home, which lies adjacent to the sculpture garden. To get here from Denver take I-25 north to the Harmony Rd. Exit (265) just south of Fort Collins. Drive east of the interstate to the zoo at **4801 E. Harmony Rd., Fort Collins, CO 80525.**

BEST HARDWARE STORE
McGuckins (Boulder)

One-stop shopping takes on new meaning when you enter this family-owned Boulder institution. Despite increased competition from chain megastores, for forty-five years McGuckins has reigned as king of the hardwares, thanks to its immense collection of eclectic stuff. The store's motto rings true: "If we don't have it, you don't need it." And customers do show up with unusual requests. One man showed up at the store with his dad's ashes in a bag under his arm, trying to find an appropriate container. He couldn't pass up a good deal on a Thermos, but it wasn't quite large enough to hold all the ashes. Before leaving, the son actually spread the remaining ashes outside of the store, saying dad would have been pleased. Yeah, right.

You don't even have to buy anything as you wander among this amassed collection of some two hundred thousand items, including everything from tools and camping equipment to wheelbarrows and toasters. Buying every variety of nails, screws and bolts (up to an inch in diameter) has never been easier, especially when you enlist the help of one of the staff's easy-to-find, green-vested employees. And, if you ever need a gift for a hard-to-buy-for relative, stop here and be guaranteed to find something to make them smile. McGuckins has one of the best collections of unusual Christmas ornaments we've ever encountered. Located inside a hangar-sized store off **23rd St. and Arapahoe Rd.; (303) 443-1822.**

☺ BEST PLACE TO SEE THE OCEAN IN COLORADO
Ocean Journey (Denver)

Looking over the Denver basin, geologists might be able to visualize the ocean that once covered the entire area. But most ordinary citizens would have a tough time with that sixty-five-million-year-old concept. So, Denver's sparkling new

The glass façade of Ocean Journey overlooks the Denver skyline from a prime Central Platte Valley perch. *Photo courtesy of Colorado's Ocean Journey.*

attraction in the Central Platte Valley fills a real void—with nearly one million gallons of water and fifteen thousand specimens.

Head out on a unique Colorado adventure. Inside the new glass-faced Ocean Journey, you follow the Colorado River from its icy beginnings at 12,700 feet. The exhibits take you on a winding excursion that condenses thousands of miles, through waterfalls and several states to the Pacific Ocean. Along the way, you'll see varieties of fish, including endangered Colorado trout—such as the humpback chub and razorback sucker—and a bit later, North American river otters and salamanders. Birdlife teems in the wetlands exhibits, alongside unusual sights and sounds emanating from the various aquarium rooms, making it a truly sensory experience.

Another river journey within Ocean Journey begins half a world apart, as you follow Indonesia's great Kampar River from its beginnings high in the rich volcanic mountain range along Sumatra's west coast. The humidity is palpable in the form of mist as you walk through the tropical environment among the massive, uniquely sculpted aquariums. Two endangered Sumatran tigers roam a four-thousand-square-foot habitat, complete with an enticing swimming area; a glass cutout nearly puts you inside of the cats' watery lair. At the end of your river journey, you find yourself in a mangrove forest growing in saltwater, and a coral lagoon. These sites soon transition to the depths of the Pacific, where you find your eyes sweeping overhead to the "smiles" of menacing sharks and colorful tropical fish.

As part of a concentrated area of attractions including the Pepsi Center, Six Flags/Elitch Gardens Amusement Park and the Children's Museum, this brilliant new aquarium is located just off I-25 (at exit 211). Surrounded by an outdoor wetlands exhibit, the aquarium lies alongside the popular Platte River Bike Path; the area is also served by the Cultural Trolley. For more information call Ocean Journey at (303) 561-4450, or visit their website at www.oceanjourney.org.

☺ BEST PLACE TO BE DAZZLED BY BUTTERFLIES
Butterfly Pavilion and Insect Center (Westminster)

Like a peaceful dreamscape filled with thousands of fluorescent, fluttering images, the domed environs of the Butterfly Pavilion create a memorable and unique experience. Pathways wind among a verdant botanical garden complete with ponds stocked with ornamental carp. The humid temperature hovers above 80 degrees, making this a perfect escape for a winter day. Benches stationed here and there encourage leisurely viewing. Take your time, look closely through the foliage and up along the ceiling nets, and you will see an array of patterns and colors created by nature.

There's nothing like a bright blue butterfly landing on your shoulder to elicit smiles from all those around. Watch your step, however, and be careful to check for any hitchhikers in the mirrored enclosure between the double sets of glass doors.

A glass case shows the butterflies emerging from their egg-shaped chrysalides, battling through the hard cases to spread their fragile, wet wings. Another room fea-

tures an interesting collection of insects. If you ever wanted to feel a hairy tarantula march up your arm, or stroke the slippery brown back of a pinecone-sized Madagascar hissing cockroach, be sure to stop here. A relatively recent addition showcases hands-on tidal pools, a real draw for the younger kids, who can touch sea stars and other clingy creatures that exist on the fringe between ocean and land.

The gift shop draws visitors inside to buy a multitude of butter-fly and insect paraphernalia, from science kits to tacky coffee mugs. Open 9 A.M. to 5 P.M. Tuesday through Sunday. Located just off the Boulder Turnpike (Hwy. 36) in Westminster at **6252 W. 104th Ave.**; (303) 469-5441.

Brightly colored butterflies can be spotted easily inside the humid, plant-laden interior of the Butterfly Pavilion. *Photo by Bruce Caughey.*

Outdoor Activities & Events

BEST OUTDOOR MUSIC VENUE
Red Rocks Amphitheater (near Denver)

Let's hope all of the recent talk about refurbishing Red Rocks Amphitheater doesn't ever cause changes that detract from its incredible natural setting. Without question, this is the finest outdoor concert hall to enjoy big-name concerts along the Front Range, if not on the planet. Since 1941, this eight-thousand-seat theater has been attracting concertgoers to shows ranging from the Beatles to Bonnie Raitt to B. B. King. It remains the musicians' choice thanks in part to acoustics perfected by Wolfgang Wagner, son of the great opera composer Richard Wagner. On summer evenings, as you listen to the music, the hard wooden bleachers hardly matter as the moon rises above the twinkling city lights. All the while you sit surrounded between immense slabs of red rock. Get concert information by calling TicketMaster of Colorado at **(303) 596-4636**.

Every Easter the sunrise service attracts thousands from across the Denver Metro area. Red Rocks Amphitheater is just part of an outdoor park that features hiking trails and great picnic spots. To get here from Denver, take I-70 west to Morrison. Then drive south to the park entrance. For more information about the park, call the **Trading Post** at **(303) 697-8935**.

☺ BEST WALKING MALL
Pearl Street Mall (Boulder)

Maybe you've heard that Boulderites, even temporary residents attending the University of Colorado, march to distinctly different drummers. It's especially true while walking down the brick-lined Pearl Street Mall, where depending on the night, you might hear African drums, steel drums or bongo drums. If that isn't enough, street guitarists, violinists and saxophonists set up in doorways or between turn-of-the-century historic buildings vying for your spare dollar.

On summer evenings you'll also catch magicians, mimes, comedians and acrobats who sometimes draw astonishing numbers of people for their short acts. All this hyperactivity happens amidst some terrific shops, galleries, cafés and restaurants. Despite all the racket, the mall really is a place to converse on one of

Even during the chilly Christmas season, talented street musicians vie for your spare change on Boulder's Pearl Street Mall. *Photo by Bruce Caughey.*

the many benches or while hanging out at a restaurant courtyard sipping a beer and taking in the essence of what Boulder is all about. One of our favorite places to catch a sunset over the Flatirons is from the rooftop tables at the **West End Tavern (between Ninth and Tenth Sts. on Pearl; [303] 444-3535).** The streets surrounding the Pearl Street Mall host more of Boulder's nightlife and shopping district. So find a parking space and wander around the entire area surrounding Pearl St. between Ninth and Fifteenth Sts.

☺ BEST PEOPLE WATCHING
Washington Park (Denver)

Although tempted to select Denver International Airport as the site of the best people watching, we decided to go for more local flavor. The heart of a city lies in its public places, and Washington Park remains Denver's pulsing lifeline, especially in summer. Whether walking around Grasmere Lake, jogging the park's perimeter trail or pedaling your bike in the park's interior, you'll encounter a rich mix of the city's inhabitants. Old couples gaze at the replica of George Washington's colorful garden at Mount Vernon while in-line skaters whir around the wide asphalt road. On warm days, volleyball nets and boundary ropes sprout by the tens along grassy areas of the park, vying for space with Ultimate Frisbee, soccer and touch football games. Everyone shares the park's beauty and diversity.

Kids love the place, flocking to a couple of large playgrounds with their parents in tow—the one adjacent to the historic boathouse blends the best aspects of a medieval castle and a McDonald's Playland. The park's outdoor tennis courts, indoor pool and gym all attract fitness buffs.

But favorite places for catching people totally immersed in their element remain the older, mostly male crowd at the dozen or so well-used horseshoe pits on the park's west side and those impeccably dressed denizens at the manicured croquet greens to the east. There's even a small section of the park reserved for the venerable sport of lawn bowling! Washington Park lies to the east of Downing St. between Virginia and Louisiana Aves.

☺ BEST AMUSEMENT PARK
Six Flags/Elitch Gardens (Denver)

As if they heard that faint tune coming from the ice-cream truck, the urge to let the inner child come out and play sweeps over drivers on I-25 as they approach the Platte Valley. They look out at an incredible juxtaposition of thrilling rides nestled

right up against the jagged skyline of downtown Denver. This sight becomes Denver, but many of us still hanker for a time when Elitch's meant heading to historic north Denver to enjoy the rickety wooden Mr. Twister, mature landscaped gardens, picnic tables and the famous Trocadero Ballroom. The old place held a quaint charm for sixty-six years that will never be replicated.

But then who could be thinking about a charming setting when riding face-first down a 125-foot drop before careening through inverted loops on the Boomerang? If you find it frightening that your eyeballs practically pop out of their sockets, you might find some comfort in knowing you're not alone. Just when you think you've had enough, the cars launch into the twisting, turning loops backward! An expanded children's area and plenty of water rides make this state-of-the-art

The Boomerang whips riders through a dizzying spiral at Six Flags/Elitch Gardens. *Photo courtesy of Six Flags/ Elitch Gardens.*

park an all-ages experience. The rides, shows, attractions and food will keep you busy all day and into the night.

In 1999 the park took on the banner of Six Flags as it entered a massive building program and added Looney Tunes and DC Comics characters such as Batman, Bugs Bunny, Sylvester, Tweety and Daffy Duck to the merchandising and marketing program. Children three and under get in free, but everyone else pays a pretty hefty admission. Located at **299 Walnut St.** From I-25, go south on Speer Blvd. (exit 212A), then turn onto Elitch Circle. **(303) 595-4386**; **www.sixflags.com/elitchgardens**.

☺ BEST BIKING AND IN-LINE SKATING
Denver Greenway Trails

A paved ribbon winds some thirty-five miles through Denver, providing bikers, walkers and bladers a welcome escape from curse-provoking traffic jams. This

well-used resource (especially on weekends and during the lunch hour) can get crowded at times, but it still flows seamlessly through the heart of the city and goes on to terrific resources in outlying areas. Historic markers, natural areas, parks and even urban wildlife areas keep every journey interesting.

The best place to begin could well be the actual beginnings of the fair city of Denver. Founders of the burgeoning towns of Auraria and St. Charles

A biker whirs along next to the South Platte River on the Denver Greenway Trail system. *Photo by Bruce Caughey.*

City thought they had it made when planning sites near the confluence of Cherry Creek and the South Platte River in 1859. Then, under the orders of General William Larimer, a new claim jumped some rights, thus creating Denver. Today the area near Confluence Park has taken on a gem quality, with many attractions and massive redevelopment, including Ocean Journey, Six Flags/Elitch Gardens, the Children's Museum, the Pepsi Center and the new REI outdoors store taking root in the former Forney Transportation Museum. Great views of Denver's skyline accompany you at the outset, as does a popular kayaking course that plies the South Platte River.

With two main branches of the Denver Greenway Trail System following Cherry Creek and the South Platte River—in addition to endless possible side trips—these routes have become an indispensable part of the city. Routes wind all the way to destinations on the outskirts of town such as Cherry Creek, Chatfield and Bear Creek State Parks. You can even link up with the Waterton Canyon Trailhead and the Colorado Trail (described in Best Trailhead on page 27). For more information and an excellent map of the Greenway Trails, contact the Colorado Division of Parks and Outdoor Recreation at (303) 866-3437. With the infusion of millions of dollars of lottery money, bikers and bladers can also find extensive trail systems in Boulder, Fort Collins, Colorado Springs and even Pueblo, along the Riverwalk.

☺ BEST "PRIMITIVE" STATE PARK
Roxborough

Jutting vertical slabs of red sandstone rise spectacularly in the diverse transition zone between prairie and mountains just forty-five minutes south of downtown Denver. Created by five hundred million years of geological turmoil combined with erosionary forces, this state park comprises a "primitive" nature preserve close to home. Having barely escaped the developer's blade, Roxborough now plays an important role in safeguarding nature for its visitors. It's an absolutely great place to escape the city, and it is so close that you only need two to three hours to get a real sense of the area's beauty.

Hikers enjoy miles of easy-to-moderate trails through nine ecotypes, including verdant meadows, thickets of Ponderosa pine and desert terrain interspersed with yucca and colored with patches of thick gambel oak. Even if you just want to enjoy a picnic at one of the close-in overlooks, this destination provides a strong connection with nature. Spiked with ever-present reddish towers of stone, some as flat as upturned serving trays, the landscape plays on your imagination. Check in at the visitors center, nestled among the rocks, to see what recent wildlife sightings have been made. They will likely include deer, mountain lion, hawks and eagles, among many other species. Talk with rangers for in-depth information about the flora, fauna and geology of the entire area. Small park admission fee.

To reach Roxborough State Park take Hwy. 85 (Santa Fe Dr.) south to Titan Rd. Turn right and proceed 3.5 miles. Follow the curve left (south) three miles to a signed entrance to the park. 4751 N. Roxborough Dr.; (303) 973-3959; www.coloradoparks.org.

Jutting red sandstone characterizes the scenery at Roxborough State Park south of Denver. *Photo by Bruce Caughey.*

☺ BEST PARK FOR A PICNIC
Chautauqua Park (Boulder)

From the sloping, grassy expanse of Boulder's Chautauqua Park, next to the jutting rocks of the Flatirons, you can lose yourself in deep thoughts, superficial musings or your favorite trashy novel. Spread out your blanket and share some gourmet treats with a special friend or dive into some PB&Js and potato chips with your kids. What you eat in this glorious setting doesn't matter much—just being here and enjoying the moment counts volumes.

After lunch head out on the miles of well-marked trails in the Boulder Open Space. A favorite afternoon hike leads up toward the Flatirons and Bluebell Shelter. Be sure to keep your eyes peeled for wildlife along the way, especially deer (and an occasional mountain lion) and, in season, a colorful spectrum of birds. You can often see technical climbers inching their way up the nearly vertical rocks with the help of ropes. Other walking trails lead to the top of nearby Flagstaff Mountain or south to the National Center for Atmospheric Research (NCAR). If you don't feel like hiking, bring along a kite; this park is often buffeted by a steady breeze. A well-designed playground, adjacent to the venerable Chautauqua Dining Hall, will undoubtedly attract young children.

To reach the park drive west on Baseline Rd. Chautauqua Park is on the south side of the street before the road curves up Flagstaff Mountain.

☺ BEST URBAN OASIS
Jefferson County Open Space

The citizens of Jefferson County showed prescient foresight when they voted to increase their taxes in 1972. Since that time, millions of dollars have bought hundreds of thousands of acres of land along the foothills. In the face of unprecedented urban sprawl, Jeffco has done us all a huge favor. Large tracts of open spaces have been preserved, protecting at least a part of Colorado's heritage from developers. As of 1999, eighteen Jefferson County Open Space Parks provide miles of hiking, mountain biking and horse trails, and nature and history programs. They also help to keep open important wildlife corridors and dramatic vistas of the Front Range.

One of the early acquisitions wasn't open space at all. The Hiwan Homestead Museum in Evergreen preserves a log home and many of its furnishings from the 1800s. Mt. Falcon Park above Parmalee Gulch was the site of an ambitious turn-of-the-century project by John Brisben Walker. Enlisting Colorado schoolkids and their penny-sized donations in the effort, he hoped to build a summer White House for U.S. presidents. Getting only as far as the cornerstone and foundation, the ruins of his attempt still lie on trails that bring impressive views of downtown Denver far below. The remains of his own stone house that burned down also sit in the park. The trails of Pine Valley Ranch Park, about five miles off of Hwy. 285 from Pine Junction, connect with trailheads of the Pike National Forest. An observatory in the park provides a perfect venue for stargazing. At the Lookout Mountain Nature Center north of I-70, scores of nature hikes and programs keep urban kids in touch with the outdoors. Lair O' The Bear offers secluded walks in the woods along Bear Creek.

New properties are being added to Jefferson County Open Space every year. Maps and other information are available at its Golden offices. **(303) 271-5925;** **www.co.jefferson.co.us.**

☺ BEST BACKYARD CAMPING
Golden Gate Canyon State Park

Close to the city, Golden Gate Canyon State Park might as well be a hundred miles from civilization. Lush meadows, aspen forests and abundant wildlife once attracted Utes, Cheyenne and Arapaho to this rugged country. City folks today find solitude and sanctuary from smog and busy streets. Urbanites escape to this close-by park to replace a skyline of tall buildings with expansive views of Front Range mountain peaks.

Located in the foothills between Nederland, Central City and Golden, the park offers camping that runs the gamut from developed campgrounds to primitive, backcountry sites. At Reverend's Ridge, you'll find more than a hundred cushy campsites with hookups. A camper services building offers hiking information along with showers and laundry machines. Summertime nature programs are held Friday and Saturday nights next to a roaring campfire in the amphitheater. Other areas in the park are reserved just for tents, and a few sites are for horse-back riders only. If you really want to get away from the city, twenty-three first-come, first-served backcountry sites are spread throughout Golden Gate. Permits can be obtained at the visitors center. In addition, four primitive shelters styled like those along the Appalachian Trail are located in remote corners of the wilderness.

Miles of trails crisscross this country through which a toll road once carried supplies to the nearby, booming mining towns of Central City and Blackhawk. Call the visitors center for more information: (303) 582-3707. Reservations should be made well in advance of your visit. Call Colorado State Parks at (303) 470-1144; www.coloradoparks.org.

☺ BEST MODERATE MOUNTAIN BIKING
Horsetooth Mountain Park and Lory State Park (Fort Collins)

Mountain biking doesn't have to be only for adrenaline junkies. Many of us appreciate the way a bike provides access to nature. The rolling landscape of these two interconnected parks provides a perfect escape only fifteen minutes from the urban trails of Fort Collins. These parks lie in a transition zone between the plains and the mountains, with dramatic rock outcroppings above (including one that looks a bit like a horse's tooth, and another famous one called Arthur's Rock) and the snaking shoreline of Horsetooth Reservoir along the eastern boundary of the parks.

With more than thirty miles of trails just behind the red sandstone hogback, riders have a great opportunity to explore a lovely area that encompasses the shortgrass prairie as well as thick ponderosa forest. As a recognized equestrian area, though, trails must be shared with horseback riders, and consideration is expected. Horses can be rented on the premises at Double Diamond Stables. Hikers also love this area.

One of our favorites is the 1.9-mile Overlook Trail. It connects with other tougher trails and offers sweeping views as it winds along the red sandstone hogback that marks the mountains' final descent into the plains. The six-mile-long Foothills

Mountain bikers share the trail with horses at Horsetooth Mountain Park just west of Fort Collins. *Photo by Bruce Caughey.*

Trail also offers a moderate introduction to the area and gorgeous views of the reservoir as it parallels the shoreline much of the way. For more information contact Lory State Park at **(970) 493-1623**; **www.coloradoparks.org.**

☺ BEST SOAKING AFTER A HIKE
Eldorado Artesian Springs (near Boulder)

Because the forbidding rock walls in Eldorado Canyon appear impenetrable, this area remains a slice of heaven close by. First things first. Take a hike on one of Eldorado Canyon State Park's many miles of trails that lead steadily upward from the canyon floor. Or, sit back next to South Boulder Creek and watch technical climbers muscle their way upward while on belay. Whatever you choose, just be sure to make your way to Eldorado Artesian Springs during the heat of the day.

This slice of vintage America has been here since becoming a fashionable spa in the early 1900s. Today, its sheen has definitely slipped from its former heights, when there was a choice of restaurants and a nice hotel, and it was, for a time, a favorite stopping-off place for Dwight D. Eisenhower. But the springs nonetheless remains a fantastic place to spend some time and soak away the trail dust. Heated by natural geothermal water more than a mile beneath the surface, the old concrete pool remains a comfortable swimming temperature. A long steel slide descends into the clear water from one corner. Sunbathers find spots on balcony overlooks or down along a narrow grassy area next to the creek. If you get thirsty or want to buy some bottles of Eldorado artesian water for the road, be sure to stop in at the snack bar.

Fee charged. Open from Memorial Day to Labor Day from 10 A.M. to 6 P.M. To get here take Hwy. 93 (Broadway) south from Boulder for 5.5 miles. Turn right on Eldorado Springs Dr. and continue for three miles to the park entrance. The pool lies off to your right just before the park entrance. **(303) 499-1316.**

☺ BEST TRAILHEAD
Colorado Trail/Waterton Canyon (Denver)

While you are pulling up to any trailhead, a sense of expectation and an openness to discovery accompany you. Whether you're out for a day hike or planning to trek along the 469-mile Colorado Trail from Denver to Durango, the Waterton Canyon Trailhead awaits.

A dusty parking area, often filled with cars left behind by day hikers and mountain bikers, announces your arrival at the beginning of the trail. Due to its location at the head of a canyon, you find yourself secluded from the city only moments after setting off on the mellow grade road. Keep your eyes peeled for the bighorn sheep that scramble along the upper reaches of the rocky canyon; beware of other wildlife sightings, including an occasional stealthy mountain lion. The initial route follows an old Denver South Park & Pacific rail bed. The train used to take Denver residents six miles up the canyon beside the South Platte River to Strontia Springs Resort. The resort no longer exists, replaced by a dam of the same name; nonetheless, this historic area remains a compelling draw to hikers, bikers and an occasional hopeful sportsperson fishing in the trout-laden waters.

The dirt road ends at the base of Strontia Springs Dam, becoming a single-track trail that after about ten miles arrives at the confluence of the North Fork of the South Platte River and the South Platte River. From here, a road continues up into Cheesman Canyon and eventually to the small town of Deckers and some of the best trout fishing near the Front Range. To reach Waterton Canyon head west on C-470 to Wadsworth Blvd. (Hwy. 121) and then south for several miles to the parking area.

☺ BEST FUN TIMES AT A RESERVOIR
Lake Pueblo State Park

Expectations don't exactly soar when you mention Pueblo, but over the years it has become a worthy destination. If you haven't been to the reservoir at Pueblo State Park, you'll first be impressed by its sheer size. Not that it competes with Lake Powell, but along the Front Range this is our favorite. Why? Lake Pueblo offers a variety of pleasant options for escaping the heat, and a starkly beautiful sixty-mile shoreline that snakes along the interior of this massive state park. It almost always finds ways to surprise and delight its increasing number of visitors.

Swimming, sailing, windsurfing, fishing and motorboating are all excellent choices at the reservoir. Set aside just below the dam and you'll find the Rock Canyon Swim Beach (open Memorial Day to Labor Day), with a sandy waterfront, shady cottonwoods and even a waterslide. Two marinas—north shore and south shore—provide mooring and boat rentals for those wanting to explore the forty-five-hundred-acre lake. Sailors love the constant buffeting wind at Lake Pueblo, especially in spring. Most motorcraft are used to day fish for walleye, large- and small-mouth bass, sunfish, catfish and good-sized trout. Windsurfing is permitted anywhere, but thanks to the snowmelt, beware of chilly water and arrive equipped with a wetsuit through May. Windsurfers should check out the designated launch area on the north shore. If you aren't into plying the water, try hiking or biking on the many miles of marked trails inside the park. Below the dam, excellent wildlife viewing opportunities can be found along the Arkansas River at the **Greenway and Nature Center** and **the Raptor Center of Pueblo**. The Greenway and Nature Center also hosts some excellent events, including the Rolling River Raft Race and one of the state's top bluegrass festivals.

Open year-round, Lake Pueblo State Park requires park passes and camping permits. Four hundred mostly cushy campsites (showers, hookups and toilets) fill up on summer weekends, making reservations essential (**1-800-678-2267**). For general information contact the Park Headquarters and Visitors Center on the south shore. To get to the "Rez," drive west of town on Hwy. 96 until you see the signs. **640 Pueblo Reservoir Rd., Pueblo, CO 81005; (719) 561-9320; www.coloradoparks.org.**

BEST ROCK CLIMBING CLOSE TO THE CITY
Eldorado Canyon (near Boulder)

Whether you are a climber yourself or one who likes to watch their death-defying antics, few earthly places match Eldorado Canyon. Climbers from around the world flock to the near-vertical fifteen hundred-foot walls of ancient rock that line both sides of South Boulder Creek. If you already think of yourself as some kind of rock jock, there's no better place to entice you and your belay partner out of the climbing gym. The "Bastille" and various routes up seventy-five hundred foot Shirt Tail Peak at the park's northern edge remain the most famous testing grounds for your climbing skills. Remember, though, this area requires proper training and equipment, so don't even think of scrambling up these rocks unless you are ready. Fixed bolts or pitons on the routes are *not* maintained, so please use caution.

If you are thinking about learning this sport, check in at the International Alpine School in Eldorado Springs. It has an excellent reputation and, thanks to its prime location, can help ensure your safety. The Colorado Mountain Club and the City of Boulder also offer climbing instruction in the canyon. For additional climbing resources and detailed information about the many popular Eldorado routes, stop in at Neptune Mountaineering in Boulder, founded by Everest conqueror Gary Neptune.

Certainly one of the best attributes of this area lies just outside the state park. Ending your climbing day by slipping into the cool, clean waters at Eldorado Artesian Springs makes for a perfect finish. No camping is allowed at Eldorado Canyon State Park. To get here take Hwy. 93 (Broadway) south from Boulder for 5.5 miles. Turn right on Eldorado Springs Dr. and continue for three miles to the park entrance. Fee charged. **(303) 494-3943;** **www.coloradoparks.org.**

BEST FOOT RACE
Bolder Boulder

Sneaker-clad feet by the tens of thousands run, plod, waddle, walk, shuffle and fly. Bodies of every shape, height, width and weight snake through the streets in a shimmering display and range of athletic ability. From serious wheelchair racers to families out for a 10K stroll; from weekend joggers to elite, world-class studs; from babes in strollers to eighty-something marvels, running aficionados celebrate this annual Rite of Spring known as the Bolder Boulder. It's a spectacle, a happening, a wonder unlike anything else in the world.

First off the start line every Memorial Day, inspiring disabled athletes whir in their low-slung three-wheelers, arms pumping like well-oiled pistons, propelling themselves around the byways of Boulder. Next, wave after wave of citizen racers bolt at the crack of the starting gun, spreading out along the winding, rolling, sometimes grueling 6.2-mile course, some running for a good time, others out for a good time. In this crazy crowd you might see Elvis gyrating in his blue suede shoes or Abe Lincoln lumbering in his top hat. Sauntering brides and grooms in gown and tux have been overheard saying "I do" to a backward-running parson. If that's not enough, spectators along the way are at least as entertaining as the main event. Belly dancers delight the passing drove, and rock bands keep a pulsing beat to run by.

On their way through residential portions of the course, overheated runners get welcome relief from garden hoses sprayed by obliging townsfolk in their front-yards. When the streets finally clear, elite runners from Europe, Africa and North and South America challenge the course, their strong strides broadcast live to a statewide television audience.

The University of Colorado's Folsom Field, filled with thirty-five thousand well-wishers, provides the venue for the dramatic climax of this annual tradition. Loud cheers greet the first elite runners on their final push, circling the field in a last triumphant lap to the finish line. Jubilation reigns in this yearly festival called the Bolder Boulder. (303) 444-RACE.

☺ BEST STATEWIDE EVENT
Colorado State Fair (Pueblo)

Despite recent financial pressures, the Colorado State Fair remains one of the state's favorite all-around special events. Beginning in mid-August, this action-packed two and a half weeks combine championship rodeo with hundreds of exhibits and a chance for visitors to see the requisite lambs, steers, hogs, horses and other animals that journey to the fair. There's no better place for salespeople to hawk their wares, including food processors that dice, chop and much, much more. Likewise, you can find any number of trinkets or some really nice western wear, especially leather hats, coats and belts.

But the real draw to the State Fair has always been its live entertainment. A free stage with local talent and regional acts remains a mainstay, but be sure to check the schedule to see who will be performing on the main stage. In past years, topflight musical entertainers have included Tom Jones, Bob Dylan, Mary Chapin Carpenter and George Strait. Kids love the children's barnyard, carnival rides and games, and adults enjoy wandering among the scores of free exhibit booths. Throughout the duration of the fair, more than a million people throng to the festival grounds, but each day is never too crowded to enjoy. To find out more about rubbing elbows with your fellow Coloradans at the fairgrounds, call the information line at 1-800-444-FAIR.

☺ BEST OFFBEAT OUTDOOR FESTIVAL
Kinetic Conveyance Challenge (Boulder)

For two decades the Boulder Reservoir has served as the site of an outrageous springtime race among comical, creative crafts crossing both land and water on nothing but human power (beer could be the other primary propulsion agent). Many conveyances feature engineering savvy with hundreds of moving parts;

others simply manage to combine the sleek simplicity of a bike mounted on a kayak.

Every year the event embraces a silly outlook that overpowers any sense of serious drive to be the quickest to the finish line. Teams win in categories such as best newcomers, engineering, perseverance, sportsmanship and looks. Ridiculous team names—such as the skunky Pepe Le Pew Eau de Parfum—match the sheer audacity of grown men and women sitting inside of an oversized toilet or wearing special reservoir-tipped hats. The fastest teams arrive at the finish merely forty-five minutes after the start, whereas others straggle in three hours later. Some don't make it past the beach or a few yards into the water. One of the highlights has to be watching teams of participants climb out of the water and over the oozy mudflats.

Top bands play high-energy sets for the assembled twenty thousand (or more) fans of this annual nonsense. Food and drink always come in bountiful supply. Be sure to bring your rain, wind and sun gear, because the weather is almost as unpredictable as the contestants. Sponsored by KBCO radio station in early May; call (303) 444-5600 for ticket and parking information.

BEST SCENERY AT A GOLF COURSE
Arrowhead Golf Club (near Denver)

Only a handful of golf courses feature the kind of dramatic beauty that actually distracts from your play. Arrowhead Golf Club, near Roxborough State Park (see Best "Primitive" State Park on page 22), happens to be one of them. The winding fairways and manicured greens have found a spectacular home nestled amid jutting red sandstone rocks that march along the eastern foothills of the Rocky Mountains. The red rock backdrop is a geological kissing cousin to Garden of the Gods in Colorado Springs and Red Rocks Park and Amphitheater.

Designed in 1970 by Robert Trent Jones Jr., the 6,682-yard, par 70 course brings tough elements into its undulating layout. Since surviving a series of financial starts and stops, Arrowhead has become a mainstay in *Golf Digest*'s top seventy-five public courses in America. It's an unforgettable golf experience, but be wary of areas of impassable scrub oak as well as seventy-six strategically placed sand traps and six lakes. The course looks deceptively open but plays rather tight.

Watch out for the 436-yard, par 4 fourth hole. "If you get out of here with a bogie, feel proud," says the pro. "The green alone can easily turn into a four putt." After a downhill tee shot, get within two hundred yards of the fast, north-tilting, elevated green, or you can almost be assured of a penalty stroke. Why? Consider the rocks and scrub oak to the left, a sand trap to the right, a gully on the left front, and, yes, water hazards on the right front. The back nine features the prettiest holes, including hole thirteen, where you drive through two jutting red rocks and encounter a ninety-foot drop. *Golf Digest* calls hole fourteen "one of the most beautiful holes on the planet."

No doubt, you must be on your game to feel good about your score at Arrowhead, but even if you end up flogging the ball, you'll enjoy the scenery. You will likely spot some birds and animals (three hundred species inhabit the area), including nesting eagles and hawks as well as foxes and deer.

Stop in at the pro shop and recently renovated clubhouse restaurant. Although memberships continue to be sold at Arrowhead, public tee times remain available (rather pricey, but worth it). You can call seven days in advance. Please use spikeless golf shoes. Located forty-five minutes southwest of Denver at **10850 W. Sundown Trail;** **(303) 973-9614.**

BEST SCOTTISH-STYLE LINKS
Riverdale Dunes (Brighton)

Brighton, best known for the Mile High Flea Market and barren agricultural and industrial development, can now be known as an excellent golf oasis. The area features two public courses: the Knolls, and the newer, longer Scottish-style Riverdale Dunes course. Designed by the father-and-son team of Pete and Perry Dye in 1986, the Dunes features 7,027 yards of gently rolling fairways and difficult, fast greens along an alluvial plain next to the Platte River.

The course was completed by bringing in thousands of cubic meters of dirt. Its length is characterized, of course, by dunes, as well as rolling mounds, swales and bunkers. With trees coming into play on only two holes, these wide-open links provide a unique set of challenges—the word "forgiving" will not enter your vocabulary often as you try to keep your score down. But the course has a high-country appeal with views of the majestic Rockies as a perfect backdrop to a day outside. Check out the award-winning pro shop and well-appointed restaurant and clubhouse. Reasonable green fees. **13300 Riverdale Rd.;** **(303) 659-6700.**

☺ BEST DISK GOLF COURSE
Edora Park (Fort Collins)

Forget the $100-plus fees and four hours it takes to play a round of golf. Pack up your favorite disk(s) and head out to our favorite course at Edora Park. You don't even have to abide by a strict dress code: Go ahead and wear your cutoffs and T-shirt. Nobody will care. But that's not to say that people who play this course are lackadaisical about their sport. Though caddies are nowhere to be found and nobody's bragging about their new set of graphite clubs, you will see serious folfers (Frisbee golfers). They're the ones carrying special sets of disks of varying weights for driving, chipping and, yes, putting. Many still like flinging their 165-gram standard Frisbee for the entire course.

The eighteen "holes" at this course can be found mounted on steel poles with dangling chains to guide the disks inward before dropping into a metal basket. You can pick up an official scorecard, which maps out the holes, at the **Wright Life Store** (1-800-321-8883) in town. A creek runs through the park, creating a decent water hazard on several holes. Watch for pedestrians who take their chances walking across your fairway. Have a most excellent time with your friends anytime between 6 A.M. and 11 P.M. The mature, beautifully landscaped park also features tennis courts, walking and biking paths, a BMX track and horseshoe pits. To get to Edora Park travel three blocks east of the intersection of Lemay Ave. and Stewart St. **(970) 221-6640.**

☺ BEST ZOO

Cheyenne Mountain Zoo (Colorado Springs)

Okay, so we really had only two contenders to choose from—Denver Zoo and Cheyenne Mountain Zoo—but it was still a difficult choice. When all things were considered, the dramatic mountainside setting of the Cheyenne Mountain Zoo set it apart. Just be sure to bring your walking shoes, unless you want to climb into one of the open-sided trolleys for a ride around the sloping roads that lead to the animal habitats. Being smallish, it doesn't take days to see all of the zoo's animal inhabitants. People, however, are lured back time and again by the richness of endangered species and the large, natural settings provided for the playful primates. Discover more than 650 zoo animals, including hungry giraffes, downcast vultures and proud birds of prey, snow leopards, lions and black-footed ferrets.

An attraction near the zoo but at a higher elevation is the **Shrine of the Sun,** dedicated to famed American humorist Will Rogers. A drive up the mountain to the Shrine of the Sun is worthwhile for the sweeping views alone. Once there, you'll also hear a taped Will Rogers monologue and see photos of his life, which ended in a 1935 plane crash. The admission fee to the zoo includes the Shrine of the Sun. Open daily 9 A.M. to 5 P.M. in summer, 9 A.M. to 4 P.M. in winter. From I-25, head south on Nevada Ave. Take a right on Lake Ave. and head to The Broadmoor. Turn right and up Mirada Rd., following signs to the zoo. **4250 Cheyenne Mt. Zoo Rd.; (719) 475-9555; www.pikes-peak.com/zoo.**

☺ BEST POLAR BEAR HABITAT
Denver Zoo

Ever since the rage over Klondike and Snow, the two bear cubs that needed to be bottle-fed by zookeepers after being rejected by their mother, this town has been polar bear crazy. Of course those cute, cuddly bundles of white fur grew into menacing, humongous adults with sharp teeth and long claws designed for ripping flesh, but they're still fun to watch from a distance. Now that Klondike and Snow have been shipped out, you'd think the attention would die off, but noooooo.

The Denver Zoo features its star cubs—Ulaq and Berit—in a terrific habitat that seems to encourage active play instead of only lazing around. Two more cubs were born in November 1999. Zoo visitors seem to pay nearly as much attention to these new white fluff balls as they did to their predecessors. Families have been lining up to watch the new cubs learn to swim and play at the water's edge. You can head down below to a window, which provides a stunning view underwater . . . at least it's stunning when the bears decide to go for a dip; otherwise it resembles a huge aquarium without fish. If you're there when papa bear swims right up to the glass, it's a sight not soon forgotten!

Besides polar bears, the zoo has become a total attraction, with the indoor Tropical Discovery (complete with colorful fish, venomous snakes, menacing crocodiles and snapping sea turtles), Primate Panorama (you kind of wonder who's watching whom in this large exhibit area, featuring our evolutionary predecessors), and the range of 1,300 other bird and animal species. Lots of programs complement the animal sights, sounds and smells. Check out the newborn animals at the nursery. Fee charged. Located at **E. 23rd St. between Colorado Blvd. and York St.;** (303) 331-4110; www.denverzoo.org.

Two polar bears lounge next to the water on a warm fall day at the Denver Zoo. *Photo by Doug Whitehead.*

Where to Eat, Drink & Stay

BEST BREW TOWN
Fort Collins

In Fort Collins, the explosion of craft brewing can be seen in the shadow of a behemoth called Budweiser. This college town manages to hold its own against Denver with a delightful mix of microbrewery and brewpub experiences alongside a fascinating glimpse at big-time corporate brewing. Pick the experience to suit your mood or your taste buds.

Don't miss the low-key factory tour (on weekdays at 2 P.M. you'll see the factory in full action) and sample the variety of excellent brews at **New Belgium Brewing Company (500 Linden Ave.; [970] 221-0524; www.newbelgium.com).** In the airy, well-appointed tasting room, the staff serves up platters of small goblets with a mouth-watering array of tastes, including the famous "Fat Tire" brand. With chairs and bar stools, this place seems to take its customers' comfort seriously. The state-of-the-art brewing facility prides itself on environmental friendliness, and employees swear this is the best place they've ever worked—after a year on the job, each employee is given a sturdy red bike similar to the one perched on their flagship brand's label. Here you can pick up a six-pack, a half-gallon "growler" or a keg.

Down the road, try out the up-and-coming **Odell Brewing Company (800 E. Lincoln Ave.; [970] 498-9070; www.odells.com).** Their popular and hoppy-tasting 90 Shilling Ale finishes clean and instantly reminds us of Scotland with its hearty flavor.

For a smaller, warehouse-style brewing operation stop in at **H. C. Berger Brewing Company (1900 E. Lincoln Ave.; [970] 493-9044; www.hcberger.com)**—try their Ault and the chocolate stout.

For a night out with food and a game of pool, head straight to the long brick room at **Coopersmith's Pub and Brewing Company (#5 Old Town Square; [970] 498-0483).**

The world's fastest-producing brewery, the massive **Anheuser-Bush Brewery** on the northern outskirts of town (at I-25 and Harmony Rd., exit 271), represents a totally different extreme. More than two thousand cans per minute roll off the line; the well-organized tour takes an hour. At the hamlet, you get a close-up look at the groomed Clydesdales before retreating to the hospitality center to sample some of the product and buy a cap or key chain. **(970) 490-4500.**

BEST COLORADO CHILES
Pueblo Chiles

At his fresh produce stand, Carl Musso lights a gas burner, pours a sackful of green chiles into a large steel drum and turns the handle like a lottery drawing, constantly rotating the hot peppers as they crackle and sizzle above the hot flame. The distinctive aroma of roasting peppers wafts to waiting noses, and stomachs begin to growl. But the mouthwatering taste of these Pueblo homegrowns does not happen by chance. Musso and thirteen other area farmers have banded together under the brand name Mira Sol to create some of the tastiest red and green chiles in the world.

Trade publication *Fiery Foods* magazine awarded Mira Sol chiles some top prizes in a 1999 international competition. Growers claim that Pueblo's hot days, cool nights and unique soil create ideal chile-growing conditions. From the first of August until mid-October, roadside farm stands along a ten-mile stretch of Business Hwy. 50 east of Pueblo brim with fresh chiles. If you run out of the fresh ones, check your local grocer for Mira Sol chiles and salsa in a jar. Devotees of this delectable vegetable celebrate on the last weekend of September each year at the Pueblo Chile & Frijole Festival. Music, dance and food make for a "hot" time in old downtown Pueblo. **Mira Sol Chile Corporation, (719) 948-3581; www.mirasolchile.com.**

☺ BEST FREE TOUR
Celestial Seasonings Tour of Tea (Boulder)

Poke your nose into the "mint room" at Celestial Seasonings in Boulder and you'll never forget the power of herbs. The strength of the aroma almost knocks you backward. During the rest of the fascinating thirty-five-minute tour, you'll discover a wide range of wonderful scents. Include the rest of the large complex, where workers mix and bag an astonishing one thousand bags of tea per minute, and an overview of all other Celestial operations, and you have the best free tour we can imagine.

The company was founded in 1969 when nineteen-year-old Mo Siegel started gathering herbs in Aspen. It has grown into an international success story. In addition to the free tour and tea tasting in the little gift shop, you can make a day of it by stopping for lunch at the Celestial Café. The factory floor gets pretty loud, so children under age five are not permitted for that part of the tour. Guided tours are offered on the hour from 10 A.M. to 3 P.M., Mon.through Sat., and Sun. from 11 A.M. to 3 P.M. From the Boulder Turnpike (Hwy. 36) take the Foothills Pkwy.

exit and follow it north through Boulder; the road automatically feeds onto Hwy. 119 (the Diagonal) and continues northeast toward Longmont. Turn right, heading east, at Jay Rd. (stoplight) and drive east one mile to Spike Rd. Turn left and continue north for a half-mile to the plant. **4600 Sleepytime Dr., Boulder, CO 80301;** (303) 581-1202.

☺ BEST CHICAGO CUISINE IN COLORADO
Mustard's Last Stand (Denver and Boulder)

We tried to keep away from oxymorons in our "best of" titles . . . really. But thinking of Chicago and cuisine in the same slightly acrid breath brings the image of a fully garnished hot dog complete with wedges of tomato, sweet relish, a fat slab of dill pickle, raw chopped onions, mustard and sauerkraut all topped with a hot pepper. When you stop at Mustard's near the CU–Boulder campus in Boulder or Mustard's II near the University of Denver campus, you'll conjure up a semblance of the Windy City, too. Especially if you order a red Vienna dog with the works and a side of perfectly cooked fries.

The stand's variations on a theme include Polish sausage, burgers and even a tasty veggie dog made out of compressed tofu. "That gets the most complaints," says the guy behind the counter. "People think we gave 'em a real dog by mistake . . . these tofu dogs are that good!"

If you want your hot dog done right, don't pressure the counter help to hurry or expect them to treat you with a subservient attitude, because this is just not the place. But when your name is called and you pick up your wax-paper-wrapped creation, you are about to enter a Chicago dimension. Check out the photo wall of official vendors of Vienna Beef products from as far away as Hawaii. Take one of just a few seats inside or, better yet, find a shaded outdoor table and watch the university students hurry by. Located in Denver near the corner of Evans and University Blvd. at **2801 S. University;** (303) 722-7936; in Boulder at **1719 Broadway;** (303) 444-5841.

The best Chicago-style hot dog can be found at Mustard's Last Stand in Boulder and Denver. *Photo by Doug Whitehead.*

BEST BEANS WITH BREAKFAST
Lucile's (Boulder)

Let the slow cooking of red beans at Lucile's set a leisurely breakfast pace for you and a special friend. If an opening exists, nab a table on the front porch on a warm summer morning, and then settle in for some chicory coffee and delicious beignets. If you head inside of the old restored house, you'll find tables decorated with faded calico napkins and nestled throughout the home's small, intimate rooms. As the coffee begins to warm you up, settle in on your breakfast entree. Lots of egg dishes entice, but nothing hits your belly better than the kitchen's special Cajun Breakfast—a hearty serving of red beans alongside poached eggs and hollandaise sauce, all served with grits or potatoes and a fresh buttermilk biscuit. You might also consider the wonderful eggs sardu. Around lunch the menu includes spicy gumbo, shrimp Creole, crawfish étouffée and blackened red snapper. You just can't miss with this reasonably priced Boulder mainstay. You can find Lucile's on a side street just off the Boulder Mall. For more than a decade it has attracted locals to its unobtrusive location, so expect a wait, especially on weekends. **2124 Fifteenth St.; (303) 442-4743.**

We should mention that **Dot's Diner**, in a converted gas station at about Seventh and Pearl Sts. in Boulder, was in the running for this category thanks to their generous servings of tasty huevos rancheros.

BEST NIGHTLIFE DISTRICT
LoDo (Denver)

In the late 1980s, LoDo could have been called NoDo. It simply didn't exist. That is, except in the minds of modern-day pioneers who had a vision of refurbishing Lower Downtown's (hence the name LoDo) turn-of-the-century brick warehouses into something unique to Denver. In an era of sameness, the LoDo area, bordered by Fourteenth St. and 22nd St. between Larimer St. and the tracks, brings a unique vibrancy to downtown Denver. Thousands have moved into the area's lofts, so, unlike most downtown areas, the streets don't roll up at night. Quite the contrary; on many nights you'll see crowds down here until the bars close at 2 A.M.

During eighty regular-season games each year, the Colorado Rockies bring hordes of nightlife seekers downtown. Most games will find corner ticket sellers offering discounted tickets to the games. Depending on your perspective, you might decide to come down here during a Rockies' game or avoid it at all costs. After scoring a parking place, you have your choice, ranging from dozens of sports

Denver's Union Station, adorned with festive holiday lights, looms over the high energy of the lower downtown district. *Photo by Doug Whitehead.*

bars and several brewpubs to dance clubs, wine or martini bars and live jazz and blues clubs. Here are our top picks for a week of nightlife:

Monday: El-Chapultepec—A good night to pull up a Naugahyde bar stool and listen to some cool, live traditional jazz at this Denver institution. **1962 Market St.;** (303) 295-9126.

Tuesday: **Denver Chop House and Brewery**—In the shadow of Coors Field, this rather dark but luxurious place serves good handcrafted beer and high-quality food. **1735 Nineteenth St.;** (303) 296-0800.

Wednesday: **Wynkoop Brewpub**—The true original, this outstanding brewpub serves up a selection of ales and features a second-floor pool hall. **1634 Eighteenth St.;** (303) 297-2700.

Thursday: **Jackson's All American Grille**—If sports pulses through your veins and you just aren't happy without TVs blaring minute-by-minute scores, dis is da place! **1520 Twentieth St.;** (303) 2998-7625.

Friday: **LoDo Bar and Grille**—A tidal wave of people head here before and immediately after Rockies games. Wander through the crowds inside and head immediately to the rooftop on a summer night. **1946 Market St.; (303) 293-8555.**

Saturday: **Soiled Dove**—Even if you're in the back row of high-back chairs at Denver's top live-music nightspot, you'll only be forty-five feet from the stage. The excellent sounds of top local and national names in rock, jazz, blues and folk music fill the room. **1949 Market St.; (303) 299-0100.**

Sunday: **Cruise Room at the Oxford Hotel**—This classy, restored art deco bar opened in the 1930s and remains the place for a perfectly shaken martini. **1600 Seventeenth St.**

BEST EXOTIC TEAHOUSE
Boulder Dushanbe Tea House

The decorative, multicolored elements of this teahouse can be attributed to the hard work of more than forty artisans from Tajikistan. They toiled for some dozen years in their homeland creating hand-carved, distinctly painted elements for this extraordinarily detailed building. Crate by crate, thousands of pieces were shipped to Boulder as a "gift" before being reconstructed as what we see today. All of this effort

celebrates the two towns' special sister-city relationship. We never did hear what gift Boulder sent in return for this elaborate gift, but suspect a truckload of Boulder's own Celestial Seasonings tea would not quite suffice.

Dushanbe's (Doo-shawn-bay) unparalleled craftsmanship can be seen in its tables, stools and columns as well as the ceiling and exterior ceramic panels. The instant you look up at the brightly colored, elaborate rectangular structure from its well-kept garden courtyard and outdoor seating area, you know a special experience awaits. But without the Himalayas looming

The careful craftsmanship of the interior of Boulder Dushanbe Tea House leaves a lasting impression on the senses. *Photo by Bruce Caughey.*

more than twenty-four thousand feet in the background, you'll have to use your imagination before you can actually see yourself traveling along the Silk Route to this destination.

The teahouse features a carefully selected menu for lunch, teatime, dinner and weekend brunch. The worldly selections borrow from cuisines ranging from Indian to Mediterranean to Mexican. Dinner entrees include Persian lamb kabobs, stew and Thai curry noodles. At other times, you'll see tofu, egg dishes, pasta and unique salads and even an excellent breakfast burrito. Depending on your mealtime, these choices are complemented by beer, wine, juices, coffee and, of course, an excellent variety of teas. The strong black teas range from classic Earl Grey to Darjeeling from India. Or try the mild, low-caffeine tastes of the green teas, with delicate flavors emerging from almost clear liquid. For a caffeine buzz from tea that is equivalent to coffee, try the Matta Latte. In nice weather, retreat to the tables alongside bubbling Boulder Creek. Otherwise, the inside beckons with a unique sensory experience even before you taste the food. **1770 Thirteenth St.; (303) 442-4993.**

BEST POOL HALL
Wynkoop Brewing Company (Denver)

When John Hickenlooper opened the first brewpub in Colorado since Prohibition ended—on the outskirts of downtown Denver in the 1980s—people thought he was crazy. Yeah, crazy as a fox. The out-of-work geologist turned legendary marketer jumped ahead of the pack by a few years, and he now enjoys one of downtown's best locations. Thanks to Coors Field and the rash of development around lower downtown (see Best Nightlife District on page 38), the Wynkoop continues to draw crowds. Hickenlooper's brewpub spawned other business ideas, but none is better than a terrific second-floor pool hall featuring the same great beer and atmosphere as the popular downstairs restaurant/pub.

So take a cue and head upstairs to the high-quality slate tables, which rent by the hour. You will find twenty-two full-sized billiard tables, five dart lanes, shuffleboard and a full bar. They are spaced so you won't get jabbed often, and the upbeat crowd makes the whole experience uplifting, in contrast to the dark, dank pool halls we have all tried at one time or another. If you get there between 3 and 6 P.M., you can enjoy happy-hour prices on pints of fresh beer (our favorite is the St. Charles E.S.B.) and a relatively quiet game of pool. When the downtown office buildings let out, people stream to this place, and long waits for tables become common. For a truly special event, reserve one of the private billiards rooms. Located at **1634 Eighteenth St.; (303) 297-2700; www.wynkoop.com.**

☺ BEST FRIED CHICKEN
Castle Café (Castle Rock)

In these days of endless salads, tofu burgers and protein drinks, we all look for the perfect place to backslide a bit to the simpler days, when we didn't know better. For family-style food, especially fried chicken done to perfection—crispy on the outside, tender and juicy on the inside—there's no better place we've found than the Castle Café. The owners gutted a historic, rundown stone building on Castle Rock's main street (Wilcox) and created a casual atmosphere with a focus on heaping servings of homestyle food. Slide into a comfortable booth, order a heavy frosted mug of beer or an icy margarita, and settle in for a meal of complete and utter decadence.

Those not in the mood for chicken might try a steak, prime rib or fish dish. The side dishes appeal almost as much as the entrees. Along with its fried chicken specialty, the Castle Café has become known for its buttery mashed potatoes, rich brown gravy, tasty slaw and hot rolls. As you lick your fingers clean, you'll keep thinking, "Dang, this is good!" If for some reason you don't get enough to eat, top off your meal with a massive serving of dark chocolate cake. Open nightly for dinner. **403 Wilcox; (303) 814-2716.**

BEST MEXICAN FOOD
La Cueva (Denver)

Now that we have sampled burritos, enchiladas and, yes, margaritas across the Front Range, we can honestly say you won't be disappointed by La Cueva. Set along a stretch of East Colfax surrounded by pawn shops lies a hidden gem called "The Cave" that has flourished for more than two decades. The Nuñoz family insists on fixing food from scratch with the freshest ingredients available, using recipes from their native home of Guanajuato, Mexico. Actually, "Papa" does the cooking and "Mama" greets the customers. "I don't cook a bean!" she laughs when asked about the food preparation. "But I promise, everything is homemade."

Regular customers told us they cannot remember one bad experience at La Cueva. If your Spanish is rusty, you may need to play a little charades to communicate with the prompt, polite servers. You will be delighted by the service and care you receive, even as you are waiting for a table to free up— which happens a lot, especially on weekends.

From the moment a black crock of fresh, spicy salsa arrives, you know you're in for a treat. The light, almost greaseless flautas topped with guacamole and sour cream are out of this world. The chicken mole and tacos al carbón remain perennial favorites, and the chile rellenos couldn't be more appealing (unless you like 'em crispy). The beef and chicken melt in your mouth; the marinated and slow-baked meat is moist, tender, and almost greaseless. A side of beans doesn't mean a side of lard here, so go ahead and chow down. Sometimes the best item on a menu is the simplest: green chili smothers the burritos or comes in a bowl with warm tortillas. End your meal with a sopaipilla, flan or an empanada and you will be back here whenever you think of dining Mexican. Located in Aurora at **9742 E. Colfax Ave.;** (303) 367-1422.

BEST BED-AND-BREAKFAST
Abriendo Inn (Pueblo)

Whether you are a business traveler or are just visiting the Pueblo area, you will appreciate the homey ambiance of this lovely and well-run B&B. Since 1989, when the restoration of this mammoth, foursquare 1906 Victorian was complete, guests have been returning year after year, often filling the home to capacity. Why do people love this place? It might be because of the decadent morning meals, or possibly it's Kerrelyn McCafferty Trent, the friendly owner. The garden setting in central Pueblo, only a couple of blocks from the Union Avenue historic district, offers another reason to stay, as does the sheer elegance of the common areas combined with the practical amenities of the rooms.

You shouldn't come to the Abriendo to get completely away from modern features; each room has them, including televisions and telephones and recently added data ports to better serve business clients. You will also discover a decorator charm, careful craftsmanship and imaginative use of space unknown to most hotels. The inn offers ten clean, comfortable bedrooms with private bathrooms. The common areas truly inspire the friendly interaction of the guests. As lace curtains filter the sunlight, guests gather in the living room for lingering moments of relaxation. On a warm afternoon, find a wicker chair on the wide veranda and enjoy the garden setting and large trees. Help yourself to a complimentary cup of tea or rummage through the fridge for a chilled soda or bottled water as you settle in and enjoy this historic home. During the holidays, each room has a Christmas tree and individually themed decorations; an eighteen-foot-tall tree decorated in Victorian-style silver and lace can be found in the living room during the season.

The sunny dining room and back patio provide a backdrop for a full breakfast. When we visited, guests walked into the dining room for freshly brewed coffee before diving into their meal of stuffed ham and cheddar French toast as well as oatmeal coffee cake with a coconut topping. The next day's offering: a breakfast enchilada with seafood. The inn discourages guests from bringing young children; pets are not allowed. No smoking. A range of reasonable rates for various-sized rooms. **300 W. Abriendo Ave., Pueblo, CO 81004; (719) 544-2703.**

BEST REFURBISHED INN
Cliff House (Manitou Springs)

The many transformations of the Cliff House have resulted in a very beautiful final stage. The smashing overhaul of this 126-year-old structure will transport you in many ways, most notably off the somewhat funky, somewhat hit-and-miss action on the streets of Manitou Springs. In short, the Cliff House appears a bit out of place. This majestic building, with its stunning interior rehab, deserves several hundred acres of gardens surrounding it—with some horse stables, a burbling creek full of hungry trout and a serene place to watch the sunrise.

Instead, the Cliff House is crushed between a hillside of houses and the busy trinket shops and arcades that give Manitou its no-snobs-allowed charm. An enchanting setting? That's a stretch. But you still need to stay here. It's a perfect spot for getting away if you don't have all day to get somewhere. It's intimate, homelike and welcoming. The rooms are beautifully appointed; indeed, the deluxe suites practically insist that you relax. Your room fee includes afternoon tea, a satisfying complimentary breakfast and travel tips from the staff. The restaurant offers a fine assortment of creative dishes, fine wines and friendly Colorado service—sincere but not too much.

This structure has endured floods, fire and multiple attempts to revive it. This time, barring a disaster, the latest incarnation of the Cliff House should be here for a long, long time. **306 Canon Ave., Manitou Springs, CO 80829; 1-888-212-7000. E-mail: inquire@thecliffhouse.com.**

BEST HISTORIC HOTEL
Brown Palace (Denver)

Since 1892 the Brown Palace has served as a tangible monument to the ingenuity and core beliefs of this ever-optimistic city. Now dwarfed by imposing steel and glass office buildings, the nine-story Brown Palace, designed by Frank Edbrooke, still deserves respect and admiration from passersby at its prime downtown location. Built of native red granite and Arizona sandstone, the unusual triangular shape and

Victorian architecture leave a distinctive mark on this most famous of Colorado hotels. Inside, six tiers of cast-iron balconies lead upward to a magnificent Tiffany stained-glass ceiling some eighty feet above. The lobby's Mexican onyx walls and white marble floor lend the hotel an elegant permanence that today's buildings rarely capture.

Now entering its second century of operation, the hotel manages to reinvent itself without forgetting the past. Comfortable furnishings can be found throughout the 230 guest rooms (and twenty-five spacious suites), which come replete with brass beds, TVs hidden inside armoires, down comforters, linen duvets and private bathrooms with brass fixtures. Rooms come decorated in an art deco style, a more traditional Victorian style and even a kind of western baroque. Famous guests of the Brown include The Beatles, who stayed here in 1964 while performing at Red Rocks. Dwight D. "Ike" Eisenhower based his 1952 presidential campaign inside the hotel and maintained the "Western White House" here during his presidency.

The beautifully adorned, comfortable lobby sets the tone for the hotel. Polished tunes from a grand piano waft by as guests enjoy high tea or, perhaps, an evening cocktail. The hotel never forgets its western roots; every January it still proudly displays the prize bull from the National Western Stock Show in the lobby. Around the perimeter of the atrium lobby, guests may choose to dine at the ultra-fancy Palace Arms, the classy Ellyngton's (great brunch) or the steady Ship Tavern nestled in the narrow prow of the building. Rest assured that the well-trained staff at the Brown Palace will make your entire stay comfortable and relaxed. Expensive. **321 Seventeenth St.; (303) 296-6666.**

BEST EXCLUSIVE NIGHT'S STAY
The Broadmoor (Colorado Springs)

Feel like royalty by checking into The Broadmoor, an exceptional, historic resort set at the base of Cheyenne Mountain in Colorado Springs. Much more than a hotel, this sprawling collection of buildings, situated around a large lake, conjures up images of Europe. As you drive toward the entrance, your view shifts from beautiful landscaped gardens to the rose hues of impeccably maintained, Italian Renaissance–style buildings. The Mediterranean feel of The Broadmoor sets the tone for the entire complex, and you feel like you have transitioned back to a timeless age—one where unhurried hospitality remains something of an art form. Sure, it's expensive, but flawless service is everywhere. That happens when you have the equivalent of two staff for each single guest room.

Built in 1918 by Spencer Penrose, a mining magnate, The Broadmoor's opulent surroundings include marble staircases, sparkling chandeliers and a fabulous collection of original art and antiques. Penrose and his wife traveled the world to find just the right mix of fine art, tapestries, sculptures and furnishings. Spacious, luxurious guest rooms include the finest toiletries, plush towels and robes and, of course, room service. Three eighteen-hole golf courses sweep in and around the complex, or you can try one of the sixteen tennis courts, three heated pools, biking and hiking trails, equestrian courses or trap, skeet and rifle shooting ranges. Check out one of the nine restaurants, ranging from the Charles Court, an elegant English country manor, to raucous sing-alongs at the Golden Bee pub. **1 Lake Ave.; (719) 634-7711.**

Northwest

Previous page: Fly fishing on one of Colorado's best rivers, the Fryingpan, is satisfying no matter how the fish are biting. *Photo by Burnham Arndt of ACRA.*

Northwest

From Grand Mesa, North America's largest flattop mountain, to the desolate river
canyons of Dinosaur National Monument and natural rock archways of Rattlesnake
Canyon, the beautiful northwest portion of Colorado resembles facets on a gem-
stone. The eye-popping beauty of some areas, however, seems impossible to imagine
in others. Massive in scope and relatively unpopulated, this area has long stretches of
open road distinct from the obvious resort highlights of Steamboat Springs, Aspen
and Vail. Stark buttes and cliffs are interspersed among a quilt of national forestlands,
soaring mountain passes, pretty river canyons and remote alpine lakes.

Once the domain of Ute Indians, the northwest portion of present-day
Colorado gradually became an appealing draw to miners, ranchers and recreationists.
As inroads and transportation networks pushed into the area, the Utes found
themselves displaced to reservations in extreme southwest Colorado and across the
Utah border. The Meeker Massacre in 1879 became the final blow to the nomadic
tribes of American Indians who had lived here for generations.

With a forty-year period of extensive oil and uranium production behind it,
much of northwestern Colorado now has become a hunters' mecca. Lower elevations and warmer climates encompass excellent cherry and peach orchards and
vineyards around the base of Grand Mesa. Stopping at roadside fruit stands in late
summer and pausing to sample Palisade's fermented produce, in the form of wine,
should be on your list of things to do. Located in the fertile Grand Valley, the
town of Grand Junction feels about as midwestern as it gets, but within a basin
of weirdly eroded plateaus offers nearly unlimited recreation possibilities.

Skiing and snowboarding the wooded glades at Steamboat Springs, sampling
the ritzy nightlife and art galleries of Aspen or soaking in the "world's largest" hot
springs pools at Glenwood Springs are just a few of the experiences you should

seek out. Above all, with thousands of acres of Routt and White River National Forests awaiting, we suggest packing up your camping gear, mountain bike and fishing pole and heading into nature. Ice fishing in the frozen expanse of North Park brings its own appeal. The many contrasts of northwestern Colorado make it difficult to describe in sweeping terms—but its differences contribute to this region's intrigue as a logical destination for curious travelers.

Cultural & Historical

BEST LOCAL ARTS SCENE
Aspen Music Festival and School

In an effort to fill a void created by the country's wracking emotional pain in the years following World War II, a group of artists and intellectuals formed a gathering in Aspen to celebrate human goodness—and nearly two thousand people showed up! The Goethe Bicentennial Convocation and Music Festival in 1949 included visits by humanitarian Albert Schweitzer and conductor and pianist Arthur Rubinstein. This effort at human renewal signaled the birth of the Aspen Music Festival and School, which still flourishes today.

The festival lasts two months, from late June to late August, and brings some of the finest musicians in the world to this mountain Shangri-la. Promising students play, practice and learn from musical masters—you get the sense from their sheer determination that many will come back someday as acclaimed artists themselves, perpetuating this worthy cycle. The town takes on a unique aura as you see bulky string instrument cases at bus stops, hear sounds of arpeggios escaping from open windows and listen to concert perfection at the renowned music tent. But the mostly classical concerts represent only one way to enjoy the music. Be sure to visit during the rehearsals, attend a workshop or stop and pause to hear the unusually talented sidewalk musicians. Even if you cannot afford tickets to the concerts, you can always find a perch on the grassy expanse outside the tent to hear the sounds.

Aspen and the arts come together with a historical depth and creative breadth that no other mountain town can touch. Here galleries, theater, music and dance are as much a part of the environment as the ever-present aspen tree. Give yourself pause, and remember how it all began five decades ago. **(970) 925-3254;** www.aspenmusicfestival.com.

During the Aspen Music Festival unusually talented street musicians perform to passersby all around town. *Photo by Burnham Arndt, ACRA.*

BEST PLACE TO EXPERIENCE COLORADO AS IT ONCE WAS
North Park

No matter at what point you drop into the immense North Park basin, you find your eyes drawn across the broad plain to the surrounding mountain vistas. Massive peaks comprising several distinct mountain chains—the Never Summer and Rabbit Ears Ranges to the south, the Park Range to the west and the Medicine Bows to the east—were created through buckling and movement of bedrock. The high valley floor shifted downward from the mountain peaks in North Park just as it did in Colorado's Middle Park, South Park and San Luis Valley. Driving across the arid plain, the views open, and you get a sense of Colorado as it once was, without the resort development so common in other parts of the state. Thousands of acres of public lands, including the Arapaho National Wildlife Refuge area, make this an appealing destination.

The Ute Indians came here initially in the 1800s following buffalo and other game on their hunts. Pioneers came here later to find furs and eventually gold, but those who stayed based their livelihoods on ranching. Hikers who want remote destinations enjoy the beautiful and secluded trails that enter the Mount Zirkel Wilderness and Routt National Forest. Fishing success can be found year-round on area streams, lakes and ponds; North Park continues to be a popular ice-fishing destination. Scores of hunters set out from North Park with one of the area's many outfitters. As you drive through North Park, take some side routes and you'll see just how much of the place remains open range. North Park has been extensively logged, but much of its forest area has healthy secondary forests coming into their own. Along the beaver ponds on Illinois Creek, near Rand, a moose reintroduction program now has the herd numbering over six hundred.

Visitors interested in history should wander among the ruins of Teller City, a town that in 1879 claimed thirteen hundred residents. One cabin has been rebuilt, and about twenty others in tumbledown condition can be seen on a short hiking loop hike into the woods. The most interesting ruin may be of the Yates Hotel, which once boasted forty rooms and furnishings such as Persian rugs and a grand piano in its well-appointed lobby. For a complete overview of North Park's history, check out the guns, antiques, tools and historic photos at the North Park Pioneer Museum (small fee). For more information call **(970) 723-4344**.

☺ BEST CANYON PASSAGEWAY
Glenwood Canyon Trail

It took millions of years of steady erosion, massive uplifting and geologic chaos to create the gorgeous, almost vertical, two thousand-foot-high rock walls of Glenwood Canyon. Today the canyon remains a wonderful resource with easy access to drivers, bicyclists, in-line skaters, kayakers, hikers and picnickers. In recent history, the canyon had remained impassable; even the Utes forsook the area for easier routes. Eventually the pull of gold and the pleasure of natural hot springs in Glenwood Springs (formerly Grand Springs) proved to be the impetus for pathways to be built through the canyon.

The sweeping views and wide open spaces of North Park bring a simpler way of life into clear focus. *Photo by Bruce Caughey.*

The first Denver & Rio Grande tracks pushed through the canyon in 1887 (thanks to the wit and audacity of David Moffat), and today trains still make frequent runs on the opposite bank. The development culminated in the completion of a four-lane highway (I-70) in 1992—truly an engineering feat that should count as a Wonder of the World.

Though early opponents of the highway expansion had cited environmental and aesthetic concerns, almost everyone agrees that the twelve-mile link success-fully achieved a balanced outcome. The stretch of smooth concrete truly repre-sents a magnificent engineering marvel with countless attractive recreational opportunities for the public to use and enjoy. From Glenwood Springs, drive east on I-70 and the canyon begins almost immediately. The Hanging Lake trailhead (a 1.2-mile uphill trek to a series of interconnected waterfalls) can be found ten miles up the canyon. From Denver, Glenwood Canyon can be reached easily by heading west on I-70 for 140 miles.

☺ BEST GHOST TOWN
Ashcroft

Back in 1879, three mining camps were quickly established in the area to accommo-date the silver-mining boom: Ashcroft, Ute City (later Aspen) and Independence, which is located high up the Roaring Fork Valley toward the famous pass of the same name. Ashcroft was named for its founder (T. E. Ashcraft, but pronounced Ashcroft), who had a knack for promotion as he laid out his site along Castle Creek at an elevation of nine thousand feet about a dozen miles from Ute City. Within two years the camp had five hundred residents, and throughout the early 1880s Ashcroft rivaled Aspen in importance as miners pulled tons of silver ore from the surrounding mountains. But as fate would have it, Aspen triumphed while Ashcroft withered away. In 1887 the Denver & Rio Grande (D&RG) railroad puffed into Aspen, dooming tough-to-reach Ashcroft to its current fate as a ghost town.

In 1949 Muriel Sibell Wolle wrote in her classic book, *Stampede to Timberline,* "Store after store lines the principal street, each in a different state of disintegration. The roof of one is caved in; the false front of another is stripped of its cornice and presents a bare upthrust palisade of boards; a third has shuttered windows, through whose cracks the interior with its counters and shelves can be seen; and a fourth has succumbed to wind and snow, and lies a pile of jumbled lumber." The passage of time has taken away much more in the past half-century, but you can still see many remnants of better days.

As you walk, bike or ski past Ashcroft's remaining shells of weathered wooden buildings, try to imagine a peak population of twenty-five hundred, two bustling main streets, three hotels, a jail and a newspaper office. If you're lucky, you'll meet the ghost of Ashcroft, a helper from the Aspen Historical Society who can help you interpret what you are seeing. However, you won't have to imagine the gorgeous views of the surrounding Elk Mountains. To get to Ashcroft from Aspen drive west on Hwy. 82 to Castle Creek Rd. Turn left and continue twelve miles along Castle Creek Rd. to Ashcroft. During summer, experienced four-wheel-drive enthusiasts can continue up and over 12,705-foot Pearl Pass and down into Crested Butte on the other side.

Outdoor Activities & Events

BEST FLY-FISHING
Fryingpan River

If you haven't heard about the great fishing on the Fryingpan, you're not listening. Regular insect hatches, big fish and long stretches of public water make this fly-fishing heaven. Unfortunately, any place so highly regarded becomes crowded, so you may want to consider some off-peak times to visit the stretch of free-flowing water that joins the Roaring Fork River at Basalt. Besides, the water flows clear and relatively low in early spring and late winter. And the scenery, with high reddish bluffs, forested hillsides and mountain views, could hardly be more beautiful.

The prime area is the mile below Reudi Reservoir, which features massive trout in the eight- to ten-pound range, thanks to the Mysis shrimp that flourish in the reservoir and tend to inhabit the waters below the release. You are likely to catch good-sized brown, brook and cutthroat trout in addition to lunker rainbows in this Gold Medal–designated stream.

To match the shrimp and drive the trout wild, try a Burton or Dorsey pattern in a 14 to 18 at the end of your (5–6X) tippet. March and April bring midges, mayflies and blue-winged olives. For almost guaranteed success, get to the river in July or August for the green drake hatch. A road runs beside the fourteen-mile length of river below the dam with numerous pullouts for easy access. A couple of good shops in Basalt can answer your questions and fill your fishing vest with all of the essentials.

BEST MOUNTAIN GOLF COURSE
Steamboat Sheraton (Steamboat Springs)

Robert Trent Jr. designed this highly regarded mountain course, which has been open since 1974. At seven thousand feet in elevation, the fairly low-lying course offers more playing days (mid-May through late October) than most mountain courses. Yet you still get to enjoy incredible mountain vistas and gentle bluegrass fairways lined by groves of fluttering aspen and sturdy pine trees. The real reason to play here remains the big views, up to the ski mountain as well as down the valley. Fish Creek winds through seven of the eighteen holes, and seventy-seven sand traps lie in wait, making for ample challenges on the 6,902-yard course.

The Sheraton offers value packages all season long, with some of the best early- and late-season deals around. One of our favorites is the weekday "Golf 'Til You Drop" package, which includes hotel accommodations and greens fees for up to thirty-six holes per day. There is even a suggestive sounding "Swinger's Weekend." The resort complex of the Sheraton features three restaurants, condo units and nearly three hundred hotel rooms. As a place to stay, the first-class rooms are pretty standard, but the setting at the base of the ski mountain is anything but. If you don't have a hotel reservation, you can walk on seven days a week, or make reservations twenty-four hours in advance—but be prepared to pay for the privilege. Clubhouse, rentals and instruction are available. **(970) 879-2220;** **www.steamboat-sheraton.com.**

BEST LAND O' LAKES
Grand Mesa

One of the world's largest flattop mountains, Grand Mesa lures travelers with its high alpine vegetation and thick forests dotted with more than three hundred lakes and reservoirs. At an average elevation of ten thousand feet, Grand Mesa soars above the surrounding valleys and provides sweeping views from its perimeter edges. It remains a most spectacular place to view in the early and late

Grand Mesa, one of the world's largest flattop mountains, provides far-reaching views from its perimeter. *Photo by Bruce Caughey.*

hours of the day, especially if a storm looms nearby. The mesa lies sandwiched between the orchards of Palisade to the west and Cedaredge to the east. Formed millions of years ago by volcanic activity, the fifty-three-square-mile mesa is situated atop a deep lava bed. The passage of geologic time with massive glaciers, steady erosion and violent uplift has created wide variations of terrain for backcountry enthusiasts.

Before the 1880s this area was an original Ute hunting ground. The Ute called the region *Thigunawat*, or home of departed spirits, and a story recounted in the *WPA Guide to 1930s Colorado* tells how the Utes saw the formation of so many lakes. The story goes that the north rim of the mesa was home to great eagles that feasted on deer and antelope and sometimes carried off Ute children. One day the chief's son was taken away to the eagle's nest, and the vengeful father climbed up, pulled out young eaglets and threw them down the hill to a giant serpent who lived at the base of the cliff. When the eagles returned, they were full of rage and suspected only the serpent. They carried it high up in the air by their talons and tore it to shreds. The dismembered body of the serpent fell to the earth with such force that it formed deep pits that later turned into lakes. Okay, so it's a bit of a stretch, but it's more interesting than any other explanation we've heard!

Fishing continues to be a major draw on the mesa, and the lakes and streams get stocked each year. The lakes with easy access draw many visitors and can be a drag for those interested in isolation. Check out the thirteen public campgrounds and reserve by calling 1-800-280-CAMP. Hikers can head out on a ten-mile circular trail providing sweeping views of the entire southwestern corner of Colorado and into Utah from high on an undulating spine on the mesa top. The seventy-eight-mile (one-way) Grand Mesa Scenic and Historic Byway and the memorable Land's End Road provide added enticements for motor travelers. For information contact the Grand Junction Ranger District Office by calling (970) 242-8211.

☺ BEST IN-TOWN RAFTING
Yampa River (Steamboat Springs)

Okay, several Colorado destinations allow you to raft, kayak and tube right through town. But the Yampa River, which flows right through the middle of Steamboat Springs, is the only one where you can pull your watercraft to the side and warm your fanny in a natural riverside hot spring. Several excellent put-ins lie along the five miles of river that flow right through town, and a bike trail also traces the river's route. The shallow but nice natural hot springs lie right across the street, »in a parklike setting, from Steamboat Health and Recreation (the developed hot springs can be found at 136 Lincoln St., with a covered waterslide and various-temperature pools; call (970) 879-1828 for information). You will see a nook of rocks from the Yampa where the hot water emerges to mix with the cold river water. Sit back and enjoy the perfect temperature—but please be sure to maintain your modesty here, unlike down the road at Strawberry Park Hot Springs (see Best Hot Springs on page 60).

For those who enjoy fly-fishing, this stretch of water can be productive, but all trout must be returned, and please restrict your tackle to flies and lures only. It's best before 11 A.M. and after 6 P.M. in summer because of the hordes of tubers that scare the living daylights out of the fish. For more information contact the Steamboat Chamber of Commerce at 1-800-922-2722; www.steamboat-chamber.com.

A young visitor warms up in the natural hot springs along the Yampa River in Steamboat Springs. *Photo by Bruce Caughey.*

☺ BEST PLACE TO SEE MOOSE
Colorado State Forest

The Colorado State Forest comprises a seventy-two thousand-acre swath of remote backcountry just north of Rocky Mountain National Park, about two hours west of Fort Collins. Its rugged beauty is complemented by views of rocky peaks, and the land encompasses a natural area with alpine lakes, trails, campgrounds and fewer visitors than you might expect. One major attraction: This is one of the few locations where moose can be found in Colorado (another is along the Illinois River in North Park). You might also see raptors, deer, elk and other smaller four-legged creatures. The Colorado State Parks' excellent website offers some interesting facts about the lovable moose. For example, did you know:

- **Moose are actually deer,** and an adult male can weigh twelve hundred pounds and stand six feet at the shoulders?
- **The hairy flap that hangs from a moose's neck is called a "bell" or "dewlap"?** Biologists are not sure of its purpose, if any. During cold winters it may freeze and fall off.

- **Moose are excellent swimmers** and spend much of their time in or near the water? They like to feed on aquatic plants and have been known to dive down to eighteen feet to feed on them.
- **Moose can live up to twenty years in the wild?**

Some thirty-six moose were introduced into the state forest between 1978 and 1987; today, the Division of Wildlife estimates the herd at five hundred. A recommended stop is the moose-viewing platform, which is located on County Rd. 41 about seven miles into the state forest. Although there are no guarantees of sightings, the platform overlooks a prime moose habitat. The lumbering creatures can often be spotted best in the low light at dawn or dusk. Look closely for any kind of motion, because moose blend in extremely well with their environment. Even if you don't see one, check for evidence in the unusual scrape marks on bark from their front teeth and antlers.

The State Park Visitors Center provides an excellent introduction to all the wildlife in the area—you'll know you're at the right place when you spot a seven-foot-tall barbed-wire moose replica near the park entrance on Hwy. 14. Stop in for a look at the interactive displays, and shop for T-shirts, posters, postcards and more. Contact the State Forest Park Office for more information at **(970) 723-8366;** **www.coloradoparks.org.**

It's best to look for moose in the Colorado State Forest during the early morning or at dusk. *Photo courtesy of Winter Park Resort.*

BEST HISTORIC MOUNTAIN BIKE (JEEP) ROUTE
Marble, Crystal and Lead King Basin

Beginning at the hamlet of Marble, along the Crystal River, a tough but gorgeous twelve-mile mountain bike loop takes you around the broad shoulders of Sheep Mountain into Colorado's past. Marble got its start back in the late 1880s, but it wasn't until 1905, when the Yule Marble Quarry opened, that the town's population boomed to fifteen hundred and train service reached the marble mill.

Today, you can visit the fascinating remains of the mill as well as a general store, campgrounds and a couple of places to stay. You can't miss the massive chunks of marble scattered like giant sugar cubes along the banks of the Crystal River. Thanks to a groundswell of protest after the four-mile road uphill to the quarry was closed, visitors can still reach the quarry area (also a recommended ride along Yule Creek). From a parking area, a short but rather steep hiking trail leads up to the cavernous one hundred thousand-square-foot pit, where marble is still being brought out by the ton. The quarry's former contents have been used for the Tomb of the Unknown Soldier and the Lincoln Memorial in Washington, D.C., as well as in many downtown Denver buildings.

Before setting out, top off your water supply for this demanding ride. The ride begins on County Rd. 314 in Marble near Beaver Lake (or if you want to skip a thigh-burning ascent, drive your high-clearance vehicle about two miles farther to a plateau where the road splits before setting out on the right fork). From the plateau, take the right fork and continue on the rest of the gorgeous, tree-lined dirt road along the Crystal River.

Just before arriving at the townsite, stop and take the obligatory (it's just that picturesque) photo of the restored Sheep Mountain Mill, an 1882 vintage power-house perched on a rocky outcropping beside the river. Crystal's dozen remaining weathered frame houses—restored as summer residences—bring out ghostly memories of the lively town's 650 residents who lived here and the newspaper, hotel, saloon and post office that served them.

After passing through Crystal, take the left cutoff for Lead King Basin on County Rd. 315. Now the uphill route begins in earnest as the views open up while you trace the southern boundary of the Maroon Bells/Snowmass Wilderness Area. In July and August, wildflowers will astound you with their color, variety and density. At one point, you'll need to fork left, crossing a bridge over a creek, and then begin a series of endless uphill switchbacks. The view gets better and better as you climb and then you enjoy a fast, bumpy ride and a couple of shallow stream crossings on the way back down to Marble. For maps and questions, contact the Sopris Ranger District Office in Carbondale at **(970) 963-2266**.

BEST ROCK ARCHES
Rattlesnake Canyon (west of Grand Junction)

Colorado's natural character remains a primary reason why many of us choose to live here and is the pull for visitors who return year after year. Thanks to the turbulent geologic past that formed Colorado's mountains, plateaus and valleys, we also have a stunning, little-known collection of natural rock archways just west of Colorado National Monument near Grand Junction. When thinking of arches, most people immediately think either of McDonald's or Arches National Park in Utah. But don't forget our own obscure local collection—the second-highest natural concentration in the world—in an out-of-the-way location on Bureau of Land Management (BLM) land called Rattlesnake Canyon.

You'll need a high-clearance SUV, a good map and plenty of gas and water to safely enjoy this beautiful area. Amid weirdly eroded Entrada sandstone canyons, hardy explorers can four-wheel, hike or bike into Rattlesnake Canyon to find twelve natural rock arches. The largest, Rainbow Bridge, spans some one hundred feet, providing a compelling sight. All of the archways reach new photogenic heights during the soft, shadow-lengthening light just before dusk. The rocks, canyon walls and archways take on even redder hues against the azure Colorado sky as sunset approaches. But because of Rattlesnake Canyon's difficult-to-reach location and intimidating name, this beautiful place has never achieved any true acclaim. You just won't ever find a crowd here. For more information contact the Grand Junction BLM Office at **(970) 244-3000**.

☺ BEST HOT SPRINGS
Strawberry Park Hot Springs (Steamboat Springs)

Since the late 1970s, this privately owned hot springs located seven miles north of Steamboat Springs has managed to escape resort development and cushy spa amenities, remaining something of an inexpensive hangout at the end of a rough road. Many will remember the teepee changing room, which provides only a modicum of privacy. Kids love the place but should be supervised, as Strawberry Park tries to be a "rest and relaxation" center, not a splash playland. And yes, after darkness falls, children are asked to leave so that adults can shed their suits if they please.

Unlike the old days, the three large, clearly defined pools, ranging from 70 degrees to 106 degrees, are now surrounded by rock terraces and sculpted gardens. In summer the place employs two full-time gardeners, and it shows! In winter the

Located just north of Steamboat Springs, Strawberry Park Hot Springs proves to be a restful retreat. *Photo by Bruce Caughey.*

backdrop changes as snow piles up on the surrounding trees, never sticking to the source waterfall that emerges at a piping hot 135 degrees. No matter the season, the mineral water doesn't smell and it feels clean against your skin. You can also slip away to a private room and enjoy a leisurely massage, or enter the pools with a trained Watsu expert who will massage you in the buoyancy and heat of the natural springs. The place stays open 365 days a year. Consider taking a tour from town or skiing into Strawberry Park in winter because the road can become treacherous, and if you slide off you may be subject to a $500 fine. To stay overnight in one of the five rustic cabins or to reserve a tent site nearby, you'll need to mail a deposit for your stay. No pets, no smoking. Call **(970) 879-0342** for information.

BEST DOG-LOVERS' SPECTACLE
Meeker Classic Sheepdog Championship Trials

It takes only seconds for the sheep to assess the dog. If the border collie shows no power, no control, the woolly mutton scoffs and pays no heed. Come to North America's largest sheepdog trials and witness the brilliance, patience and tenacity of canines bred for centuries and trained for years to herd large flocks of sheep on the open range. Here in Meeker, organizers of this event could never have guessed that what they started in 1987 would eventually draw as many as twelve thousand onlookers to this small town of two thousand people.

"There is no good flock without a good Shepherd and there is no good Shepherd without a good Dog." This ancient motto of the International Sheep Dog Society reflects the tone of the five-day trials. The handler's whistle commands his dog to approach a group of six sheep 450 yards distant. Onlookers in the stands sit captivated, groaning or booing at a wrong move by sheep or dog, or cheering a job well done. Under the keen eye of the judge, the winning pair works in concert, directing the flock through a series of gates within time constraints, demonstrating supreme skill and control.

Even before nationwide interest was spawned by the success of the movie *Babe,* in which a pig performs a sheepdog's job, the Meeker Classic had begun to grow. By 1999, 126 entrants entered the trials, representing at least seventeen states from California to Virginia, and even Alberta, Canada. The Meeker Classic Sheepdog Championship Trials take place every September on the weekend after Labor Day. For information, call Gus Halandras at **(970) 878-5483** or the Chamber of Commerce at **(970) 878-5510**. Or write to organizers at **P.O. Box 225, Meeker, CO 81641**.

BEST MULTIDAY RAFT TRIP
Dinosaur National Monument

If dam builders had had their way in the 1950s, the river canyon country within Dinosaur National Monument would now be a standing reservoir. Fortunately the dams were never built, and you can still experience the richness and variety of wilderness while floating the Green and Yampa Rivers. The marks of man are nonetheless present, but in the form of ancient rock art that depicts the game they hunted as well as primitive rituals and ceremonies. Go back much further in time, 140 million years to the Jurassic period, and you will begin to understand the netherworld of massive prehistoric beasts that used to roam the land. Combine this with a sometimes wild, sometimes calm river passage and you have all the makings of a great multiday river trip.

Beginning at the popular and imposing Gates of Lodore, most rafters put into the flat, calm waters with a heightened sense of discovery. You cannot see beyond the bend; two massive rock gates mark your entry point. The first foolhardy boaters who navigated this area in 1825 as a kind of shortcut to the western gold mines took massive risks and were lucky to walk away alive. In 1869 the famous one-armed explorer Major John Wesley Powell kept journal entries and created detailed maps during his daring adventures down the Green and Yampa. He managed to name many of the prominent landforms, including Echo Park and Steamboat Rock.

The waters can still be treacherous, but with solid equipment, good maps and 150 years of experience, it has become a fairly safe voyage. Be sure that if you take the trip during spring runoff you'll have your share of white water. So hire a good outfitter and head into the great unknown. Lean back on your raft while crossing calm water and just listen to your remote surroundings. When emerging at the Dinosaur Quarry in Utah three days later, you again see the trappings of modern life but will be fascinated by the paleontology of the area. Getting away from it all takes on a new perspective while eating, drinking and sleeping in a free-flowing river canyon. **(970) 374-3000.**

BEST DOGSLEDDING
Krablooniks (Snowmass)

The approach to Krablooniks, with its chorus of yapping huskies, gets you in the mood for what's to come. And when is the last time you visited a place named for "bushy eyebrows," as *Krablooniks* means in Eskimo? But for a select few, dogsledding happens to be one of those "once-in-a-lifetime" adventures. You will gather at the restaurant before settling into your wood sled, covered in warm blankets for a gorgeous ride upvalley from Old Snowmass. The musher stands behind you barking orders to his troops and getting enthusiastic barks in response and a strong team pull. And you're off on a half-day ride that includes homemade food in a gorgeous setting. You feel a bit guilty chowing down as the huskies huff and puff out steam in the cold mountain air, but soon

Krablooniks' dogs bring you on an unforgettable adventure up an isolated valley from Old Snowmass. *Photo by Gregg Adams.*

realize they are enjoying the day almost as much as you are—it's as if they were built for this task.

Even if you cannot spare the rather expensive fee for dogsledding, be sure to visit Krablooniks for lunch or dinner. The five-star restaurant features some of the finest game dishes you'll ever taste. Absolutely, no matter what, try a bowl of the rich wild mushroom soup—it's incredibly good. You can get to Krablooniks by car or cross-country skis. Reservations necessary for dogsledding or dinner. **(970) 923-3953.**

BEST HUT SYSTEM
10th Mountain Division Hut System

No question, really: The finest hut skiing in Colorado can be found along the hundreds of miles of trails in the scenic mountain area between Leadville, Vail and Aspen. Named for the famous World War II ski troops who trained in the area before going overseas, the 10th Mountain Division Hut System has grown to include seventeen overnight accommodations. Each hut comes provisioned with the basic necessities, including a wood-burning stove, firewood, electric lights, cookstoves and cookware. Outhouse facilities and sleeping quarters with mattresses make for comfortable stays, and some even feature an opportunity to sweat in a sauna.

Although the word "hut" implies a small building, most are surprisingly large, with an attractive two-story, wood-frame design that sleeps sixteen people; a couple of privately run lodging options also fit into the trail system. The absolutely stunning views will bring you back again and again, with standouts being the Shrine Mountain Inn and Fowler/Hilliard huts.

Originally built for skiing, this extensive hut system now entices guests year-round who hike or ski into these backcountry destinations. Well-marked, well-used trails follow recommended routes to the huts, but a maze of side routes veer away and surround the basic trail system, providing unlimited opportunities for discovery. Just be prepared and stay within your experience level. Very reasonable costs (this system is managed as a nonprofit), but reserve your huts early to avoid disappointment. To reserve, call **(970) 925-5775.**

The on-mountain experience at Aspen can be eclipsed only by the many options in this ultimate ski town. *Photo by Carl Yarbrough.*

BEST SKI TOWN
Aspen

Despite all the hot air ski resorts create about their on-mountain experiences, we'd like to highlight another aspect: the town. The ultimate ski town can be found in the Roaring Fork Valley, thriving 120 years after it was founded during the silver mining boom. Yes, its reputation conjures up all sorts of images, some fond, others full of bile, but the fact remains that no other place truly compares.

The town has maintained its cultural, historical roots better than most places on the planet. And despite endless controversies over development, transit and furs, Aspen residents do have a real town, and they care deeply about it. It may not feel that way when you walk among upscale galleries and boutiques and realize the average house costs more than you are likely to make in a lifetime of working. But the heart of a real town beats strongly, and the sheer beauty of the surroundings at this true destination more than make up for petty comments on its shortcomings.

Visitors get to take in a slice of it just by showing up. Plus, in winter, they can choose from four different on-mountain experiences: Aspen Mountain, Aspen Highlands, Buttermilk and Snowmass. For convenience, visitors should head straight to Snowmass for a range of ski-in, ski-out condos. But for the joy of wandering around, taking in a play, browsing the racks of a good bookstore, checking out a restaurant or partying all night, stay right in the town of Aspen. The accommodations and dining tend to be expensive, but certain places do cater to the non-Gold Card set. And many activities rely on community property: The surrounding White River National Forest brings out people who like to hike, mountain bike and fish for endless outdoor fun. In summer, you can even camp overnight not too far from town. For information on lodging, start with Aspen Central Reservations, 1-888-290-1325. For more information on Aspen Skiing Company, try their website at www.skiaspen.com.

BEST BOWL SKIING AND BOARDING
Vail

Wide vistas of white powder stretch out in front of you in a space so vast, no adequate comparisons can be made. You become conscious of your own labored breathing as you look down at the snow crystals sparkling on the slope, watching as it falls quickly downward, away from the intense blue sky above. You've worked hard to be ready for this frozen moment of pure pleasure in Colorado's best wide-open ski and snowboard experience. With 87 percent of its back bowls classified as expert terrain, but much of it suitable for strong intermediates, you'd better have your legs under you before setting out. Nothing compares to the adventure of the nearly four thousand acres of Vail's back bowls on a powder day. Nothing.

Locals know each of the seven back bowls has its own distinct personality and times of day when it shines. Sun Down and Sun Up bowls make it obvious when to delve into their delights. But to really get to know the bowls, you need to venture out to China, Siberia, Inner Mongolia, Outer Mongolia and Tea Cup. Nothing in North America comes close to the mostly ungroomed experience of this terrain. Not that it's always picture-perfect, either. The conditions can vary widely from chopped blocks of half-melted crust on the fringe to big bumps down the spine of the ridge. Find a powder day, and you'll never want to go anyplace else. Boarders love carving fat turns on the open sides of the mountain, swinging from wall to wall.

The sheer scale, combined with the stunning mountain backdrop, makes it seem more reminiscent of Europe than of North America. So even if you are not totally taken by the nouveau Bavarian village of Vail below, this backside of the mountain is sure to satisfy. And even if you stay for a week, you'll not finish exploring the rest of this massive area, with its complex range of peaks, valleys, glades and chutes, all served by thirty-one lifts. Great ski school, too. For more information contact (970) 476-5601 or www.snow.com.

☺ BEST FAMILY SKI AREA
Sunlight Mountain Resort
(near Glenwood Springs)

Only ten miles from Glenwood Springs, Sunlight Mountain Resort appeals to families in need of mostly mellow slopes and affordable lift ticket prices. With few lifts and a map that an eight-year-old can read, you can all go skiing or snowboarding on 2,010 vertical feet of mostly beginner and intermediate trails. You won't find high-speed, detachable quad chairlifts, but you will find an unpretentious, friendly environment. And the lift ticket prices have held for years. Sunlight provides all the necessary amenities despite its small size. There are even some ski-in, ski-out accommodations (Brettelberg Condominiums; 1-800-634-0481). Call Sunlight Mountain Resort for information at **1-800-445-7931**.

After a chilly day on the slopes, you can't miss a chance to go swimming in the hot springs in downtown Glenwood. After a chilly day on the slopes, nothing feels better than slipping through a veil of steam into the 104-degree hydrotherapy pool, especially on a snowy night. However, tiptoeing across the frozen concrete from the lockers can be a shock to one's system! Kids absolutely love the mystical experience of swimming outdoors in winter and will beg you to come back every night you stay in town. Fee charged. **(970) 945-6571**.

BEST TREE SKIING
Steamboat Springs

When the light filters through the bare aspen trees, nothing compares to dodging in and out of a forested, pick-your-own slalom course. Tree skiing takes a certain amount of raw nerve, quick reflexive timing and skill. Here at Steamboat, because of the generous spacing between immovable tree trunks and ample snowfall, skiers can practice their moves and build some confidence. Without lower branches, aspen glades provide the perfect venue. With nearly three thousand acres of runs at the massive resort, including 1,149 acres of skiable/ridable glades, Steamboat remains the king of tree skiing. The best tree runs in our book have long been Shadows and Twilight in the gorgeous Priest Creek area. In addition to planned runs, the area features 1,790 acres of in-bounds timber bashing for adventuresome souls. Nothing could possibly make you smile more than making turns here on a perfect powder day. For complete skiing information on Steamboat, call **(970) 879-6111**; www.steamboat-ski.com.

Where to Eat, Drink & Stay

☺ BEST WHOLESOME BREAKFAST AND LUNCH
Daily Bread Café (Glenwood Springs)

For years the Daily Bread has been a planned stop on the way to skiing in Aspen or Sunlight. It's definitely a local's favorite, too, as you will almost always encounter morning waits for one of the few tables. The restaurant has been given kudos in the *Mobil Travel Guide* and was named by locals as the "Best Place for a Healthy Meal." Evidently Glenwood residents consider rich, wonderfully fattening fare to be healthful—perhaps for your mental health! All of the food is lovingly prepared from scratch, and you won't want to skip the baked goods. Hot entree specials on a recent visit included artichoke quiche, blueberry coffee cake and crab Benedict. You get the idea that the cooks here enjoy creative combinations that are sure to please. Lunches consist mainly of massive salads, homemade soups and sandwiches. Leave room for a slice of freshly baked pie after your meal. Open for breakfast and lunch only. Located next to the bridge at **729 Grand Ave.; (970) 945-6253**.

BEST BRUNCH
Redstone Inn (Redstone)

It seems an unusual sight as you reach the south end of Redstone, a coal-mining town turned artisans' community. There lies a distinctive Tudor-style inn with a square clock tower, modeled after a Dutch inn. Back in 1902, John Osgood, a paternalistic coal-mining baron who ruled the town with a velvet glove, built this place for his unmarried coal workers as part of a model industrial village. It has long since been transformed into luxury accommodations, just

The distinctive Tudor style of the Redstone Inn creates a perfect ambiance for a leisurely brunch. *Photo by Bruce Caughey.*

like Osgood's former house, a true castle situated on the Crystal River two miles upvalley. Even if you can't stay overnight, don't miss a chance to enjoy the Redstone Inn's classic Sunday brunch.

With bold colors, the inn and its well-regarded restaurant preserve Old European charm for its guests. Here you'll find attention to detail, from the friendly wait staff to the carefully folded linen napkins and tasteful place settings. A cold buffet offers beautifully presented fresh fruits, baked goods (including cherry croissants on our visit), salmon mousse and fresh tomato slices topped with fresh basil and mozzarella. Hot entrees ordered from the menu include eggs Benedict, ricotta crepes and potato tatin layered with prosciutto. People from miles around make a special trip here to enjoy the setting and the food. Redstone is located about seventeen miles south of Carbondale on Hwy. 133. For information and reservations call **(970) 963-2526.**

BEST UNUSUAL DINING EXPERIENCE
Pine Creek Cookhouse (Ashcroft)

As the moon slowly rises from the east, a gathering of thirty to forty people gets a demonstration of how their cross-country ski bindings and headlamps work at the base area for the Ashcroft Ski Touring Center. The center maintains thirty-eight kilometers of cross-country trails for day use, but unlike most touring centers, it receives an influx of guests as the sun sets. Outside the ghost town of Ashcroft (see Best Ghost Town on page 53) the activity reminds you of an era past. Now you are about to ski to dinner. It's common to hear languages from several different countries and feel a natural camaraderie among the group. A 1.5-mile trail leads gently uphill to the Pine Creek Cookhouse, a backcountry restaurant where soft candlelight, a roaring fire and a gourmet dining experience await.

Once there, your ski guide transforms into your food server, taking orders from the full bar (remember, you've got to ski back down!) to start off your meal. Enjoy a good glass of wine before turning your attention to your feast of salmon, chicken or wild game cooked up in a creative Colorado style. For nonskiers, a horse-drawn sleigh also makes the leisurely trek to the cook house. This unique restaurant also serves lunch, but dinner remains the most special excursion. This is the kind of place you visit once and remember for a lifetime. It's also open June through October for drive- and hike-in guests. For reservations call **(970) 925-1044.**

ELBOWS-RUBBING WITH RICH AND FAMOUS
Aspen

To improve your chances of meeting up with a movie star, rock musician or at least someone with a few Texas oil wells, head to Aspen. This former gold-mining town is Colorado's best destination, per capita, to meet and mingle with an elite crowd. When the average home price approaches two million bucks, and the largest—Prince Bandar's—manages to fit nineteen bathrooms in a fifty-five thousand-square-foot monstrosity, you have a pretty good shot at rubbing elbows with the rich. In addition to a host of vacationing glitterati, longtime resident celebrities Don Johnson, Hunter S. Thompson, Goldie Hawn and Glen Frey may be sighted among the crowd.

You'll have to develop your own look before you join in the fun. Choose your destination, and then decide on *biker hip* with Lycra shorts and wraparound sunglasses, or *evening chic*, with expensive Gucci accessories. Any listing of the hottest party spots should begin with former Playboy Bunny Barbi Benton's annual pajama party. But, because security guards keep out most ordinary citizens (except caterers and valet attendants—hey, anyone got an extra black bow tie?), you may want to have a backup plan. Here are three places we'd suggest:

Caribou Club—This members-only nightclub offers weeklong memberships with a price tag that'll make you wince. (Tip: To fit in, try not to show your financial discomfort and do not haggle.) Once past the snobbish hostess, you'll see a relaxed and exclusive crowd hanging out on overstuffed furniture, drinking at the bar or dancing in the smallish but lively disco room. **411 E. Hopkins; (970) 925-2929.**

J-Bar—Part of the legendary Hotel Jerome (see Best Historic Hotel on page 72), this historic bar still packs 'em in. Enjoy drinking at the same spot where John Wayne brawled and playwright Thornton Wilder got totally liquored up on a regular basis. The gorgeous back bar and pressed tin ceiling all add to the atmosphere. **(970) 920-1000.**

Woody Creek Tavern—Hunter S. Thompson lives down the street— need we say more? For a game of pool, a burger and a cheap beer (or the house drink, the Biff), stop by this low-key, downvalley location. Nice patio in summer and absolutely great buffalo wings. Located in the town of Woody Creek, near Aspen. **004 Woody Creek Plaza; (970) 923-4585.**

BEST WINE TASTING
Palisade

Few people realize that in northwest Colorado you have your choice of wine-tasting rooms. Yes, it's a long way from Napa Valley, but when you find yourself amid the hundreds of acres of vineyards in Palisade, near Grand Junction, it feels like a special discovery. And you most likely won't be intimidated by snooty, swirling, sniffing wine aficionados or haughty attitudes from the local vintners. What you will find are a half-dozen relaxed places to enjoy award-winning, locally produced wines. With its hot days to build sugar in the grapes and cool nights to provide a distinctive crispness, the Grand Valley along the Colorado River serves as a perfect location for growing and harvesting many varieties of grapes. So, hop into your car or grab your bike and tour the green, carefully tended Palisade vineyards surrounded by the reddish cliffs and arid mesas.

Vineyards started in this area before the turn of the century but were squashed in 1920 when Prohibition came into effect, and the vines were ripped out by authorities. It's taken a long time to rebound, but the industry has boomed in the past decade. Palisade has long been a destination for people who love its flavorful peaches, but today the area's rising star has become the grape. Slowly but surely, wine makers have expanded their varieties from the ever-popular chardonnay and merlot varieties to more exotic syrah, sangiovese and viognier strains. They have also added drip irrigation, high-tech monitoring equipment and comfortable tasting rooms for visitors. In our view, the top three Palisade vineyards to visit are as follows:

A range of wine styles, including Meritage red, are there for your tasting at Grand River Vineyards in Palisade. *Photo by Bruce Caughey.*

Plum Creek Cellars—Since 1984 the owners of Plum Creek have been producing some of the state's most consistent chardonnay and merlot wines. Nice tasting room, store and outdoor picnic area. **(970) 464-7586.**

Grand River Vineyards—The airy interior of the facilities here allows the vintners to stack casks of wine in the back storeroom. You will find many varieties, including the distinctive Meritage red and Barrel Select chardonnay. The tasting room, store and picnic area make a great stop just off I-70. **(970) 464-5867**.

Carlson Vineyards—Parker and Mary Carlson push the humor limits with whimsical wine names like Tyrannosaurus Red, Prairie Dog Blush and Pearadactal. With colorful labels and these offbeat names, you might be tempted to buy this wine just to surprise and amaze your friends. It tastes great too! **(970) 464-5554**.

During harvesttime in mid-September, try to attend the Colorado Mountain Winefest. Tour the area's wineries, sample the wines and kick back for some music and appetizers. No tickets necessary. **1-800-704-3667**; **www.coloradowine.com**.

☺ BEST CINNAMON ROLL
Winona's (Steamboat Springs)

Some travel writer proclaimed that Johnson's Corner near Fort Collins had the best cinnamon rolls in the country, but they must have missed stopping off at Winona's restaurant in Steamboat Springs. This small, well-appointed place on Lincoln Ave. attracts a mix of locals and tourists for its delicious selection of pastries. Full breakfasts include eggs Benedict, lox omelets, a killer breakfast burrito and fluffy pancakes. Still, the cinnamon roll remains the menu's standout with its soft swirls of buttery cinnamon pleasure finished with a calorie-laden honey and cream cheese frosting. *Bon Appetit* magazine calls it a "Plump Perfect Cinnamon Roll," and we're not going to argue. More than a decade ago, Winona started this restaurant with her favorite recipes, and the small restaurant has been sustained by strong business ever since. During high season you are pretty much guaranteed a wait for breakfast, although lunch and dinner are not quite as packed. **617 Cincola Ave.; (970) 879-2483**.

BEST HISTORIC HOTEL
Hotel Jerome (Aspen)

When you visit Aspen, the town's history becomes paramount to your experience. So let it guide your selection of a place to stay. The Hotel Jerome maintains a stately Victorian elegance as the three-story brick anchor of the town's silver-mining past. The hotel opened on Thanksgiving Day in 1889, after mining magnate and former Macy's president Jerome B. Wheeler decided to pour his time and funds into making this hotel one of the best of its day. Since that time it has had some ups and downs, but a massive one-hundred-year renovation in 1989 recaptured the hotel's splendor. The original building houses twenty-seven luxurious rooms, and a new wing, seamlessly built behind the hotel, offers an additional sixty-seven guest rooms.

Each spacious room features period floral wallpaper, antique brass and cast-iron beds and Eastlake armoires in a way that blends comfort with convenience. Modern touches have been gracefully added, including robes, telephones, televisions, and even hair dryers in the oversized bathrooms. The pool on the west side of the hotel, with patio seating at umbrella tables, can be quite a scene in summer. Room service, valet parking and a ski concierge round out the services, though the staff can sometimes seem aloof to requests. Even if you don't splurge on a room at the Jerome, spend some time plopped comfortably on a sofa in the historic lobby with its high glass ceiling, or stop in for a drink at the always popular J-Bar. Expensive. 330 E. Main St.; 1-800-331-7213.

BEST RUSTIC LODGE
Trappers Lake Lodge (east of Meeker)

Arthur Carhart was sent to scout the area east of Meeker for homesites in 1919. Faced with a sparkling mirror of a large lake reflecting the deep blue sky and surrounding mountains, he had a change of heart. He thought everyone should enjoy this beautiful country, and thus was born the wilderness preservation movement in the United States. Trappers Lake lies at the edge of the Flat Tops Wilderness, a legacy to Carhart's foresight. No houses were ever built, but a historic log structure sits tucked in a corner of the White River National Forest near the lake. At ninety-five hundred feet in elevation, the Trappers Lake Lodge today serves as a rustic gateway for explorations into this pristine wilderness.

You won't be pampered here on your overnight stay. Sixteen log cabins contain beds, table and chairs and a gas furnace and woodstove for heat; there is no plumbing. A communal bathhouse at the lodge at least offers the modern convenience of a hot tub. The restaurant serves hearty meals, and the fireplace makes for a perfect setting for storytelling around a roaring fire at night. You come here, though, for the outdoors. You can rent boats or canoes to fish on the lake or take horses on the many trails to numerous glacial lakes in the Flat Tops. Wildflowers proliferate, and mushroom pickers find several varieties along the banks of Trappers Lake. Huge elk herds draw hunters in the fall, and cross-country skiers and snowshoers are never at a loss for snow in the winter. A sixteen-mile ride in a snow coach carries winter visitors from the end of the plowed road up to the lodge.

The area lies fifty miles east of Meeker. Follow the White River along the Flat Tops Trail Scenic Byway east from Meeker and look for the turnoff to Trappers Lake. For reservations at the reasonably priced Trappers Lake Lodge, call (970) 878-3336 or log on to www.trapperslake.com.

BEST CHAIN HOTEL
Hyatt Regency (Beaver Creek)

As you drive up to the horseshoe-shaped entrance, with its heated brick pavers, the realization comes over you that this hotel—no, this entire village—represents a carefully crafted departure from your day-to-day existence. You just don't see anything unless it's tasteful and upscale, and the Hyatt represents the best of the best. So, suspend your view of the world, get into vacation mode and enjoy this European-style hotel for all that it offers: convenience, style, romance, warmth and Old World charm. It doesn't feel anything like a chain, and that's why we selected it. Its sandstone and rough-hewn wood interior in tasteful combinations, numerous wood-burning fireplaces—some with massive, wall-sized mantles (in winter the hotel retains a full-time fire tender)—and plenty of little nooks and alcoves invite intimate conversation. Oh, and something magical comes over you as you sit back in the large outdoor hot tub filled by a steaming cascade of water coming down a rocky slope.

In summer or winter—or in between with some great package deals—the Hyatt remains a very special hotel, one that looks out for your every need. From the coffeemaker in the bathroom, to the fluffy bedcoverings, to the logic and convenience of the design, the 276 guest rooms assume a masterful decadence. Speaking of which, the ski concierge's assurance that your gear is ready and waiting takes a lot of hassle away from the sport, as does the convenient slopeside location. The peaceful Feng Shui ambiance of the on-site Allagria spa with its full-service salon, massage, wraps and body scrubs can be a perfect time-out from strenuous outdoor activities. Pamper yourself a bit before you need to return home, preserving your time here as a memory. Camp Hyatt will take care of your kids at times, so you can all enjoy the vacation. Children (two under eighteen years of age) may stay in their parents' room free of charge or, if available, in an adjoining room at half price. Three on-site restaurants. (970) 949-1234.

☺ BEST DUDE RANCH
Latigo Ranch (North Park)

Sit back, close your eyes and imagine a true western experience: You and your family are being transported to an isolated ranch in a beautiful forest setting, and you have your very own horse to ride each day. You feel comfortable in jeans and boots, and you make lasting friendships over hearty meals. Your kids run and play with others their age, yet you still share many wonderful times with them. Snap out of it! It's not a dream, it's Latigo Ranch, which accommodates a small number of guests (about thirty-five) in its tailored, year-round vacation programs.

Over the years, the two families who own and run Latigo have been pleasing guests with their attention to detail. With the help of a well-trained and caring staff, they have found a way to strike a balance between a ranch experience and vacation comfort. Their low-key approach without intrusiveness helps you enjoy simple, memorable times without daily hassles. Small duplex cabins tucked into the woods bring a welcome degree of comfort without being overly plush. After spending all day building your appetite, you'll truly enjoy sitting down for gourmet food in the common dining room. You won't go away hungry.

In summer the ranch focuses on horseback riding, with wranglers who manage to match your riding skills with one of their sixty horses. Be sure to try a breakfast or sunset ride sometime during your stay; experienced riders should inquire about going on an actual cattle roundup. Other summer activities include fishing, white-water rafting, hay rides and nature walks—however, guests are not railroaded into participating if they'd rather just hang out by the pool and enjoy the setting. In winter, cross-country skiing on thirty-five kilometers of groomed trails and snow-shoeing on backcountry trails remain the most popular activities. Special photo workshop and other programs are available. **(970) 724-9008 or 1-800-227-9655; www.latigotrails.com.**

North-Central

Previous page: Mountain bikers enjoy cross-country thrills at Winter Park Resort. *Photo by Rod Walker for Winter Park Resort.*

North-Central

For it was here on May 6, 1859, that John H. Gregory's discovery of a rich vein of gold-bearing quartz gave the state its first real rush. Other strikes followed quickly, and within a few months Gregory Gulch was swarming with thousands of frenzied gold seekers.

—Kent Ruth, from *Colorado Vacations*,
regarding the famous gold strike
on Clear Creek near Central City

High mountain passes, jagged peaks and vast stretches of open space come to mind when one thinks about the diverse landscape in the northern middle of the state. This rich area started out as a haven for miners and loggers in the mid-1800s and eventually transitioned into an enmeshed collection of nature preserves, mountain vistas and booming resort communities. Stretching south from the Wyoming border to the vast spaces of North Park to the foothills beside the eastern plains, the region's above-timberline centerpiece is Rocky Mountain National Park. Containing some seventy peaks over twelve thousand feet and providing a perfect habitat for an abundance of wildlife, this national treasure embodies the best attributes of an already remarkable region.

Consider the range of year-round outdoor experiences you can have in north-central Colorado. You won't be disappointed by visiting the awesome landscape while traveling among the communities of Estes Park, Grand Lake, Summit County and Central City. The forty miles of free-flowing water in the often-raging Cache la Poudre River Canyon provides excellent grounds for fishing and kayaking. The excellent snow and friendly mentality of Winter Park, a laid-back Colorado resort stalwart, has been a major draw since the T-Bar first brought skiers up the mountain in 1940. The three-mile tracks of the Georgetown Loop Railroad and belching black smoke of the restored railway still recall the engineering tenacity it took to bring ore down from the mines above Silver Plume. The Central City Opera brings out our common cultural heritage and stands as true historic preservation in the midst of gaming and massive development.

Much of this part of the state—especially those rounded, heavily forested mountains that lie just north of Rocky Mountain National Park—remains undisturbed and relatively unknown. So, depending on the season, break out your hiking boots, mountain bike or cross-country skis and find the beauty and isolation of this scenic area. If heart-pumping outdoor activities are not your thing, then hop in your car and tour some of the places that served as the impetus for the settlement of the West.

Cultural & Historical

BEST OPERATIC EXPERIENCE
Central City Opera

We heartily recommend the Central City Opera House in the foothills west of Denver. The understandable, witty, vibrant operas have always drawn crowds, and the vintage 1878 opera house remains a stable Victorian-era anchor in a town that has been transformed by gambling over the past decade. Serious opera aficionados should check out Opera Colorado, but for most of us the Central City experience fits the bill. During the hall's construction, the *Rocky Mountain News* declared it "the most beautiful auditorium to be found between Chicago and San Francisco." In this small setting you can actually catch the nuance of voice and expression of the performers, making the experience memorable even for those who are not fans of opera. With the new padded, theater-style seats it's a complete experience (the seats used to be on a par with the cold metal benches in the south stands at Mile High Stadium).

The nation's longest-running summer opera has been performing shows annually since 1932, and here's why: the high-powered talent, popular productions and a tasteful, intimate setting. The talent runs the gamut from regional stars to Sylvia McNair, one of the world's finest lyric sopranos, who performed a 1999 concert of the music of George Gershwin. You feel as if you have been transported back to the town's mining-era heyday, for operagoers still tend to get gussied up for the show. Feeling the energy of the crowd in this historic opera house also seems to propel the performers to new artistic heights. In addition to full operas, visitors can reserve tickets for opera dinners, salon recitals and shortened "à la carte" performances. Children under six are not allowed. Each show tends to sell out early, so be sure to call in to reserve seats for the summer season program. (303) 292-6700 or 1-800-851-8175; www.centralcityopera.org.

☺ BEST PLACE TO CELEBRATE A DEAD HERO
Buffalo Bill Museum and Grave (near Golden)

In his day, William Frederick Cody (a.k.a. Buffalo Bill) managed to achieve folk-hero status in distant parts of the world, thanks largely to the spectacle of his traveling Wild West Show. But before turning into a famous frontier personality, "Bill" rode for the Pony Express, served as a scout in the Army and killed far more buffalo than he should have—including 4,280 buffalo in one eight-month period. The mythology of his persona can be difficult to sort out from the reality, but nobody questions that Buffalo Bill captured the imagination of millions.

In the narrow shadows of radio transmitter towers on Lookout Mountain above Golden, Buffalo Bill and his wife are buried under a rock marker. Sweeping views east to the plains mesmerize visitors, and from lower down the trail, an equally expansive mountain view lies to the west. A small museum commemorates the man and the myth. A huge gift shop sells the usual mix of everything from fake tomahawks to shot glasses.

Inside the museum, be sure to catch the video on Buffalo Bill and his life, which began in 1846 and ended in 1917. Displays capture some of what made him famous, including a collection of shotguns, lots of buckskin clothing and some Native American artifacts. Reflection brings into question Buffalo Bill's hero status in terms of his relationship with the people who were here first. Did he kill many, or was he "kind and decent to Indians" as the video claims? The truth no doubt lies somewhere in between; with the benefit of the passage of time, we can all be the judge. Small admission fee. Located off I-70 and Lookout Mountain Rd. Follow the signs. Take your picnic lunch next door to the tables set up in sixty-six-acre Lookout Mountain Park. **(303) 526-0747.**

☺ BEST WAY INTO THE MOUNTAINS WITHOUT DRIVING
The Ski Train from Denver to Winter Park

Leave the driving to a train conductor. The trip into the mountains becomes even more of an adventure when you hear the whistle blow while departing Denver's Union Station. For nearly sixty years, Denver residents and visitors have enjoyed this direct route to the slopes of Winter Park, which bypasses Berthoud Pass on Hwy. 40 and crosses the Continental Divide via the 6.2-mile-long Moffat Tunnel. Winter Park is the only resort in the United States with direct train service. The Ski Train takes about two hours each way and runs every Saturday and Sunday from mid-December to mid-April and Fridays in

February and March. Service has recently been expanded to include weekends in other seasons, too—especially during festivals and for fall foliage tours. For information on the train call 1-800-729-5813.

☺ BEST SHORT RAILROAD TRIP
Georgetown Loop Railroad

Passengers load into open-air cars, some covered, some not, for a brief ride into the past. On narrow-gauge track, more than a foot closer than today's standard rails, the train begins its trip from the well-preserved Victorian confines of Georgetown with a loud blast of its whistle. The route begins by crossing a curving span of steel called Devil's Gate as it chugs its way up the steep grade. It travels past the Lebanon Mine, where riders can disembark for a mine tour, on a steady winding route to Silver Plume. The six-mile round-trip takes only slightly more than an hour, just as it did when the route was completed in 1884.

Along the way, the railcars cross the roily white water of Clear Creek four times. The slow but powerful steam train could never have made the trip at all if it were not for the engineering effort to overcome the impossible 6 percent gradient between the towns. By building the winding track with a series of curves—hence the name Georgetown Loop—the grade was sufficiently reduced. In another feat

Rebuilt in 1984, the historic Georgetown Loop Railroad plies a winding route to Silver Plume and back. *Photo by Bruce Caughey.*

of human tenacity, the entire route was rebuilt in 1984 with help from the Colorado Historical Society; the original tracks were sold for scrap in 1939.

Now riders can catch the train at the Georgetown or Silver Plume depots many times daily through the warmer months. Keep your eyes peeled for bighorn sheep, which inhabit the rocky crags adjacent to I-70. Since the train was retrofitted to burn oil instead of coal, passengers need to worry less about cinders, but the primary engine still belches huge blasts of smoke along the route. Be sure to bring jackets, gloves, and raingear, as even seemingly clear summer mornings can turn rainy, windy and cold in a Rocky Mountain minute. For information and reservations call (303) 569-2403.

Outdoor Activities & Events

BEST SAILING
Lake Dillon (Dillon)

Surrounded by three mountain ranges, with constantly shifting wind directions, the huge body of water called Lake Dillon has always been a challenge to sailors. "You can be sitting on the lake when it's as flat as glass," says hard-core sailing aficionado Roy Burley. "Then five minutes later, forty-knot winds kick up and can rip your head sail off!" Sailors come here mostly because of the pristine environment and terrific views. "If you can sail here, you can sail any place in the world," says Bob Evans, harbormaster of the Dillon Marina.

Because the reservoir serves as a main water source for Denver, the deep, cold waters are off-limits for swimming, waterskiing, jet skiing and other immersion activities. You can, however, still head out on a charter cruise, pontoon or motorized fishing vessel if you don't want to count totally on wind power. No matter what you choose to get you around the lake, you'll be amazed by the panoramic views and the beauty of countless small side channels. If your craft has running lights, you'll get to enjoy midnight sailing at its absolute best.

With its unpredictable winds, however, the reservoir does not cater to novices. Afternoon brings about rapid changes in wind direction, including some breezes that seemingly sweep straight down off the surrounding mountains. On a warm day the water remains a chilly 40 degrees, and it's two hundred to three hundred feet deep in places. "Bodies and boats lie at the bottom of this reservoir," Burley

Golf Pro Kim Anders surveys the scenery at Pole Creek near Fraser, one of Colorado's best public courses. *Photo by Bruce Caughey.*

confides with a serious tone. "If you don't know what you're doing, get off the lake before the afternoon winds invariably kick up."

Two marinas serve the boating population and provide rentals. **Dillon Marina** (**970-468-5100; www.dillonmarina.com**) on the northeast shore remains the best; it sponsors regular competitive regattas on the lake and even a sunset cruise with five-course gourmet dinner. To the west, **Frisco Bay Marina (970-668-5573)** provides services, boat rentals (including canoes) and boat-launching ramps.

BEST PUBLIC GOLF COURSE
Pole Creek (near Fraser)

"Verging on holy" is the way Kim Anders, longtime pro at Pole Creek Golf Course, describes the vistas from his favorite tee box on hole number nine. Here, the green rolling fairway drops 130 feet, and sweeping views of the Continental Divide distract from the stated reason you're here: getting that small white ball in the hole in as few strokes as possible.

At an elevation of 8,600 feet, the ball flies 12 percent farther than at sea level, according to Anders. That advantage disappears when you try to find a level lie in this undulating environment, and you begin to learn that the ball tends to break toward Pole Creek, which runs right through the middle of the course. *Golf Digest* just loves this place and has named it the number-one "place to play" in Colorado, among other accolades, over the years. If you want to beware of any one hole, watch out for the 570-yard hole number seven. "You need three well-placed shots in a row to have any hope," says Anders.

The eighteen-hole course just expanded to include nine new holes. Course architect Dennis Griffith, who was inspecting his work when we visited, says this new area is "a wonderful palette." He worked hard to match the landforms surrounding the greens to the strikingly beautiful mountain horizon. Thanks to the thick woods, he says, "golfers feel a simultaneous sense of openness and isolation." Griffith's care to blend the course into the environment while building memorable holes must be working, because golfers are lining up tee times earlier each year, making it harder to get last-minute slots. For a fee, golfers can reserve choice times a month or more in advance. Pole Creek features a well-positioned clubhouse (great deck), putting green, driving range and pro shop. Though fees do not compete with the big resorts, they're not cheap either. Located eleven miles northwest of the town of Fraser, on Hwy 40. Call **1-800-511-5076** for information.

BEST DESTINATION TO BAG FOUR FOURTEENERS
Mounts Democrat, Cameron, Lincoln and Bross

A peak bagger who wants to get a head start on capturing all fifty-four fourteen-thousand-foot peaks in Colorado may well want to begin with a full day in the Tenmile and Mosquito Ranges. There, Mounts Democrat, Cameron, Lincoln and Bross can be found towering just above the tiny burg of Alma in South Park. In addition to being interlaced with trails that rise and fall with the mountain's saddles, in effect shortening each hike, these routes to the summits are fairly gentle. Nonetheless, any travel by foot in high elevations requires stamina and knowledge. These popular peaks require no technical mountaineering skills, but hikers should be prepared for all sorts of elements and beware of the altitude. Get an early start to avoid the storms and give yourself some leeway—oh, and have fun too!

Several approaches and combinations of routes may be taken to bag these four nearby peaks. The easiest and most popular route begins at Kite Lake and completes the ultimate up-and-down cirque to each of the high summits. A popular route begins up the east ridge to the 14,148-foot summit of Mount Democrat before descending east to the saddle between it and Mount Cameron. Hike up the top of 14,238-foot Cameron before heading northeast to Mount Lincoln (14,286 feet) and then back to the saddle between Lincoln and Cameron. The final leg begins here up the gentle southeast slope to the flat summit of 14,172-foot Mount Bross. This aerobic outing will put your

Stairmaster workouts to shame. Keep your eyes peeled for well-adapted mountain goats, and be nice to the other humans who have decided to make this same popular trip. For more detailed route information, check out the excellent guidebook *Colorado's Fourteeners* by Gerry Roach (Fulcrum Publishing, 1999).

BEST MOUNTAIN BIKING SYSTEM
Winter Park and Fraser

Who wouldn't love the adrenaline rush and intense focus that come over you when powering your bike up and down single-track trails, darting around obstacles and splattering through the mud? You feel like a kid again, maneuvering your bike with balance and dexterity, building your confidence and speed as the day wears on. Hopefully you haven't been a couch potato lately, because this sport requires muscle and stamina. Also, though you may be able to negotiate your old Schwinn most anywhere, you'll appreciate the gadgetry—including clip-in shoes and front shock absorbers—of modern mountain bicycles as well as tried-and-tested accessories like fingerless bike gloves and padded shorts (a must!).

Since debuting its on-mountain trails in 1991, Winter Park Resort has continued to expand its marked trails to accommodate all skill levels—although first-timers should stick to the valley floor. Riders take their bikes up the ski lift (for a reasonable fee) and then get to skip most of the thigh-burning uphills. Stop in for an energy-boosting lunch and glorious views from 10,700 feet at the massive log-hewn Sunspot Lodge. In addition to the down-hill experience at the ski mountain, riders can access more than six hundred miles of marked, mapped trails throughout the valley. A couple of favorites: the mellow six-mile Northwest Passage, and the more difficult twelve-mile Zoom Loop. Families tend to migrate to the area's miles of dirt roads and the paved Fraser River Trail, which winds along for five mostly forested miles between Winter Park Resort and Fraser. Thousands of additional miles of unmarked trails and dirt roads, most of which started out as logging roads, get frequent use by in-the-know locals.

The annual Fat Tire Classic in late June remains one of the top fund-raising events (for the American Red Cross) anywhere. Winter Park is also a regular stop on the National Off Road Biking Association (NORBA) series. For information and updates on trail conditions, contact 1-800-903-7275; www.skiwinterpark.com.

BEST PLACE TO MAKE YOUR RELATIVES GASP
Mount Evans Road

Coloradans sometimes take for granted that we have fifty-four mountains topping fourteen thousand feet in elevation, right in our backyard. Instead of just gazing up at them, pack up a picnic lunch, hop into your car and journey up to the top of 14,264-foot Mount Evans, enjoying incredible views along the way. Aunt Edna and Uncle Bert and all the little cousins will need to acclimate for a few days before you whisk them into oxygen deprivation at nearly three miles high. This famed Scenic and Historic Byway also captures the prize as the highest paved automobile route in North America. Please share the road with countless road bikers huffing their way to the summit.

As the dominant peak dwarfing the Denver skyline, Evans provides memorable sights, including an ancient bristlecone pine forest, scenic vistas and ample wildlife. You can also veer off the road to explore more than one hundred miles of hiking trails. The first stop on the driving route is beautiful Echo Lake, with its roadside fishing, campsites and picnic tables. After Echo Lake, pay your entrance fee and get ready for countless ooohs and aaahs the rest of the way. Keep your eyes peeled for yellow-bellied marmots (also called whistle pigs because of their distinctive call),

The glorious setting of Summit Lake makes a good stop on the journey to the top of Mount Evans. *Photo by Bruce Caughey.*

bighorn sheep, pikas and mountain goats. Volunteers from the Division of Wildlife set up an interpretive stand during summer weekends at Summit Lake. The parking lot leaves a quarter-mile hike to the mountaintop, where you'll enjoy an unparalleled panorama below. The Clear Creek Ranger District operates a visitors center in Idaho Springs that offers publications, including a Junior Ranger Adventure program as well as an excellent taped audio tour. For more information call (303) 567-2901.

☺ BEST WILDLIFE VIEWING
Rocky Mountain National Park

The eerie bugle of elk in the fall and the sight of a little pika scampering about the rocky tundra represent two vastly different wildlife experiences. Add agile bighorn sheep and the bulbous-nosed moose, along with an entire range of other mammals and birds (from ptarmigan to large birds of prey), and this 415-mile wilderness becomes the best wildlife viewing in the state. More than sixty peaks above twelve thousand feet and the massive slopes of Longs Peak (14,255 feet) dominate the park. It encompasses a glorious natural area with lakes, waterfalls, grassy meadows and vast stretches of above-treeline terrain. Even with three million annual visitors, Rocky Mountain National Park brings an important, accessible slice of nature to those who seek it out.

Many area residents drive to the park in late September and early October each year to see herds of elk and watch as the bulls put on quite a show for a bevy of cows. They sometimes fight, locking racks in mock battle, but mostly they strut their up-to-eleven hundred-pound frames among the herd and emit a loud bugle (which ranges from a distinctive low roar to a high-pitched squeal) in a fascinating mating ritual. People bring out their lawn chairs to sit, watch and listen to this natural phenomenon, which occurs most often at dawn and dusk. The elk can be counted on to congregate in Horseshoe Park, Moraine Park, Kawuneeche Valley and Upper Beaver. Just minutes from the busy main street of Estes Park, you can enjoy the wildlife experience of a lifetime. For more information contact the National Park Service at (970) 586-1206; www.nationalparks.org.

☺ BEST PLACE TO PRETEND IT'S THE SIXTIES
Rocky Grass Festival (Lyons)

In late July, time-traveling backward into the tie-dye haze of the 1960s becomes easy in Lyons, even if the participants seem to sport more gray hair each year. Next to the St. Vrain River, a permanent stage brings nationally acclaimed bluegrass musicians together for three days of jamming in a superb outdoor setting. The rapid strains of traditional music fit perfectly in this natural setting at the base of a high rock cliff. Throw down your blanket and your low-slung chair and settle in for a dynamic mix of music and the best people watching anywhere.

The river flows along one side of the concert green, enticing audience members to head in for a little wading or tubing; many take the flagstone rocks from the river bottom to create impressive rock pylons as the day wears on. Others prefer to laze in a hammock and listen to the live music under the shade trees at river's edge. At the back of the concert green, twenty or more gyrating hips attempt to keep hula hoops aloft in rhythm to the music.

A veritable marketplace springs up with international food sellers and arts and crafts. There's no better place to buy a toe ring, micro beer or veggie wrap. The sweet kettle popcorn entices customers by its scent and is served delightfully warm. Concertgoers can reserve a three-day pass (or just a day at a time) and a nearby campsite. Just be sure you call early to buy tickets, because this show is limited to thirty-five hundred and it sells out earlier each year. Kids under twelve are free. (303) 823-0848; www.bluegrass.com.

At Lyon's Rocky Grass Festival, one of the many participating groups entertains the crowd. People return year after year. *Photo by Bruce Caughey.*

Kayakers test their skill on a summer afternoon on the free-flowing Cache la Poudre River. *Photo by Bruce Caughey.*

BEST WILD RIVER
Poudre River

The ancient granite rock walls of spectacular Cache la Poudre Canyon have been cut over time by the powerful passage of water rushing down from the Continental Divide. Thankfully, one of the last free-flowing rivers along the Front Range, just west of Fort Collins, has never been dammed (some bumper stickers still scream, "Don't Damn the Poudre"), and thanks to its Wild and Scenic status it is likely to stay that way. The river crashes downhill from the high reaches of Rocky Mountain National Park, through the canyon toward the plains, mellowing in the flatlands before becoming subsumed by the South Platte. The Poudre's journey has formed a historical and geological thread that creates understanding and appreciation of the entire area. And, because the river is paralleled much of the way by Hwy. 14, you can easily enjoy the canyon and river from many scenic vantage points. Numerous excellent campgrounds and picnic areas lie along its forty-mile length. The small Cache la Poudre Wilderness Area caters to those who want to explore the more peaceful higher reaches of the canyon.

The unusual name, meaning "Hide the Powder," came in the mid-1800s when some French trappers didn't want to continue carrying heavy barrels of gunpowder—so they stashed them at the river's edge. For many years the river represented a shared route into the mountains by both Indians and trappers, but when gold hunters flooded the state, they never really made any significant discoveries here. Over the years, the area became a popular tourist route and transportation route. The river proves to be an excellent fishing destination (for smallish browns and rainbows), including some stretches of designated Wild Trout water. It has also become a magnet for thrill-seeking kayakers and rafters. The variety of courses and put-ins provide water to suit various skill levels, but all enthusiasts should beware: You can't just float here and hope to come out the other end of these sometimes dangerous waterfalls, huge rocks, boulders, suckholes and other dangers. So hire an experienced guide, go with people who know the river or just be supercautious in your planning.

☺ BEST PROGRAM FOR DISABLED
National Sports Center for the Disabled (Winter Park)

"A feeling of freedom so profound I can't begin to describe," wrote one participant about the National Sports Center for the Disabled at Winter Park. You can see confidence and joy spreading across the face of a blind skier, or the sheer determination of a man paralyzed from the waist down making turns on a specially equipped mono ski. Since its inception in 1970 with twenty-three amputee children from Children's Hospital in Denver, this program has taught forty-five thousand students with physical and mental disabilities. Tens of thousands of volunteer hours are logged annually as area residents reach out to make a difference in someone's life.

The popular winter program includes skiing (downhill and cross-country), snowboarding and snowshoeing. Hal O'Leary, founder of the program, has been singled out as one of "the best 100 things to happen to skiing" by *Ski* magazine. The successful competitive program offers regional, national and international experiences that were once reserved for a select few athletes to those with disabilities.

Of late the winter program has been expanded to offer a range of year-round recreational opportunities. Summer programs include rafting, therapeutic horseback riding, hand-crank and tandem biking, camping, rock climbing and sailing. In addition to the sports center programs, casual disabled visitors appreciate the area's wheelchair-accessible trails: The Bonfils Stanton Trail, located across from the Winter Park Resort entrance, features a boardwalk that winds into nature and strategically placed picnic tables along the way; the Fraser River Trail offers five miles of "champagne pavement" winding through the forest between the town of Fraser and the ski resort. For more information on disabled recreational opportunities, contact the center at (970) 726-1540; www.nscd.org.

☺ BEST SLEDDING

Winter Park and Fraser

As you drive up and over Berthoud Pass, the treacherous vertical landscape makes sledding seem nearly impossible. But once you settle into the valley floor, many places seem perfectly suited to that new wood toboggan, odd-shaped inner tube, or molded plastic sled. One of the prime sledding hills for all ages lies about a half-mile beyond the entrance to Mary Jane on the right side (or about four miles south of Winter Park Resort on the left side). This slope, about the size of a horizontally situated football field, has various setting-off points—it features longer, hair-raising runs as well as much mellower runs better suited to younger kids. The entire hill features a perfectly flat landing, and there's ample parking, so you can run back to your vehicle to stock up on hot chocolate between runs. So, hike up and enjoy the ride down.

If you are not much into hiking uphill, consider taking a shuttle to Fraser to try snow tubing at Fraser Winter Sports. At this commercial operation you can fly down the fairly steep, snow-covered slope on a rental tube and enjoy the ride back up to the top by a primitive but effective rope tow. The warming house atop the hill has a fire in its hearth and a snack bar ready to get you and the kids buzzed on sugar before heading back into the cold. **(970) 726-5954.**

Sledding and tubing are guaranteed to bring on smiles at two prime Winter Park/Fraser locations. Photo courtesy of Winter Park Resort.

☺ BEST OUTDOOR ICE-SKATING
Evergreen Lake

Like the small town of Evergreen, with its wooden sidewalks and false-fronted shops, ice-skating on Evergreen Lake evokes memories of simpler days. Denver families have made the traditional twenty-eight-mile trip up to this popular winter activity. Evergreen Lake's uneven ice may not compare to an indoor arena, but the uplifting mood can't be beat. On the recent 50-degree day we visited, the place was packed with laughing kids and adults all enjoying the Colorado sun and pretty, if not spectacular, mountain views.

Families with infant children skate in tight knots with small plastic sleds in tow or even bring strollers onto the ice. Young kids spread their coats to catch the breeze so that it propels them across the frozen expanse. Couples circle the immense skating area holding hands, while groups of adolescents play hockey on adjacent makeshift rinks. Grandparents and others watch from the deck of the impressive log Lakehouse.

Evergreen Lake helps you forget about everyday stresses of city life and zero in on what's truly important. Small admission fee. Snack bar and hearth can be found inside the Lakehouse; rental skates available by the hour with a picture I.D. (expect a long wait on weekends, especially during nice weather). Occasional closures due to bad ice and weather conditions. Call the hotline at **(303) 512-9300** before heading out.

BEST BUMP SKIING
Mary Jane (Winter Park)

So you want to batter your body by tackling deep, well-carved bumps, some the size of Volkswagens? There's no better place than "the Jane," with its steep pitches of moguls that seemingly go on indefinitely. As one of four interconnected ski mountains at Winter Park Resort, Mary Jane challenges the best skiers and thrashes the rest. Opened in 1939, Winter Park remains the oldest continuously operated resort in the country, and Mary Jane has steadfastly hung onto its mantle as the state's bump heaven. With 60 percent of its slopes classified as "Most Difficult" and only 3 percent beginner terrain, you won't run into many newbies on these long runs, which stretch to 4.5 miles in length.

Mary Jane's generous 2,610-foot vertical drop and separate base area lie five miles away from all the new residential development at Winter Park's base area. Another good stop for experts who want to explore a variety of terrain besides mogul fields can be found in the ungroomed, off-piste conditions of Vasquez Cirque. A complex at the Mary Jane base features cafeteria food and full-service dining (outstanding mud pie at the Club Car restaurant), rentals and tickets. If the bumps beat you up, consider signing up for a coaching session with an expert bump skier; the more skiers who sign up, the more time you get for your money. For snow conditions, call **1-970-SNOW** or from Denver, **(303) 572-SNOW**; www.skiwinterpark.com.

BEST EXPERT RUNS AT A SMALL SKI AREA
Berthoud Pass

High atop 11,315-foot Berthoud Pass, just a twenty-minute trip off I-70, experienced skiers and boarders can find lift-served extreme skiing and numerous powder caches. It's one of the few places you can still find soft snow hours and even days after it has come down from above. Some gentler slopes lie just beneath the chairlifts, but the real reason to ski here remains the expert pitches. The area has always been a haven for backcountry enthusiasts who for years have been taking their chances on the steep, avalanche-prone pass, hiking and hitching when necessary.

Recently the area has again found its financial footing, with the owners of the much gentler Silver Creek Ski Area about thirty miles away. The owners have realistic plans for operating the small area, and tickets between their two resorts are interchangeable. The area's well-trained ski patrol does avalanche control within the boundaries, but you still get the thrill of a somewhat controlled back-country experience by heading through the access gates. In all, the area provides access to seventeen hundred acres of terrain and a top vertical drop of twelve hundred feet.

Berthoud's glade skiing/boarding is tough to match. When the views open up, they're huge, and the powder lasts longer here than virtually anyplace else we've been. Part of the adventure comes from dropping down below the pass summit and taking one of the frequent shuttles back up. Long, narrow bump runs lie in wait on the vast terrain on the west side of Hwy. 40. With a slightly enlarged parking lot, the area accommodates a whopping fifty more cars near the day lodge (rentals, gift shop, food, warming hut), but you will still not encounter any lift lines even on weekends. And, yes, lift tickets here remain a bargain. For information call **1-800-SKI-BERTHOUD**.

BEST LATE-SEASON SNOW
Arapahoe Basin

Always a rebel in terms of its outlook, Arapahoe Basin takes full advantage of its high alpine perch near the Continental Divide on the west side of Loveland Pass. So what if it's the smallest area in Summit County? A-Basin remains one of the state's best places to challenge your skills. A low-key but demanding day area, A-Basin's slopes provide 90 percent intermediate and expert terrain, so beginners beware. Thanks to the country's highest summit, at 13,050 feet, and 360 inches of annual snowfall, skiers and boarders can ride here much later in the season than anyplace else in Colorado—sometimes past the Fourth of July! Due to A-Basin's astonishing summit elevation, lowlanders should give themselves a few days to acclimate before tackling this area.

Without a condo anywhere nearby, Arapahoe offers views of a more natural environment and access to some of the finest steeps and above-timberline skiing anyplace. The spring snow isn't usually reminiscent of February powder days, and the 490 skiable acres tend to dwindle as the days get longer, but with fantastic views, pushing turns through morning crust and afternoon mashed potatoes still adds up to a great day on the slopes. So, cop an attitude, lather up with sunscreen and don some strange attire—on nice days, a bikini top for the ladies or Hawaiian shirt for the guys is perfectly acceptable. Rentals, child care and a cafeteria are offered. Located several miles east of Keystone on Hwy. 6 on the western slopes of Loveland Pass. **(970) 496-7077.**

BEST COLLECTION OF SKI AREAS
Summit County

Named Summit County for a reason, the spectacular landscape just west of the Continental Divide, conveniently located off I-70, features some of the finest skiing and snowboarding anywhere—lots of it! Arapahoe Basin, Breckenridge, Keystone and Copper Mountain comprise the four separate Summit County resorts, each with a distinct personality. In a nutshell:

> Arapahoe Basin—Geared toward expert and strong intermediate skills, this rather small day-use area attracts a younger, more aggressive crowd of boarders and skiers. The snow here tends to pile up faster and stay longer thanks to its extreme 13,050-foot summit elevation and majority of above-timberline terrain. See previous entry for more information. **(970) 496-7077.**

Breckenridge Ski Area—With a quaint Victorian mining town at its base and a range of modern condos and hotels for destination travelers, Breckenridge lays a strong claim to full resort status. A mix of slopes on a quartet of interconnected peaks attracts a broad range of skiers and boarders to its sixteen hundred acres of terrain. Advanced skiers enjoy the double black diamond challenges—such as the forbidding pitch of Devil's Crotch—on Peak 9, while beginner and intermediate skiers find enjoyment gliding down other areas. **(970) 453-5000.**

Keystone Resort—The consummate learning area, Keystone has continually improved its stature by adding steeper terrain at North Peak and the rollicking, ungroomed slopes of the Outback. With excellent service and a planned resort community at its base, Keystone provides a "no-surprises" experience especially suited to families. Extensive snowmaking equipment allows Keystone to capture the prize as the first or second area in Colorado to open each fall. Nightskiing is offered too. **(970) 468-2316.**

Copper Mountain Resort—A ready audience of skiers and boarders appreciate the distinctly separate areas of terrain suited to all skill levels. In most cases, the unsteady, unpredictable turns of beginners don't conflict with the lightning-quick turns of experts. And everyone seems to enjoy Copper Mountain's vast 2,324 acres and 2,760-foot vertical drop. With its planned base area finally growing to suit the mountain, destination skiers now have shopping, dining and accommodations to match a longer stay. **(970) 968-2882.**

The vast terrain of Breckenridge Ski Area with The Village at Breckenridge in the foreground. *Photo by Bob Winsett, from The Village at Breckenridge.*

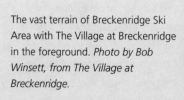

Where to Eat, Drink & Stay

☺ BEST HOT DOG STAND
Coney Island (Aspen Park)

It feels like something out of a nightmare as you walk inside a giant pink hot dog with all of the trimmings. In fact, this oblong restaurant in Aspen Park, about twenty miles southwest of Denver on Hwy. 285, really does serve up great dogs as well as greasy fries and burgers from its cluttered counter. You can sit inside at one of the few tight booths or, better yet, get your food to go and find a spot at one of the outdoor picnic tables. Regardless, you (and your kids) will forevermore be practically forced to say "There's the hot dog!" as you drive past. Open year-round. **(303) 838-4210.**

BEST INTIMATE DINING
Alpine Café (Breckenridge)

A sophisticated atmosphere permeates the various rooms of this cozy, four-level restaurant located inside a Victorian-style home a half-block east of Main Street in Breckenridge. Chef/owner Keith Mahoney puts a major emphasis on creative cuisine made with fresh ingredients and an extensive well-chosen wine list. The attention to detail can be found in the folded linen napkins and an extraordinarily well-trained and knowledgeable wait staff. A fire glows in the corner, original contemporary artworks line the walls and you can see the vast wine selection of mostly French and California vintages displayed in racks around the lower-floor dining room and tiny bar area—the Alpine Café has earned *The Wine Spectator* Award of Excellence every year since 1994.

The eclectic menu cannot be described in detail because every day new specials appear and four times yearly it undergoes a complete revision. "The changing menu adds excitement in the kitchen and is good for our wait staff," says one employee. "Educating customers becomes a nightly ritual and builds anticipation for the meal." Despite the menu's changeability, locals swear this place has consistently great food. The fish entrees when we visited included jerked salmon with smoked rock shrimp and mango salsa, and roasted halibut with red curry sambal; or choose lamb, beef tenderloin or wild game. All dishes come with odd pairings of wonderful sauces and side dishes. The range of cuisines represented and the expertise in the

Canvas umbrellas on the outdoor deck of the Alpine Café create a natural ambiance to complement the wonderful food. *Photo by Bruce Caughey.*

kitchen create a distinctive, memorable dining experience. For lighter appetites, the second-floor tapas bar should be your only stop. A chef behind a glass-encased counter whips up everything from sashimi to Chesapeake Bay crab cakes. Don't skip dessert, especially if you enjoy delicious, mouthwatering bread pudding. Tapas bar seating is first-come, first-served; the main restaurant requires advance dinner reservations. For summer lunches, try the nice outdoor deck with its rattan chairs and canvas umbrellas. **106 East Adams Ave.; (970) 453-8218.**

BEST HOME-COOKED MEALS
The Happy Cooker (Georgetown)

Who has time to cook from scratch anymore? The owner/chef at The Happy Cooker does, and tourists and locals alike come out in droves to enjoy the hearty food at this restored Victorian house. Breakfast might tempt you anytime, especially the egg dishes or fluffy waffles, which come with your choice of maple, strawberry or blueberry syrup. To really blow your diet, go for the special waffle, complete with fruit, hot fudge and a topping of whipped cream.

For a meal later in the day, you really cannot err by ordering one of the wonderful soups, served with thick slabs of homemade bread (the yogurt dill bread is out of this world), or a triangular slice of a specialty quiche. Other options include creative salads, generous sandwiches and a bowl of tasty vegetarian chili. The excellent pies are also freshly home baked (another dessert option involves walking to the shop directly across the street for a hand-packed ice cream cone).

You will likely have ample time to enjoy the artwork and photos for sale on the wall, because service tends to be on the slow side—coming here with young, hungry kids would be a bad idea. On warm days the large front patio fills up with people soaking in the sun and the ever-present historical atmosphere of Georgetown. **412 Sixth St.; (303) 569-3166.**

BEST VIEW FROM A PORCH SWING
Grand Lake Lodge

"People compare it to Switzerland and Austria," says Sue James, longtime proprietor of the Grand Lake Lodge. Walking up to the National Historic Landmark—established in 1920 and surrounded on three sides by Rocky Mountain National Park—you know it's a special place. Parked before the large log main lodge, four restored Model As catch your interest and set the tone. On the covered front porch, people just plop down in one of the many swings to enjoy an extraordinary view out over Grand Lake, the state's largest natural lake and the headwaters of the mighty Colorado River. Your panorama includes the broad shoulders of Shadow Mountain, the distinctive profile of Byer's Peak and the Gore Range off in the distance. If you decide to stay in one of the lodge's rustic cabins, you'll be able to enjoy the same bird's-eye view from a poolside chair—an excellent option.

A majestic, boat-laden view of Lake Granby looking into the heart of Rocky Mountain National Park. *Photo by Bruce Caughey.*

A couple of miles from the town of Grand Lake, this lodge has long been a destination for visitors. Once inside the lodge, pull up a bar stool and see how the glass back bar opens to a mountain vista.

If you decide to come for dinner, lunch or brunch, call to reserve a choice table on the covered part of the porch. The view here simply doesn't stop. If your schedule permits, seek out the Sunday champagne brunch, with fresh breads and pastries, roast-carving stations, specialty eggs and peel-and-eat shrimp. Dinners include gourmet mountain favorites from elk to trout, skillfully cooked in an open kitchen. Simple, reasonably priced lunches are a good bet, too. For information and reservations during summer call (970) 627-3967; during the off-season, call (303) 759-5848.

BEST TRANSFORMATION OF A HOT SPRINGS
Hot Sulphur Springs Resort

For those who visited this hot springs in years past, you may have memories of a petri dish gone bad; the place was musty, moldy, dingy, smelly, dirty and run-down. Thankfully, Charles Nash came along with a vision for restoring the resort into a low-key and satisfying destination. Nash made his money in Denver converting obsolete historic buildings, including churches, schools and gas stations, into architecturally unique structures for people to live and work in. Nash says the waters here cure all kinds of ailments, and the resort remains an important historic asset for the area. In fact, when the renovation was complete, Ute Indians blessed the waters that their ancestors once used and received an open invitation to come and "take the waters."

People expecting a five-star resort spa may not find their Shangri-la. But those who want to experience unfiltered mineral-rich water in twenty different pools (some with privacy doors, others built into an open hillside) will appreciate the soothing design and bathing options. One word of warning: The sulfur smell remains on your skin and in your bathing suit long after departing, especially if you skip a shower to let the touted minerals improve your skin. Those with sensitive nostrils should shower off vigorously with perfumed soap.

Some 210,000 gallons of natural hot water flow from the 123-degree source and flow downward. Lupe's Pool, the hottest, varies from 109 to 112 degrees. As you move down the hill to other pools, the water gets cooler. Decks and walkways connect the pools, and intermittent benches provide perfect spots to kick back and enjoy the view to the Continental Divide. The perennial favorite, called Ute

Pool, features a natural rock overhang with a steaming waterfall. A filtered, kidney-shaped swimming pool lies in front of the complex. Kids are relegated to the lower, cooler pools, but adults can wander the entire premises. Suits are required except in the privacy areas. In addition to hot springs, fourteen spa rooms serve up various massages, herbal wraps and mud-bath treatments. You can stay in one of the twenty small, clean, motel-style rooms (sans TV and phone) with unlimited use of pools. A newly refurbished cabin and an upper-floor apartment near the pools remain the choice romantic spots. **(970) 725-3306;** **www.hotsulphursprings.com.**

BEST ROMANTIC BED-AND-BREAKFAST
RiverSong (Estes Park)

With the multiple time demands on most couples, finding relaxing hours for romance and reconnections can be difficult. So, when you do arrange to break away, you want everything to be just right. Owners Gary and Sue Mansfield designed RiverSong specifically to create spaces for couples to enjoy a certain spark from their surroundings.

Located on twenty-seven wooded acres close to the entrance of Rocky Mountain National Park, the natural environment of this B&B couldn't be nicer. Whether you are newlyweds, couples celebrating thirty years together or those considering an elopement (Gary can marry couples on the spot), the warmly decorated, elegant rooms fulfill your expectations.

The Meadow Bright Suite brings tactile western furnishings to the fore with its hand-hewn log bed underneath a cathedral ceiling and Navajo rugs on the gleaming wood floor. The smooth river-rock fireplace can be seen from both sides of the wall—one side in the bedroom area, the other next to a whirlpool tub built for two. Chiming Bells, the largest bedroom, creates a different ambiance with Victorian furnishings and a sunken oversized tub and redwood shower built for two. Each of the nine rooms feels private and secluded, and some are located in separate cabins with private decks. The quiet settles in easily without the distractions of telephone and television. Enjoy your clean and elegant surroundings without regard to hurrying anywhere.

A full, hearty breakfast with a hot entree is served in the sunny common room each morning; candlelight dinners are available by request. No smoking. Expensive and worth it. Minimum stay requirement. **P.O. Box 1910, Estes Park, CO 80517;** **(970) 586-4666.**

BEST VIEW FROM A LODGE
Lodge at Breckenridge

You might think it's an exaggeration when they call it "Top of the World" in their printed literature. But in fact, the Lodge at Breckenridge is situated on the edge of a forested cliff, up the Boreas Pass Road, just five minutes away from the ski town. With a full-service spa and forty-five well-appointed guest rooms, this upscale place should be on your list for a special occasion—or if you have room in your budget, any occasion! Spectacular mountain views seemingly go on forever from large picture windows in the bedrooms (be sure to ask for a mountain view) and common areas. Pricier rooms and suites offer private balconies to better enjoy sights of the ski mountain and out to the Tenmile Range, Hoosier Pass and Mount Baldy. Hand-hewn log furniture and carefully selected western-themed appointments help make this a unique destination.

In summer the outdoor pool, hot tubs and deck area offer the same sweeping views as the best rooms in the lodge. The spa area features luxurious facials, massages, herbal wraps and other replenishing holistic and fitness-based body treatments. Comfortable common areas and a nice on-premises restaurant with floor-to-ceiling windows entice you to stay and relax awhile. For more information about this gorgeous retreat, contact **1-800-736-1607; www.thelodgeatbreck.com.**

Glistening at the center of Breckenridge lies an ice-skating rink and balloon luminaria. *Photo by Bob Winsett, from The Village at Breckenridge.*

☺ BEST PLUSH DUDE RANCH
C-Lazy-U (near Granby)

If you desire a down-to-earth, rustic kind of ranch vacation, then do not book a week at the C-Lazy-U. This place brings the ranch experience up several notches in terms of sheer luxury. From the cowboy-hat-topped bellman to the monogrammed terry-cloth robes in the cabins and lodge rooms, you will enjoy the mix of five-star city hotel with traditional ranch activities. An emphasis on horsemanship separates the C-Lazy-U from many ranches: Expert wranglers assist you in finding the perfect horse for the duration of your stay. Visit the pool area, soak in the oversized hot tub, play tennis, go fishing or participate in many other organized activities. You can also head to the game room or just enjoy reading the latest novel in an overstuffed leather chair.

Kids have their own separate ranch experience, which seems odd when planning a vacation, but reveals its logic when in the midst of it—for example, the kids really do enjoy playing after-dinner games with a ranch hand while you and the other guests enjoy coffee or a brandy after a gourmet meal. Of course the real reason to come here is to enjoy the beautiful natural environment and views of the peaks along the Continental Divide. This amenity-laden ranch brings a certain plushness to the entire experience. The activities and dining encourage a camaraderie among the guests, who tend to return year after year. The accommodations bring a western charm to the forefront without skimping. For more information call the ranch at **(970) 887-3344**.

Previous page: The ornate exterior of Bloom Mansion hints at Trinidad's rich and colorful past. *Photo by Doug Whitehead.*

Eastern Plains

It is perfectly plain, destitute of every thing, even grass, the great reliever of the eye, and making it painful to the sight.

—Shelby Magoffin, July 1846, from *Bent's Fort on the Santa Fe Trail*

People generally drive through eastern Colorado, not to it. What can be seen out the window of your car does not inspire awe. The South Platte and Arkansas Rivers will never be mistaken for the mighty Mississippi, and the Pawnee and Comanche Grasslands look nothing like a National Forest. The gently rolling landscape can't hold a candle to the soaring Rocky Mountains. But poke around a little here and take a little time there and pretty soon a fascinating picture emerges from the grasslands, farms, canyons and waterways. On your way to somewhere else, the "other half" of Colorado has just hooked your imagination. Exploring this region of the state takes motivation, an eye for the subtle, a backroads mentality, an appreciation for the history of the high plains.

Along I-70 alone, we found several places you'd consider worth the stop. Stretch your legs and make the kids happy at the Kit Carson County Carousel in Burlington, or pull off the road in Limon with all its services for motorists and a museum full of railroad history. I-76 is your link to immeasurable grasslands, over centuries the domain of Native American tribes. And the roadside fresh produce stands along Hwy. 50 are a good excuse to get off the main road and continue to explore this area once traversed by the Santa Fe Trail.

From ancient dinosaur footprints and bones of the woolly mammoth to once-vast herds of buffalo; from the frontier days of Kit Carson and the Santa Fe Trail to the tragic days of Colonel John Chivington, Chief Black Kettle and the Sand Creek Massacre; from sweet melons and spicy chiles to the delicacy of Rocky Mountain oysters, eastern Colorado beckons those willing to look beneath the surface, around the corner and off the beaten path. In fact, not counting I-70, I-76 and U.S. Hwy. 50, no beaten path exists. Intrepid travelers discover migrating birds on the boundless prairie, age-old drawings on isolated canyon walls and faded wagon ruts along the banks of dried-up streams.

Inhabitants of the region, rooted in the soil and seasoned by the vagaries of an agricultural economy, genuinely welcome city slickers and other passersby. Custodians of fertile ground, a proud heritage and a prehistoric past, the people of eastern Colorado watch as the world zooms through in a hurry. Slow down and look around.

Cultural & Historical

BEST EQUINOX PHENOMENON
Picture Canyon (near Springfield)

In a remote corner of southeastern Colorado, only a mile from the Oklahoma border, curious souls gather before sunrise under a gnarled tree silhouetted against the early-morning glow. Standing on the west side of Picture Canyon, several people bend down to enter a narrow slot in the rock wall. Inching their way a short distance through this slender crevasse, they crouch down into cramped quarters where only four people fit. At 6:08 A.M., the sun peeks over the eastern horizon and shines its golden light directly into Crack Cave. For twelve minutes, a cryptic inscription on an otherwise darkened rock wall is the only spot illuminated by the sun's rays. Our modern travelers witness an age-old phenomenon: This ancient calendar verifies a twice-a-year occurrence—the vernal and autumnal equinoxes.

There are at least two theories about who scratched this long-ago message on a rock panel no bigger than a notebook. Most likely it was nomadic Indians of the Southwest who inhabited these lands for centuries. Rock art depicting their way of life is widespread throughout the canyon. It's said that their intimate knowledge of nature's rhythms led to the recognition that the sun's position in the sky foretold a change of season. Others speculate that the ancient Celts from Europe somehow made their way thousands of miles inland on the North American continent. It's thought that the markings in Crack Cave do not conform to the style of art in the surrounding area. They conjecture that the writings in the cave resemble Ogam, the written language of the Celtic people. By their reckoning, the translation from that extinct tongue reads, "On the Day of Bell, the sun strikes here."

That this ancient marker heralds the equinox is not in dispute. We are left to ponder who understood the significance of this natural event so long ago. Picture

Canyon is located in the Comanche National Grasslands, about thirty-five miles southwest of the town of Springfield. It's open all year long; check with the U.S. Forest Service office in Springfield for detailed directions, (719) 523-6591. A locked gate protects the entrance to Crack Cave, which is opened only for tours. Springfield hosts an Equinox Festival every spring and fall to celebrate the phenomenon; call (719) 523-4061 for information.

☺ BEST VIEW OF LIFE ON THE SANTA FE TRAIL
Bent's Old Fort National Historic Site (near La Junta)

Pull in to the parking lot and leave your car and modern life behind. There in the distance sits Bent's Old Fort right along the Arkansas River, much as it looked when it was built in the early 1830s. Long before Denver was even on the map, this trading post was an important way station on the Santa Fe Trail. Orient yourself to the past during the five-minute walk to the entrance of the fort. Enter the gate with the American flag flying high above. Adobe walls enclose the plaza inside, the size of a small town square. Imagine Mexican and American traders; Comanche, Cheyenne, Apache and other Plains Indians; French trappers; slaves and assorted mountain men gathered here in a cacophony of languages and spirited barter. This two-story "Castle on the Prairie" was the only stop between Independence, Missouri, and Santa Fe, then a northern city of Mexico.

Bent's Fort was a trading center for only fifteen years; eventually its ruins crumbled to earth, rendering it but a faint memory in some history books. But in 1975 a near replica of the original was reconstructed in the exact same spot just north of the Arkansas River, the onetime border between United States Territory and Mexico. Today, it's a living museum with people wearing period garb. They regale visitors with first-person accounts of life in this Old West melting pot. You'll meet Charlotte Green, a slave of William Bent who was respected far and wide for her good cooking and strong spirit. A blacksmith demonstrates his skill in fashioning wagon parts, horseshoes and other essentials of the trail that kept the shop busy twenty-four hours a day. The gift shop sells only 1840s-vintage goods like beads, beaver hats and blocks of Chinese tea. Up on the second level you can stand guard in the two bastions used as lookout towers. (Bent's Fort was never attacked.)

Bent's Old Fort is open all year long. It's located several miles east of La Junta on Hwy. 194. The Santa Fe Trail Encampment is held in late July and early August. It re-creates the hustle and bustle of life as it was during the trapping and trading days on the Santa Fe Trail. (719) 383-5010.

BEST LITTLE-KNOWN HISTORIC SITE
Boggsville (Las Animas)

A wooden sign frames the site where modern agriculture has its roots in Colorado. *Photo by Doug Whitehead.*

In the days when the Santa Fe Trail was still carrying pioneers and traders to the Colorado Territory, the town of Boggsville had its moment in time. Acquiring the land through a Mexican land grant, Thomas Boggs and his partner John Prowers began raising sheep and cattle along the Purgatoire River just south of present-day Las Animas. They provided agricultural products to a burgeoning population during the mining boom of the 1860s. This was the beginning of modern agriculture in what would become the state of Colorado.

At its height, the settlement had more than twenty-five buildings, including a general store, post office, schoolhouse and stage stop right along the Santa Fe Trail. Today, only the Boggs house and one wing of the Prowers house remain. As the town looked toward the future, it was also a crossroads of the past. In 1867, the legendary frontiersman Kit Carson had fallen quite ill. He moved to Boggsville to be near the post doctor at Fort Lyon, just three miles downstream on the Purgatoire River. Living in a house built earlier in the decade by Thomas Boggs, Kit Carson died in November 1868. A chapter of the Old West had closed.

When the railroad came through the area in the 1870s, the town that became Las Animas was built just a mile to the north. That spelled the end to Boggsville. Though ranching operations lasted for a while, the town disappeared. Today, the site is open to visitors from May through September, and the buildings are open from 9 A.M. to 4:30 P.M. each day. To get here, head east on Hwy. 50 from Pueblo to Las Animas. Go south two miles on Hwy. 101 and look for signs to Boggsville. **(719) 456-1358.**

☺ BEST INDIAN MUSEUM
Koshare Indian Museum (La Junta)

By the early twentieth century, the Native American way of life was vanishing. As the elders were dying off, so too were their age-old traditions. In the early 1930s, a concerned Buck Burshears created an organization to help preserve the colorful and rhythmic dances of Plains and Southwest tribes. The Koshare Indian Dancers have been performing ever since.

They do not pretend to be Indians. The dancers come from Boy Scout Troop 232 in La Junta, Colorado. Each boy must research the dance, make his own authentic costume and perform only when his creation passes muster with his group. Under the large log roof of the ceremonial Kiva, dances are performed every Friday and Saturday night at the Koshare Indian Museum throughout the summer. The group has performed all over the country and in different parts of the world. As the reputation of the Koshare Dancers grew over the years, so did Burshears's collection of Indian artifacts gathered during his extensive travels. From ancient pottery and arrowheads to war bonnets and moccasins, the museum holds an impressive array of articles.

When Buck Burshears died in 1987, he was an adopted member of the Blackfeet tribe and a blood brother of the Chippewa. He was highly respected in both the Anglo and Indian worlds that he brought together. Reach the Koshare Indian Museum by taking I-25 to Pueblo and heading east to La Junta. Go south on Colorado Ave. and follow signs to the museum. (719) 384-4411.

BEST REMINDER OF LABOR STRUGGLES
Ludlow Memorial Monument
(north of Trinidad)

Miners in the coalfields around Trinidad, Colorado, were restless. In the early years of the twentieth century, Mother Jones, a union agitator from the South, visited the area several times to offer support. The tense atmosphere between miners and mine owners erupted into the Colorado Coalfield War. The Colorado militia was sent, ostensibly to keep the peace. Some miners and their families set up a tent colony at Ludlow, about fifteen miles north of Trinidad.

On the morning of April 20, 1914, they awoke to find machine guns set up on hills above the tents. The militia fired into the camp, setting it on fire. Women and children had been sent down into cellars for safety. The flames spread throughout the encampment above. When the smoke finally cleared, the devastation to the tent colony was complete. And in a cellar meant to keep them safe from harm, the bodies of eleven women and children were found. They had suffocated from the smoke.

In all, twenty-four people died, including a militiaman and three mine guards. Today, a poignant monument stands where those lives were lost. Open a creaking metal door to reveal steps leading underground to the small space where innocents lost their lives. Bleak and desolate surroundings mirror the sad history it tells.

Erected by the United Mine Workers of America, this memorial hopes to remind the world that they did not die in vain. As a result of what became known as the "Ludlow Massacre," labor laws in the United States changed. During summer months you'll likely find archaeologists digging for artifacts that might further reveal the story of this American tragedy. Get here by taking I-25 south past Walsenburg. Take the Ludlow exit and follow a dirt road west about a mile. No phone.

☺ BEST PLAINS HISTORY
Centennial Village (Greeley)

"Go West, young man!" screamed the headlines in Horace Greeley's New York newspaper. It was an admonition that helped populate a utopian community in Colorado called Union Colony. Joined by his partner Nathan Meeker, Greeley created a planned town based on temperate ideals. Adventurous easterners flocked to the northern plains of Colorado. Modern-day visitors get a sense of that turn-of-the-century life by exploring twenty-five historic buildings, most of them moved and restored from surrounding towns and ranches. Centennial Village re-creates the spirit of Union Colony.

German, Swedish and Russian immigrants were the first to farm the area, primarily growing sugar beets. Examples of their simple dwellings can be visited at Centennial Village. Tour guides lead visitors through the church, blacksmith shop, newspaper office and other buildings that tell the story of these early settlers on the plains.

Kids especially relate to the one-room schoolhouse, where they can sit in old-fashioned, straight-backed desks lined neatly in a row. Adults take special notice of the Stevens house, a well-furnished Victorian home of the time. An Indian teepee, a trail-worn chuck wagon and even an outdoor (nonworking) privy add to the authentic feel of history.

Walking the well-manicured grounds from one building to the next gives the distinct impression of strolling through a real town. On special occasions throughout the year, the town comes to life with demonstrations, farm animals and volunteers in period costume. Centennial Village is located on the north side of Greeley. A ticket to Centennial Village also gains entrance to Nathan Meeker's historic house in downtown Greeley. **(970) 350-9224.**

BEST EVIDENCE OF DINOSAURS
Picket Wire Canyonlands (south of La Junta)

Trudging through the marshy edges of an ancient sea, the feet of multi-ton animals sank deep down in the mud. A hundred and fifty million years later, those footprints still stretch out before inquisitive eyes, beckoning the mind toward an almost unfathomable past. Here on the Purgatoire River south of La Junta lies one of the longest dinosaur trackways in the world.

Researchers have counted thirteen hundred footprints of at least one hundred individual dinosaurs crisscrossing the rock ledges along the banks of the river, a one-time gathering place for herds of herbivores and carnivores. Depressions larger than two human feet were made by the huge brontosaurus (now called "apatosaurus"), and the three-toed prints of a theropod even show claw marks. Step from print to print and imagine the gait of these beasts as they searched for food in the shallow reaches of an inland sea, buoyed by the water much like a hippopotamus today.

Cacti and rattlesnakes inhabit this stark canyon cut by the Purgatoire River as it flows toward the Arkansas. Cowboys couldn't pronounce the French, so the "Purgatoire" became the "Picket Wire." Called the Picket Wire Canyonlands, this remote landscape in the Comanche National Grassland reveals the sweep of time. Rock art etched on sandstone boulders and inside natural cave shelters offers hints

of ancient Native American lives in the canyon. The remains of a church built by Hispanic ranchers and farmers in the 1880s include hand-carved inscriptions on the headstones of an adjacent cemetery. And buildings still stand at the old Roarke Ranch, a huge cattle operation that lasted into the 1970s.

Picket Wire Canyonlands is not accessible by car. Stop at the Comanche Grassland office of the U.S. Forest Service in La Junta for directions to the trailhead, which is about an hour's drive south of town. They offer guided tours of the area on Saturdays during spring and fall. (719) 384-2181.

Footprints from the past reveal the wanderings of an ancient apatosaur along the banks of the Purgatoire River. *Photo by Doug Whitehead.*

☺ BEST ROADSIDE STOP FOR KIDS
Kit Carson County Carousel (Burlington)

Sounds from the restored Wurlitzer Monster Military Band Organ carry so far, you'd think you could hear it all the way across the eastern plains. Here, under a white gazebo among the trees, the happy music lures children, parents and grandparents for an old-fashioned spin on the Kit Carson County Carousel. Riding a menagerie of hand-carved, hand-painted wooden animals, you whirl back to a nostalgic past. Built in 1905, this carousel has survived the passage of time. There are fewer than 150 of its kind left in the United States.

Back in 1928, county commissioners purchased the carousel from Elitch Gardens, the famous Denver amusement park. After the Depression, the carousel got new life and has been operating ever since. Today, it remains the pride of Burlington, a well-placed oasis on I-70 where road-weary travelers make a welcome stop. They get more than they bargained for in this community near the Kansas border. A fishtailed horse, a glass-eyed tiger and all the other colorful critters of the carousel pique your imagination as the monotony of the highway melts away for only a quarter a ride.

If you've got the time, take a wagon ride over to Old Town in Burlington. Walk the streets and visit this collection of vintage buildings. Stop in at the rowdy saloon (no beer), where dancing girls kick their legs high, or check out the melodramas staged during the summer months in a big red barn. Between the carousel and Old Town, you just might have to adjust your travel schedule to give yourself a little more time. **(719) 348-5562.**

DARKEST MOMENT IN COLORADO HISTORY
Sand Creek Massacre Memorial

Certainly "best" isn't the most precise word to describe this simple, yet hauntingly affecting memorial to the brutal and unjustified murder of American Indians by U.S. troops, but the event without question merits consideration.

Colorado's state historian, David Hallas, calls it the "My Lai of the Nineteenth Century," referring to U.S. soldiers' massacre of villagers during the Vietnam War. On the morning of November 29, 1864, Colonel John Chivington led an attack by roughly eight hundred heavily armed U.S. volunteer troops on five hundred Cheyenne and Arapaho Indians camped along Sand Creek. Ignoring a white flag and a U.S. flag flown by Chief Black Kettle, the advancing soldiers left more than one hundred sixty dead, mostly women, children and the elderly.

Perhaps more than any other event of the time, the Sand Creek Massacre changed the course of history.

Tensions were running high in the summer of 1864. In Denver, the Hungate family had been butchered by Indians, and white settlers were calling for revenge. Politically motivated Colonel Chivington was happy to oblige. After the news of his unconscionable act spread, even some of the most anti-Indian crusaders cringed at its brutality. Three separate investigations condemned the attack, but Plains Indian tribes knew that the United States had declared war. For the next decade and a half, warfare raged on the plains, led in part by the notorious Cheyenne Dog Soldiers. By 1876 and the Battle of the Little Bighorn, the Cheyenne were fighting some of their final conflicts. In retrospect, Sand Creek was the beginning of the end for the traditional Native American way of life.

Today, a small stone monument on private land marks the spot where blood stained yet another chapter in the history of the American West. Bitterness endures—understandably so—in descendants of those killed at Sand Creek. Visitors are not allowed at the site, but efforts are under way to determine how this historic land in Kiowa County might be utilized in the future. Check out the Colorado History Museum at Thirteenth St. and Broadway in Denver for more information. (303) 866-3681.

BEST VICTORIAN OPULENCE
Bloom Mansion (Trinidad)

Two houses sit side by side and about twenty years apart in the heart of historic Trinidad. Beginning in the early 1860s, Felipe Baca, one of the founders of Trinidad, lived with his family in a two-story adobe residence right along the Santa Fe Trail. A rancher, merchant, trader and entrepreneur, Baca owned one of the fanciest and most expensive homes of the region. Tour it today and you'll see a comfortable, simple design with Greek Revival architectural elements brought from the East mixed with Hispanic folk art from the South. Built right next door, the ornate three-story Bloom mansion tells the story of what happened in the span of twenty years.

When the wagon trails of Baca's time were replaced by railroads, Frank Bloom's burgeoning cattle operations could sell to far-flung markets. Spreading his empire to New Mexico, Montana, Texas, Arizona, South Dakota and even Canada, Bloom built his mansion to befit a cattle king. Standing proud yet worn, the building reveals life in the boom days. Furniture and fixtures from the era, including a grandfather clock that once belonged to the Bloom family, fill the home. When the house was being restored by the Colorado Historical Society in the early 1960s, granddaughter Alberta offered valuable information about what the original wallpaper and curtains looked like, as well as family anecdotes and history.

Housed in the original Baca barn, the Santa Fe Trail Museum transports you from the days when Native Americans occupied the land, to the eras of trading, railroads, coal mining and into modern-day Trinidad. The entire historical complex is open May through September and by appointment. **(719) 846-7217.**

☺ BEST RAILROAD MUSEUM
Limon Heritage Museum and Railroad Park

Railroad buffs revel in the nostalgia of a colorful era gone by. Vivian and Harold Lowe's passion for that past glows at this small Limon museum. From manicured grounds to well-maintained railroad rolling stock, these caretakers of history work endlessly to preserve stories from Limon's heyday.

The Rock Island Rocket from Chicago used to split up in Limon, one half heading to Denver and the other to Colorado Springs. The Union Pacific and Rock Island lines once shared the Union Depot, which now houses photographs and artifacts from the days when trains were plentiful. One old photo shows a moveable chapel, hauled free of charge by the railroads from town to town to hold services. Money raised from offerings helped build permanent homes for local congregations. Limon's First Baptist Church credits its origins to a car called the "Evangel." A small "N-scale" working railroad runs through a model of Limon, depicting how it looked back in 1942. On tracks behind the depot sit several cars you can walk through. Sit on stools at the lunch counter in the dining car that was hauled out to crews working to clean up wrecks or repair the rail. It looks like an old main street diner complete with a working stove.

The museum plays a role in Limon's two big summer events: the Limon Western Festival and Parade in mid-June and the Heritage Celebration in early August. The museum is open from 1 to 8 P.M. Monday through Saturday from June through August. Limon lies ninety miles east of Denver on I-70. **(719) 775-2373.**

☺ BEST ODDBALL ATTRACTION
Genoa Tower and Museum

If one man's junk is another man's treasure, then Jerry Chubbuck is a wealthy man. From ceiling to floor on every available inch of space in twenty-two dusty and claustrophobic rooms, his riches provide an endless stream of wonder and

The old Union Depot houses a museum where Limon's railroad past will not be forgotten.
Photo by Doug Whitehead.

bemusement. You'll find weird stuff sprinkled among a myriad of old bottles, dishes, tools, arrowheads, postcards, coins, devices, instruments, rocks and oh so much more. Oddities include a stuffed two-headed calf, a white rattlesnake and a one-eyed pig preserved in jars; rooster glasses to protect the birds' eyes from being pecked out; and a compass mounted on a cowboy's saddle. Chubbuck points to a World War I helmet with holes in it and says, "I'll bet that guy got a headache!" He shows off one room that used to be a dance hall. The stage tilts backward, he says, so "if the band got drunk, they wouldn't fall into the crowd." You get the idea. This rambling repository is riddled with the strange, the gaudy, the bizarre, the mundane, the gimmicky, the one-of-a-kind.

Long before I-70 came through, C. W. Gregory built a tower in the 1920s along the old Route 24 in the hamlet of Genoa. He advertised it as the highest elevation between Denver and New York. When Chubbuck acquired the tower in 1967, he realized you could see six states from its summit. Climbing the narrow stairs to the top, he claims on a clear day in Colorado you can see all the way from the Grand Tetons in Wyoming to New Mexico, Kansas, Nebraska and South Dakota. In desperate need of new paint, the tower stands as a lofty landmark on an agricultural landscape.

Jerry Chubbuck is no Johnny-come-lately to the collection business. While searching for arrowheads in 1956, he discovered the remains of a prehistoric mammoth in the nearby town of Kit Carson. The tusks and bones of his find are on view in the museum. Follow signs to the tower from Genoa, exit 371 on I-70 east of Limon. It's open all year long. Small admission fee charged. **(719) 763-2309.**

☺ BEST OUTDOOR ART
City of Loveland

His strong arms stretch out and drape over the wooden yoke he carries on his shoulders. Buckets of water dangle by rope from either end as his wife helps him with his burden. "The Water Carriers" stand proud, surrounded by eastern Colorado cornfields. Greeting motorists heading west toward Loveland on Hwy. 34 from I-25, this larger-than-life bronze sculpture by nationally known local sculptor Herb Mignery symbolizes the resolute settlers who toiled to live on this land. This monument to Colorado pioneers serves as a gateway for what's to come.

The city of Loveland is a City of Bronze. At city hall, bronze violinists and flute players form an orchestra whose music you'd swear you could hear. Drive around the south end of Lake Loveland and you'll find a happy troupe of children balancing on a log. Then there's Benson Park. Back in the late 1970s, a few sculptors asked a local foundry to pour some molds. Their resulting works were erected in Benson Park. Each year since, more and more figures from different artists began to inhabit the park. Today, the bronze population exceeds fifty statues, from the whimsical to the profound, from laughing kids on sleds to a chiseled, proud Native American face. Even if you're the only person walking through Benson Park, you don't feel alone. Human emotions exude from hard, cold metal crafted by talented hands.

Loveland now has three foundries, unheard of in a town its size. Sculptors move here from all over the country to be part of this thriving artistic community. Every year in early August, the Sculpture in the Park weekend brings artists and buyers together for one of the most prominent shows of its kind in the nation. For more information call the Loveland High Plains Arts Council at **(970) 663-2940.**

Outdoor Activities & Events

BEST PRAIRIE
Pawnee National Grassland
(northeast of Greeley)

Pawnee Buttes rise like twin towers three hundred feet above the prairie floor, standing as the only natural landmark in otherwise gently rolling, unbroken, wide-open spaces. In *Centennial*, his novel about Colorado, renowned author James Michener called them Rattlesnake Buttes. (He wasn't kidding about the rattlesnakes. Watch your step!) North, south, east or west, the scene hardly changes. Cut by mile after mile of dirt road, the short-grass prairie extends as far as the eye can see. Earth meets sky on a horizon dotted only by the occasional windmill or remains of an early-century homestead. Checkerboarded in a patchwork of private holdings, the Pawnee National Grassland preserves a landscape once ravaged by the Dust Bowl of the 1930s.

For all its hundreds of square miles of unceasing expanse, the Pawnee Grassland can also be experienced by what you find right underneath your feet and just in front of your nose. Grasses carpet the earth's surface, and yucca and prickly pear cactus sprout out of the ground, joined by a variety of colorful wildflowers and small shrubs. Pronghorn antelope can be seen by the hundreds. At Crow Valley, birders congregate every spring to count as many as they can of the 284 species of birds that migrate through here. The lark bunting is a plains bird. It was named the State Bird in 1931, giving recognition to the "other" half of Colorado not in the mountains. In recent years, bones thought to be thirty-five million years old have been found in the Pawnee Grassland. Camels, three-toed horses and turtles are just some of the animals discovered in the layers of this ancient seabed. Seasonal streams and creeks hold water for only a portion of the year, if at all, directing the waters of periodic rain squalls toward the South Platte River.

Developed campsites are available at Crow Valley near Briggsdale. The vast grassland lies north of Hwy. 14 between Greeley and Sterling. Stop in Greeley at the Pawnee National Grassland office for maps and information. **(970) 353-5004.**

BEST PRAIRIE LINKS
Hugo Golf Club

At first glance, barbed-wire fences and the occasional Black Angus bull are just about all you see. Then the slogan printed on the hats of players makes it clear: "Sage, Cactus, Buffalo Grass and Sand Greens." Here in Hugo, along the old Smoky Hill Trail where settlers once rode covered wagons, they've been playing golf like this since the turn of the century. A longtime member of the golf club explains, "If you can't play in the wind in eastern Colorado, you're not gonna play much golf!"

Rubber-carpeted tees and heat-shimmering views to a far horizon greet avid rural duffers who appreciate this local nine-hole course. Through natural, unmanicured "fairways," the ball finally comes to rest on brown "greens" made of sifted sand from a nearby creek and oiled to keep it from blowing away. Players smooth a path between ball and hole with a flat-edged rake. The par 5 fifth hole presents the biggest challenge. It's a big dogleg to the left with cedar trees and railroad ties placed strategically to keep you from trying to take a shortcut. Out in this dry country, volunteers water what few trees exist from a surplus U.S. Army water tank. Inside the red A-frame clubhouse you'll find members playing pool or a game of cards; the old Westinghouse refrigerator is filled with pop, beer and candy bars. Members pay $40 for annual privileges at the Hugo Golf Club, and visitors are invited to play the course for a $5 greens fee.

A golfer prepares to make a putt on this sand "green" at Hugo Golf Club on the eastern plains. *Photo by Doug Whitehead.*

Take I-70 to Limon and head south on Hwy. 40/287 thirteen miles to the golf course. It's one of six sand green courses left in Colorado. You don't need a tee time in Hugo. **(719) 743-2492.**

☺ BEST STATE PARK AND PUTT
Lathrop State Park (Walsenburg)

Two lakes nestle in the piñon and juniper forest in sight of the imposing Spanish Peaks that serve as a natural landmark for miles in every direction. As you whiz by on Hwy. 160, you could easily miss the simple entrance to Colorado's first state park. Opened to the public in 1962, Lathrop State Park somehow remains one of the least known of Colorado's forty outdoor recreation preserves.

In the midst of yucca and prickly pear cactus, waterfowl and small game, everything you might expect can be found here: boating, fishing, waterskiing, windsurfing, swimming, camping and hiking. All this makes Lathrop ideal for a family vacation. But there's something else you would not expect to find in a Colorado state park: a nine-hole golf course. With the backdrop of Martin and Horseshoe Lakes just below and the twin Spanish Peaks to the south, the grandeur of the Walsenburg Golf Club rivals any course in the state. As you stand on the first tee, lush fairways fall away to a pastoral palette of varying shades of green. Every year on the last weekend in June, the Walsenburg Invitational draws duffers and hackers to the area's premier golfing event. Nowhere else can you enjoy such a unique combination of the raw outdoors with the more sublime pursuits of the links.

In nearby La Veta, check out the Grandote Golf and Country Club. This eighteen-hole course is considered one of the top public courses in the state. Lathrop State Park is located three miles west of Walsenburg on Hwy. 160; call (719) 738-2376 for park information. Contact the golf course at (719) 738-2730; www.coloradoparks.org.

BEST WAY TO GET "IN THE MOOD"
Glenn Miller Festival (Fort Morgan)

An audience of at least five hundred cheers as the band begins playing what broadcaster Dave Garroway once called the national anthem of World War II: "Moonlight Serenade," which wafts through the Imperial Onion Warehouse. Dinner tables empty as couples flock to the dance floor. Under a bright chandelier and a ceiling full of stars, feet shuffle softly and bodies sway with a precision that

Glenn Miller fans in World War II garb wait outside the Imperial Onion Warehouse for the music to begin. *Photo by Doug Whitehead.*

comes from decades of practice. This is the music of their lives, cemented in their psyches by the emotions of their youth, war and by everlasting, deeply rooted memories. The annual Glenn Miller Festival continues to grow in Fort Morgan, the onetime hometown of the world's greatest big band leader.

The festivities begin on a Friday night at a dance where celebrants get "in the mood" with a string of Glenn Miller tunes. The audience fills out ballots for best dancers and vintage costumes. The next day, a historic tour of town takes you by homes Miller lived in between 1918 and 1921, places he worked—such as the Great Western Sugar Company—and the cemetery where his parents are buried. World War II airplanes fly in to the Fort Morgan airport, where pilots in period military uniforms offer rides in classic aircraft. The Little Brown Jug 5K/10K race takes runners and walkers through town. Here, teenager Glenn Miller's talents playing trombone, composing and arranging flourished. Nearly twenty years later, he would achieve heights no musician—neither Elvis, nor The Beatles—has equaled: forty-five hits at the top of the charts, during 1942.

Glenn Miller's sudden disappearance in a plane crash over the English Channel in December 1944 left his multitude of fans the world over in shock and disbelief. On Saturday night, the Glenn Miller Orchestra, sanctioned by his family in 1946 to continue under their lost leader's name, faithfully reproduces the big band sound, still popular today. For information about this festival, which is held during the last two weeks of June, call **1-800-354-8660**.

Where to Eat, Drink & Stay

BEST DINNER AND A SHOW
Brush Livestock Exchange/Drover's Restaurant

The rapid-fire utterings of the auctioneer are unintelligible to the uninitiated, and the bids of the buyers are almost indiscernible. But stop in at the Brush Sale Barn on a Thursday or Friday and you'll get an earful and eyeful of livestock being bought and sold in eastern Colorado.

Before taking a seat in the arena, buyers look over an array of ear-tagged cattle from the narrow gangway that stretches over the corrals out back. Taking their notes inside, they know which animals to bid on. Either individually or by lot, the livestock is paraded before this gathering as the auctioneer works quickly, pointing back and forth with the forefinger of each hand like shooting pistols at competing bidders. With a nod of the head or flick of the wrist, the price goes up until someone finally prevails. Just as soon as the sale is made, that steer or heifer is moved out of the way for the next one's fate to be determined.

The spectacle continues throughout the day, so folks get hungry. Just across the hall from the entrance to the arena, the tables of Drover's Restaurant are almost always full—and for good reason. If the daily specials don't bring 'em in (like prime rib for $5.95), the locals know they can always get a bottomless cup of coffee for only a quarter. The manager says they'll sit for hours, drinking one refill after another, visiting with neighbors and sharing the farm and ranch news of the day. If you walk in and don't see an empty table, just ask if you can join someone at theirs. The friendliness is genuine. Though the meals are not for the weight-conscious diner (and there's no such thing as a "nonsmoking" area), the portions are hearty, the food is fresh and the pies are homemade.

The Brush Livestock Exchange and Drover's Restaurant are located on Hwy. 34 just east of the town of Brush. (970) 842-4218.

☺ BEST CHICKEN-FRIED STEAK
Fireside Junction Restaurant (Limon)

"This ain't chicken!" exclaim tourists not familiar with this uniquely western beef dish. Joe Martin, the owner of this family restaurant in Limon, says the recipe is "ridiculously simple." His secret? Bread the beef cutlet just before it's dropped in the fryer. Most places, Joe says, just buy them prebreaded and frozen. When this chicken-fried steak arrives at your table, it's just as crispy as grandma's fried chicken fresh from the kitchen. Smothered in a creamy country gravy, it's the best-selling entree on Fireside Junction's menu.

Sitting at a crossroads of highways, Limon is known for its hospitality to motorists. There are plenty of places to eat. Surrounded by McDonald's, Arby's, Subway and Rip Griffin's Truck Stop, Fireside's niche is fresh, home-made food. They make their own bleu cheese and Thousand Island dressings, the dinner rolls are homemade and the mashed potatoes are real. Be sure to try their fried pies for dessert. Apple, cherry or peach filling is folded up in an empanada-like piecrust glazed with a sugar coating. Yum. Fireside Junction is located at Limon's western exit on I-70, about ninety miles east of Denver. (719) 775-2396.

Fresh produce, including famous Rocky Ford cantaloupe, brims from this farm stand along Highway 50 on the west side of town. *Photo by Doug Whitehead.*

BEST COLORADO MELONS
Rocky Ford Cantaloupe

If you ignore the farm stands along Hwy. 50 as you whiz through small eastern Colorado towns in August or September, you're missing the chance of a lifetime. Open up a melon picked from the field just hours ago and treat your taste buds to the sweetest cantaloupe you've ever eaten. The reputation of melons from Rocky Ford has grown over more than a hundred years.

Back in 1876, George Swink developed a seed that, planted in the fertile soil of the Arkansas River Valley, thrives on the hot days and cool nights of a Colorado summer. Brian and Gail Knapp still raise the sweet fruit on Swink's original farm. They also grow a variety of vegetables that fill the shelves of their roadside farm market on the east end of Rocky Ford. Sweet corn, tomatoes, peppers, beans, onions and all sorts of other veggies come from the same ground that grows the famous melons. The Knapps run just one of many farms in the region, producing fruits and vegetables sought by consumers from around the state who make a point of traveling here every year to stock up.

When George Swink gave away his first watermelon crop to his neighbors back in the 1870s, he began a tradition that continues to this day. Every year at the Arkansas Valley Fair held mid-August in Rocky Ford, the Watermelon Pile giveaway draws melon seekers from far and wide. Rides, rodeos and food stands give you a reason to stay a little longer at the fair. For more information call the Rocky Ford Chamber of Commerce at **(719) 254-7483**.

BEST RESTAURANT FOR UNUSUAL LOCAL CUISINE
Bruce's (Severance)

Whatever you call 'em—bull fries, Rocky Mountain oysters, swinging steaks—they always make for a memorable conversation between bites. Despite the cringe effect on the squeamish, they really do taste great. You might even venture away from the bull-harvested variety and try tender turkey oysters for a change of pace. Whatever you decide, co-owner Betty Schott will encourage you to "have a ball!" If you can't even imagine doing that, then why not settle for a perfectly cooked steak, some deep-fried seafood or a reasonably priced burger?

Bruce's remains a great place to take guests from out of the country for a truly cultural experience and a chance to sample some specialized Colorado cuisine. Located in the former recreation center of the aptly named town of Severance, just northwest of Greeley, Bruce's still caters mostly to a local crowd. Pull up a chair at a booth, or share a long wooden table, which seats about twenty, with some new-found friends. Western dress, cowboy hats and boots are the norm. And when the country-and-western band kicks off its first set on Friday and Saturday nights, you'll know that this is the only place to swing. **(970) 686-2320.**

☺ BEST MEMORABLE NIGHT'S STAY
Elk Echo Ranch Bed-and-Breakfast

Through large windowpanes that rise two stories high in the living room of this log home on the plains, the view of gently rolling grasslands stretches eastward to a faraway horizon. As your eye takes in the wide vista, your mind adjusts to a seemingly incongruous sight. Inhabiting the nearby landscape are small herds of two large beasts once common to the western prairie but at least a century disappeared from these lands. Elk and buffalo lope and lumber as they graze, unaware that their presence here evokes romantic images of a time long past.

Craig and Noreen McConnell have deep roots in these parts. Their great-grandparents homesteaded just miles away, and cattle raising remains in their blood. But in 1992 Craig says he got a funny idea in his head, and he's been raising elk and buffalo ever since. Elk Echo Ranch lies on two thousand acres adjacent to the Pawnee National Grassland. To this remote location come guests looking for a little peace and quiet. Visitors sleep comfortably in any of several simply but elegantly appointed rooms in the house. The main attraction, though, comes from the cookbook of Noreen's grandmother. Noreen carefully and lovingly prepares dinner and serves several homemade courses in the cozy dining room. When you

Craig McConnell offers a snack to one of his elk at his ranch in northeast Colorado.
Photo by Doug Whitehead.

make your reservation, she'll ask you what kind of pie you'd like her to bake! (We had apple and chocolate.)

After a deep slumber in the stillness of a prairie night, the smell of Noreen's breakfast draws you easily out of bed. During your stay, Craig will take you on a tour of the ranch, giving you close-up encounters with the animals. Some of the elk will walk right up and let you touch them. Craig explains that the soft, velvety antlers are harvested for the medicinal qualities their extract can provide. He says Asians have used elk antler products for centuries to relieve arthritis and the effects of menopause, boost the immune system and provide more energy.

Elk Echo Ranch is located between Greeley and Sterling, five miles north of Hwy. 14, about thirty miles north of Brush. For reservations call **(970) 735-2426**.

BEST REST IN THE OLD WEST
Chicosa Canyon Bed-and-Breakfast (north of Trinidad)

If you had visited W. C. Riggs's place way back in this rugged canyon, you might have rubbed shoulders with Kit Carson or Bat Masterson. Riggs mentions them and other historical figures in a detailed diary he kept at the ranch he homesteaded in 1870. The sturdy stone home and fences he built survive today on sixty-five acres in Chicosa Canyon as a quiet, remote and unique bed-and-breakfast.

In the cool confines of the original house, three individually appointed rooms are furnished with period antiques, quilts and comforters. Photographs of the

Riggs family and their original ranch adorn the walls of the western-style living room. A recent addition to the structure contains a solarium and hot tub for relaxing. In the restaurant business in Denver for years, innkeeper Keena Unruh knows how to get your day off to a great start with an elegant breakfast. The bunkhouse for the cowboys on Riggs's ranch has been renovated as secluded quarters for guests looking for privacy and romance. The original wood-slat exterior has been preserved while the interior was gutted to build a cozy room with a queen-size bed, a kitchen, a loft for two single beds and a porch with views of the canyon.

In keeping with the rustic nature of Chicosa Canyon, horse lovers can board their animals in the old red barn on the ranch. Riders explore miles of scenic trails through sandstone canyons where whispers of the Old West blow on a nostalgic breeze. The ranch's proximity to Trinidad (about fourteen miles to the southeast) encourages guests to spend time investigating the museums, restaurants and shops of a historic town on the old Santa Fe Trail. **(719) 846-6199**.

BEST BED-AND-BREAKFAST
Sod Buster Inn Bed-and-Breakfast (Greeley)

Something of an apparition, this 1997-vintage, octagonal inn somehow blends into the Historic Monroe Corridor of central Greeley. Not far from the campus of the University of Northern Colorado and the downtown shopping district, the

Keena Unruh stands in the solarium of her Chicosa Canyon Bed-and-Breakfast. *Photo by Doug Whitehead.*

Sod Buster's convenient location combines with a well-considered design and personalized service to make it an obvious choice.

"Unique" is too tame a word for the ambitious open interior design of the Sod Buster, with its massive main floor great room and ten lovely guest rooms. A curvilinear staircase descends from three interior floors to a comfortable common area with plush couches, an entertainment center and separate dining area, where breakfast and evening refreshments are served. Coupled with the 360-degree, wrap-around verandah and its many rocking chairs, the Sod Buster provides many opportunities for guests to mingle—or to get away for a private conversation.

The guestrooms blend classic country, American folk art and antiques into the decor, with touches that may be a tad feminine for some guests. King or queen beds, private bath rooms, desks and telephones can be found in all rooms; if you'd like a television, jetted tub or double shower, request a special room. Innkeepers Bill and LeeAnn Sterling provide a warm, but not overbearing welcome, as does their distinctive inn dog Mamie, a happy-go-lucky bulldog with a special perch under the check-in desk. Bill cooks a terrific full breakfast (e.g., egg casserole, sausage, cornbread, fruit, juice and coffee) at two set times in the morning. You really cannot go wrong with a stay at this fine inn. **1221 9th Avenue, Greeley, CO 80631; (970) 392-1221 or 1-888-300-1221.**

South-Central

Previous page: An unlikely Colorado resident thrives in thermal waters of the San Luis Valley at Colorado Alligator Farm, north of Alamosa. *Photo by Doug Whitehead.*

South-Central

Unique and distinct geographic domains sprawl through southern Colorado, where wide basins and broad river valleys fit together like pieces of a puzzle. Headwaters of the South Platte, the Arkansas and the Rio Grande originate here, draining snowmelt from extensive mountain ranges and flowing into many states beyond. The twin Spanish Peaks cast a formidable landmark between Trinidad and the Cuchara Valley. At the heart of secluded, forested country, the rolling Wet Mountains open up to sweeping alpine views. From the top of Kenosha Pass, South Park drops away dramatically, a vast bowl with a far horizon, ringed by rocky peaks. From Leadville, the Arkansas River begins with a trickle, then quickly gathers momentum as it rushes south past a curtain of fourteen-thousand-foot snowcapped summits before veering east to cut the Royal Gorge. And from Poncha Pass, the immense San Luis Valley stretches and spreads to the New Mexican border, its eastern wall a jagged spine called the Sangre de Cristos, to the west the rugged San Juans.

Colorado's hardrock history seeps from the vanishing ghost towns and dilapidated mining structures of this region where gold and silver fueled a fever for riches. Hordes of people fled the destruction and economic ruin of the Civil War and poured west on wagon trails, filling mining camps and creating new towns almost overnight. Fairplay's South Park City preserves remnants of that past in an authentic Old West town, and Leadville's Route of the Silver Kings winds through the mining district that produced the wealth of Molly Brown and Baby Doe Tabor. Much of southern Colorado's past, however, comes not from the east, but from the south. San Luis, Colorado's oldest town, and the valley of the same name date to the days of the Spanish empire. After wiping out the Aztecs in the early 1500s, the Spanish expanded north, eventually claiming Ute Indian territory all the way up to the Arkansas River and the San Luis Valley. Mexico continued the trade routes through Colorado when it won independence in 1821 before ceding the area to the United States in 1848. That five-hundred-year legacy is reflected today in the lives and traditions of residents of the southern reaches of the state.

Mountain biking along the Continental Divide and rafting on the Arkansas River provide access to incredible vantage points you won't reach any other way. And you'll cover lots of miles in your car to experience the "best" of this wide and varied country.

Cultural & Historical

BEST RELIGIOUS SHRINE
Stations of the Cross (San Luis)

On a hill overlooking Colorado's oldest town, an age-old story unfolds. Following a narrow, winding path uphill from the small town center of San Luis, pilgrims stop to reflect at each of twelve bronze sculptures telling of the crucifixion, death and resurrection of Jesus. At each Station of the Cross, inspired images crafted from the hands of local sculptor Huberto Maestas are set against a backdrop of town

below and mountains beyond. Shadows from the sun accentuate a crown of thorns, a weary face, the hammer nailing Jesus to the cross. A flower might be placed in His hand. Rosaries, candles and other offerings lie at the base of each depiction of Christ's passage. With every step nearer the crest of the hill, Christ's story nears its crescendo until, at the top, you reach the figure of His ascension into heaven. This representation of Christianity's defining moment is matched by the grandeur of the San Luis Valley and its surrounding mountains.

The drama of Christ's crucifixion is captured in bronze at Stations of the Cross in southern Colorado. *Photo by Doug Whitehead.*

This project was inspired by local parish priest Father Pat Valdez, helping to fulfill his dream of making San Luis an artistic and spiritual destination. Catholicism has been rooted here for four hundred years, and the Stations of the Cross are just the latest manifestation of Catholic faith in this area. When the Church lost influence in the far-flung reaches of the Southwest during the 1800s, the faith was preserved in towns like San Luis in the "moradas" or small chapels of the Catholic brotherhood known as the Penitentes. And while visiting Colorado for World Youth Day in 1995, Pope John Paul II became the most notable visitor to San Luis and these Stations of the Cross.

Reach the Stations of the Cross by taking I-25 south to Walsenburg. Go west on Hwy. 160 to Fort Garland and then south sixteen miles on Hwy. 159 to San Luis. For additional information call Sangre de Cristo Catholic Church at (719) 672-3685.

BEST SPIRITUAL CONVERGENCE
Crestone

Like individual streams combining to create a mighty river, assorted spiritual paths converge in Crestone to form an irresistible magnet for mind, body and soul. At the eastern edge of the world's largest alpine valley, below the majestic spine of the Sangre de Cristo Mountains, this remote burg offers sanctuary to seekers of all kinds of truth. From ancient observances to New Age rites, a medley of mysticism, Eastern thought and Christian tradition plays to a host of spiritual wanderers. Here is just a partial list of what can be found in Crestone:

The Spiritual Life Institute at Nada Hermitage—The contemplative life is practiced by the monks, men and women of this Carmelite monastery created in the Roman Catholic tradition. As at similar hermitages in Ireland and Nova Scotia, private weeklong retreats offer solitude and reflection close to nature. Write to **Nada Hermitage, P.O. Box 219 Crestone, CO 81121;** www.spirituallifeinstitute.org.

Haidakhandi Universal Ashram—Here you can join the daily activities of a spiritual community based on the teachings of Haidakhan Babaji, a teacher from India. Prayers are sung twice a day at the Divine Mother Temple. An energy-efficient "earthship" and straw-bale greenhouse are examples of followers' attempts to live with sustainable resources. Witness a sacred fire ceremony offered on the full and new moons. (719) 256-4108.

Crestone Mountain Zen Center—For six months out of the year, cloistered Zen Buddhist monks train in the tradition of Shunryu Suzuki-roshi. During the "guest season" from May through October you can visit, among other things, a statue of Sho Kannon, the bodhisattva (similar to a saint) of infinite compassion. The only other statue like it sits in the rotunda of the Hiroshima Peace Museum in Japan. Overnight accommodations are available. **(719) 256-4692.**

Karma Thegsum Tashi Gomang—This center for the study and practice of Tibetan Buddhism offers instruction in meditation, teachings and prayer activities. A "stupa," or traditional Tibetan shrine, serves as a symbol of enlightenment. **(719) 256-4694.**

☺ BEST ONGOING CONSTRUCTION PROJECT
Bishop Castle (north of San Isabel)

The engine of an old, green Dodge pickup truck strains loudly as Jim Bishop lurches it back in reverse. A rope tied to the front bumper tightens over a pulley hitched from scaffolding more than two stories high. On the other end, a bucket full of rocks hoists into the air level with the wooden planks that run like a gangway around a portion of an outside wall. Setting the brake, the lean and muscular Bishop climbs like a man half his age up steel supports, balancing precariously on this rickety perch, carefully laying each boulder in place, adding yet a few more pieces to the thirty-year-old puzzle he calls the world's largest one-man construction project.

It is big. You can see parts of Jim Bishop's castle through the trees as you make the short walk from the highway. The enormity of his medieval monstrosity hits you only when you stand before it, neck craned skyward, taking in the sight of this unlikely concoction of iron and stone in the heart of the Wet Mountains. Bishop's enthusiasm for his castle has not diminished one bit since he began putzing around in the summer of 1969. If anything, it has grown with each addition to his dream-in-progress. On ground level you pass under stone arches and through narrow passageways to dungeonlike rooms. Climb the stone steps of a cramped, spiral staircase to the second level, where it feels like a giant cathedral with stained glass and high ceiling, a monument to the unceasing vision of this ornamental-iron worker from Pueblo. All the while, Bishop explains the details of what he has created so far and his intricate plans for the future. Shaking your head in awe, you continue the ascent to higher levels, stepping out on narrow ledges looking out over the turrets and spires, trees and mountains that surround this Colorado

Jim Bishop's work-in-progress rises high in the Wet Mountains, an enduring monument to his unceasing vision. *Photo by Doug Whitehead.*

Camelot. Back on the ground, Bishop excitedly points out an inspired touch. Sitting high atop his creation is the steel head of a dragon gleaming in the morning sun. Disappearing for several minutes, Bishop negotiates the back ways of his three-story-high labyrinth until he reappears on the uppermost roof. Crawling out on the mythical beast, he reaches into its mouth and lights a propane torch. Rising up and waving like a schoolboy, Bishop stands untethered and laughs as the dragon spits orange fire into the blue Colorado sky.

There is a gift shop next to the castle. Bishop does not charge admission but gladly accepts donations. Park along Hwy. 165 along the Frontier Pathways Scenic Byway. You'll see signs for Bishop Castle several miles north of San Isabel. It's open every day. **(719) 485-3040.**

BEST SCENIC·BYWAY
Highway of Legends
(southwest of Walsenburg)

They've been known by several names: Home of the Gods, Huajatolla, or "Breasts of the World." Legend says the wife and baby of a Tarahumara Indian named Grandote died in these mountains ages ago. He had a dream to return to this magical place to be reunited with his family. Today, the twin Spanish Peaks tower as the centerpiece to a scenic byway that explores the history and geology of southern Colorado.

The Highway of Legends begins in the old coal town of Walsenburg. Traveling west on Hwy. 160, you soon drop down to historic La Veta on Hwy. 12. The two rugged, thirteen-thousand-foot Spanish Peaks loom above this quaint town. The Fort Francisco museum holds, among other items, Kit Carson's will. Continuing south, drive past radiating walls of ancient volcanic lava that once pushed its way into cracks in the earth. Over millennia, erosion has left long, thin spines like Profile Rock. Some claim to see Thomas Jefferson or a leaping horse in the formations. The road climbs to the small town of Cuchara, where businesses have survived by catering in the winter to skiers from the nearby resort. In summer, wildflower hikes extend from the highway that continues up and over Cuchara Pass. The road drops over into rugged, remote country that supports the state's second-largest elk herd. Take in the geologic features of Stonewall and drive on to Cokedale. The streets of this National Historic District take you past the homes of coal miners. Just south of town, the old coke ovens still stand, looking like beehives where this busy coal-mining town once bustled twenty-four hours a day. At the end of the byway in Trinidad, the history of the Santa Fe Trail, coal barons, railroads, industry and agriculture acts as an anchor to this latter-day boom town (see Best Victorian Opulence, Eastern Plains, on page 115).

In a state where scenic byways abound, the Highway of Legends stands apart as a window to a region unknown to much of the rest of Colorado. For more information call the Colorado Welcome Center in Trinidad, (719) 846-9285.

BEST COLLECTION OF SCENIC DRIVES
Cañon City Area

Drive your car from Cañon City toward almost any point on the compass, and within minutes you'll find yourself in another world. Each route presents its own special history and landscape. Following are some of the best day tours in the region. Call the Cañon City Chamber of Commerce for more information, (719) 275-2331.

Gold Belt Tour—As the crow flies, it's about twenty miles between Cañon City and the historic mining towns of Cripple Creek and Victor. Three distinct, winding routes connect the two areas. Several miles east of Cañon City from Hwy. 50, Phantom Canyon Road follows a narrow railroad route that once hauled out the rich ore from the thriving mines. Remnants of those days remain along the way, including a tunnel, high trestle and ghost town. The Shelf Road leaves Cañon City and leads to the Garden Park Fossil Area, where the world's most complete stegosaurus skeleton was uncovered. Farther along, the red sandstone formations of Red Canyon Park remind you of Garden of the Gods in Colorado Springs or Red Rocks Park in Denver. Following the narrow road on a shelf high above the streambed, drivers reach the Shelf Road Recreation Area, where rock climbers scramble up more than one hundred routes in a series of limestone canyons (see Best Rock Climbing on page 145). The High Road, farthest west on the Gold Belt tour, follows a more mellow, rolling course with views of the Royal Gorge Bridge below.

Temple Canyon Park—Heading south on First St., a maintained dirt road leads about seven miles to this Cañon City mountain park. Only about one square mile in area, the park is filled with steep rock walls, sage-covered arroyos and a roaring springtime creek that seems deeper than it is wide. Native American legends of the area make this an interesting exploration.

Skyline Drive—In the early 1900s, convicts from the state penitentiary in Cañon City built a rolling road along the hogback above town to create a scenic drive originally traveled by horse and carriage. The one-way route turns off Hwy. 50 just a couple of miles west of Cañon City. The road climbs quickly and follows an undulating spine with far views falling off in both directions. The ten-minute drive offers a view into the prison yard before dropping back down into a residential section of town.

Royal Gorge Bridge—Travel west on Hwy. 50 and follow signs to the world's highest suspension bridge, towering 1,053 feet above the thundering Arkansas River. On the road out to the bridge, Buckskin Joe traps tourists at a Hollywood-eye view of the Old West. The carnival atmosphere continues at the bridge with rides, cotton candy and a miniature train ride.

☺ BEST OLD WEST TOWN
South Park City (Fairplay)

The honky-tonk sounds of a player piano burst through the swinging doors of the saloon and drift down the main street past the bank, the jail, the blacksmith shop and the livery stable. In fact, you'll see just about anything you'd expect to find in a thriving mining town of the 1800s. In South Park City, the past oozes from every nook and cranny.

The buildings have been salvaged over the years from ghost towns with names that read like an obituary from Colorado's past: Dudley, Leavick, Garo, Ophir. Restored from various stages of deterioration, more than thirty buildings now form this two-block re-creation of an Old West town in present-day Fairplay. Furnished with items from the times, each spot tells a rich story. Implements from the dentist's office would scare anyone with a toothache today, and grandma might remember products from when she was a kid stocked on the shelves of the Mercantile. Wandering down the wooden boardwalk from place to place, you can spend an entire afternoon in South Park City and never get bored. Because it's run as a museum rather than as a tourist trap with "gunfights" in the street, the experience rings authentic and the history real. It doesn't take much to imagine yourself living in those rough-and-tumble times.

South Park City is located one block off of Hwy. 9 in downtown Fairplay. It's closed in the winter. **(719) 836-2387.**

The remains of old mines are all that's left from Leadville's heyday in the mining district above town. *Photo by Doug Whitehead.*

BEST HISTORIC MINING DISTRICT
Route of the Silver Kings (Leadville)

It all happened quite by accident. Two prospectors looking for gold up California Gulch found silver in 1875, and the Leadville mining boom was on. Today, a patchwork of dilapidated remains lie scattered as if a tornado had ravaged the hillsides. Legendary fortunes were born where you drive past the ruins of broken dreams on the Route of the Silver Kings.

Turn east on Fourth, Fifth or Seventh Sts. from downtown Leadville, and within minutes you're in the heart of a mining district that transformed the high-altitude hamlet into a thriving cultural center of the West. James J. Brown's Ibex Mine created the wealth enjoyed by Molly Brown. The Little Pittsburgh reaped riches for Horace and Baby Doe Tabor, and the Robert E. Lee produced more silver than any other mine in the area. The reign of the silver kings, however, did not last long. When silver prices crashed in 1893, Horace Tabor, the king of the silver kings, lost everything but the Matchless Mine. Upon his death he instructed Baby Doe, his socialite wife, to hang on to it in the belief that it would one day produce wealth again. For thirty-five years, Baby Doe lived in increasing poverty at the Matchless. In the winter of 1935, a delivery man found her frozen body in the cabin. Her tragic death starkly symbolized the end of an era.

On the Route of the Silver Kings, you can visit the Matchless Mine and the many other ruins of the Leadville Mining District. You can also explore the area on your bicycle as you pedal the 3.5-mile loop of the Mineral Belt Trail. Pick up maps at the Leadville Chamber of Commerce on **809 Harrison Ave.; (719) 486-3900; www.leadvilleusa.com.**

☺ BEST STEAM ENGINE TRAIN RIDE
Cumbres & Toltec Scenic Railroad (Antonito to Chama, New Mexico)

Black smoke belches from a vintage steam engine as America's highest narrow-gauge train chugs through high mountain meadows filled with wildflowers. Taking in the views, passengers are in no hurry on this sixty-four-mile, six-and-a-half-hour trek from Antonito, Colorado, to Chama, New Mexico. Time melts away riding these historic rails, which were first laid down in 1880 to haul gold and silver out of the San Juan Mountains.

Almost everything about the Cumbres & Toltec Scenic Railroad contributes to an authentic ride. Classic steam engines and railroad cars roll along the original route, including an exhilarating adventure 137 feet above Cascade Creek. When the old wooden trestle was first built before the turn of the century, one railcar apparently derailed high up on the bridge. Not to worry: The railroad insists it has never happened again!

Winding up and over the 10,015-foot summit of Cumbres Pass, the train crosses the Colorado–New Mexico border seven times before arriving in the Old West charm of Chama. Passengers who make the entire trip are driven back to Antonito; others opt to stop halfway and return on the northbound train coming from the other direction. Any way you ride it, the Cumbres & Toltec is a must. Reservations are highly recommended. Runs mid-May to mid-October. (719) 376-5483 in Antonito or (505) 756-2151 in Chama. Check out their website at **cumbresandtoltec.com.**

☺ BEST REESTABLISHED TRAIN ROUTE
Royal Gorge Route (Cañon City)

When they heard the train was running once again through the "Grand Canyon of the Arkansas," many old-timers immediately conjured up the last time they rode the railroad through this stunning canyon. It had to be over thirty years ago. On July 27, 1967, the train ceased operations. No longer could passengers hug the banks of the wild Arkansas River through this narrow chasm and gaze up at the famous Royal Gorge Bridge towering a thousand feet above. But today, memories are being made anew.

In summer 1999, the refurbished Royal Gorge Route started boarding passengers again at the historic Santa Fe Depot in Cañon City. The two-hour, twenty-four-mile round-trip winds along what was once described as "the most arresting single scenic site in all of American railroading." Passing rafters and kayakers seeking white-water thrills on waters channeled through the narrow passage of the Royal Gorge, the train skirts the banks of the Arkansas. The train stops below the bridge, allowing tourists the chance to move to the open-air car to take photographs in the narrowest, most rugged portion of the gorge. The train continues to Parkdale and then makes the return trip to Cañon City as the storied history of the route is told by well-versed conductors.

The Royal Gorge Route runs three times a day from mid-May through mid-October. At $24.50 for adults, ticket prices are a little steep, but the trip is worth it. 1-888-RAILS-4-U; www.royalgorgeroute.com.

BEST WEAVINGS
Eppie Archuleta's Studio (Capulin)

"My dad was a good teacher in every way—how to pray good, farm right, cook right and how to weave right." Eppie Archuleta's family has been weaving as far back as anyone can remember. She says she was born in the loom. Today, five generations still weave, including Eppie's mother, who's over a hundred years old. Tradition runs deep in the San Luis Valley, where almost every weaver was taught at one time or another by the person *National Geographic* magazine once called "a national treasure."

Piles of wool fill Eppie Archuleta's studio in the small town of Capulin. She washes it, runs it through her mill, spins it and dyes it. Now, standing at a nine-foot loom, Eppie weaves yet another masterpiece from her pure, 100 percent wool. She is surrounded by her works: a traditional "Corn Dance" weaving, a picture of the Statue of Liberty, the portrait of a woman, a beautiful rose. With natural-dye colors and tightly woven wool, Eppie paints, with a palate of yarn, intricate designs so rare and of such exquisite quality that the Smithsonian Institute in Washington, D.C., contains some of her pieces. Her reputation as a folk-art master led to an invitation to President Clinton's inauguration in 1993.

Weaving lies at the core of Eppie Archuleta's heart and soul. With help from her daughters, granddaughters, great-granddaughters and students, this homespun art form will not fade away in the modern world. In a metal building on Hwy. 15 in Capulin, southwest of Alamosa, Eppie's studio carries on the tradition. Stop in and say hello, or consider buying a work of art. (719) 274-5019.

Eppie Archuleta dries wool that she will spin into yarn and weave into one of her exquisite creations. *Photo by Doug Whitehead.*

BEST MONUMENT TO A SPORTS HERO
Jack Dempsey Museum (Manassa)

In a small log building where "The Manassa Mauler" was born, mementos, newspaper articles and photographs from a celebrated boxing career adorn the walls. Display cases hold memorabilia, including gloves from the Firpo fight and shoes from the Tuney fight. These prized possessions were given to the small museum by a bigger-than-life sports hero, Jack Dempsey. Known early in his career as "Kid Blackie," the budding boxer fought in small towns all over Colorado. As Dempsey went on to capture the Heavyweight Championship of the World, author Damon Runyon dubbed him "The Manassa Mauler" after the town where the champ grew up.

The sleepy town of Manassa in southern Colorado has never forgotten its favorite son. In summer 1999, in front of the museum, local sculptor Bob Booth unveiled a life-sized bronze likeness of Jack Dempsey in a fighting pose. Dedicated to Dempsey's mother, to whom he lovingly gave credit for raising him with strong values, the sculpture honors a small-town kid who made it big. As the guest book in the museum attests, supporters from all over the world have made the pilgrimage to his hometown. Well off the beaten path, Manassa hopes to continue luring fight fans here with this statue that immortalizes the power and grimace of a backwater fighter who became an American hero.

The Jack Dempsey Museum, open 9 to 5 Memorial Day through the end of September, is located on Hwy. 142 in Manassa, south of Alamosa. Call Manassa Town Hall for information, **(719) 843-5207.**

"The Manassa Mauler" stands in an eternal fighting pose in front of the champ's one-time home that now serves as a museum. *Photo by Doug Whitehead.*

☺ BEST HISTORICAL CROSSROADS
Fort Garland

The West of the 1800s was in flux. Lands traditionally held by Native American tribes were changing hands from the Spanish to the Mexicans to the Americans. Historical forces brought them all together in a restless mix of competing interests. Over a period of twenty-five years, from 1858 until 1883, Fort Garland became a cauldron of cultures in Colorado's San Luis Valley. Today, within the original thick, adobe walls of this old western outpost, a museum tells the story of the last surviving nineteenth-century military fort in Colorado.

Entering each building of the four-sided fort, visitors explore detailed dioramas, maps and displays of historical artifacts. Troops mustered here for the Battle of Glorieta Pass, the Civil War battle that saved Colorado for the Union. The famous scout Kit Carson commanded Fort Garland in 1866 and 1867. His negotiating skills, knowledge of the Ute language and friendship with Chief Ouray led to a period of relative peace in the region. And the museum sheds light on an often overlooked chapter of the American West: the all-black regiments that became involved in the Indian campaigns following the Civil War. One, the 9th Cavalry, was stationed at Fort Garland from 1875 through 1879, where it served the U.S. Army with distinction. Indian foes regarded the black troops' skills with respect, calling them "buffalo soldiers." Several buffalo soldiers received Congressional Medals of Honor for their service.

The Fort Garland Museum today is an important cog of Los Caminos Antiguos Scenic Byway, a route that winds through the history of the San Luis Valley. The museum's bookstore contains an impressive collection of books about the West. It's located in the town of Fort Garland on Hwy. 160 between Walsenburg and Alamosa. **(719) 379-3512.**

Outdoor Activities & Events

BEST RAFTING
Arkansas River

Technical, steep and continuous rapids through huge boulders in the Pine Creek section of the upper Arkansas River leave no margin for error. Make a mistake in this

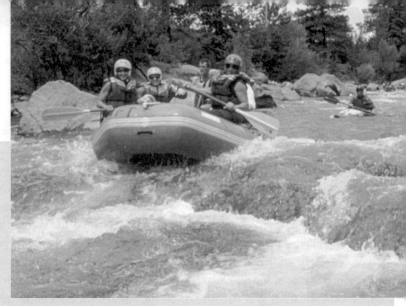

Rafters negotiate a stretch of rapids on the Arkansas River north of Buena Vista.
Photo by Doug Whitehead.

Class V white water and the consequences are severe. But you do have alternatives. In an outdoor sport that classifies its degrees of difficulty by how likely you are to damage your health if you mess up, rafters flock to the Arkansas for good reason. For every terrifying, exciting Class V run like Pine Creek, the Numbers or the Royal Gorge, long sections of more moderate, Class III waters attract floaters of all abilities. Add scenic beauty, easy accessibility and incredible variety and you have one of the premier rivers in the country for white-water rafting.

From narrow canyons where the view goes straight up to wide vistas of the Collegiate Peaks and the Sangre de Cristos, the Arkansas River cuts a silver swath through Colorado's midsection. Some of the state's pioneer river outfitters set up shop along its banks, offering anywhere from half-day to multiday adventures.

Just as soon as winter's snow starts melting from high peaks and valleys, you'll find someone paddling on the Arkansas. Anglers take to the river in early May during the famous caddis hatch. With the warming weather, these flying bugs fill the air, providing brown trout with a ready meal. Around mid-June, Salida's long-running "FibArk" (First in Boating on the Arkansas) river festival celebrates the region's lifeline with a weekend of music, arts and crafts and races on the river.

The Arkansas Headwaters Recreation Area regulates use of the river and provides put-in and take-out facilities along the 148-mile stretch from Leadville to Pueblo. Call **(719) 539-7289**. The Arkansas River Outfitters Association lists member outfitters; check out their website at **www.aroa.org**.

BEST SINGLE-TRACK BIKING
Monarch Crest Trail

On trails once traversed only by foot, mule or horseback, Colorado's backcountry today is made accessible by the ubiquitous mountain bike. It's the conveyance of choice for a whole new generation of lovers of the outdoors. Quite a few books are available that document a web of trails all over the region, but we think one trail is hill and dale above the rest for beauty, challenge, length, accessibility and single-track purity: the Monarch Crest Trail.

Beginning at 11,312 feet on the summit of Monarch Pass, park your car, grab your bike and hit the trail. Following the venerable Continental Divide, the Monarch Crest Trail rises gradually at first through a forest of Douglas fir and ponderosa pine. The narrow path leaves just enough room for only one set of fat tire tracks at a time. After a few short but steep climbs, you're already riding through rarefied air above treeline, trekking through fragile tundra that demands you keep your bike on the trail. One scar on this delicate high-altitude landscape can take years to heal. Nearby thirteen-thousand-foot peaks come into view as your bike hugs the ever-rising contours of this awesome alpine ribbon. The higher the elevation, the wider the vista. Famous Colorado mountain ranges appear in all directions: the Sawatch Range, Sangre de Cristos, San Juans and West Elks.

After fourteen miles in this top-of-the-world environment, you arrive at Marshall Pass, whose dirt road you follow down to Hwy. 285 and back to Poncha Springs. The amazing thing about this trail is that a family of intermediate ability can do this ride if they're not in a hurry, or a hot-shot mountain biker can cover it in a couple of hours. Mountain bikers should always defer to horses and hikers on the trail. Check with the High Country Shuttle in Poncha Springs at **1-800-871-5145; www.monarchcrest.com**. They'll haul you and your bike to the top of Monarch Pass to begin the trail.

BEST ROCK CLIMBING
Shelf Road Recreation Area
(near Cañon City)

With knuckles taut and curled, a climber's hand grips a crack in the rock surface with nothing but his fingertips. Belly to the wall and neck craned upward, one leg swings carefully as his foot searches blindly for its next toehold. Sensing an infinitesimal perch, he pushes himself another six inches higher, spread-eagled like a spider on a sheer stone face. He is but a speck in a labyrinth of limestone canyons known to rock climbers around the world as the Shelf Road Recreation Area.

Given names like Lizard with a View, Not So Killer Bees and Primal Scream, hundreds of routes have been pioneered since the mid-1980s on cliffs called Sand Gulch, the Gallery, the Dark Side and the Gymnasium, to name a few. Located in a banana belt, this climbing area in the piñon-juniper forest is accessible all year long. With an extensive network of cliffs and walls, climbers never feel crowded. A well-coordinated effort between aficionados of the sport and the Bureau of Land Management has led to more than four hundred established climbing routes in this landscape between Cañon City and Cripple Creek. Strategically placed expansion bolts open up all manner of technical pitches, bulges, cracks and slabs. Climbers spend little time getting to these easily accessible routes and most of their time climbing them.

Although some climbers have moved on to the more remote Penitente Canyon north of Del Norte, the Shelf Road remains one of the premier choices in the state for variety, challenge, accessibility and scenery. The area is located about nine miles north of Cañon City on County Rd. 9, part of the Gold Belt Tour Scenic Byway (see Best Collection of Scenic Drives on page 136). BLM campsites are available in the canyon area, or more refined accommodations can be found in nearby Cañon City or Cripple Creek. For information about the area, call the Bureau of Land Management in Cañon City at **(719) 269-8500** or the Sport Climbing Center in Colorado Springs at **(719) 260-1050**.

BEST ANIMAL SANCTUARY
Mission: Wolf (near Gardner)

Howls carry through the still air of an otherwise silent night, awakening primal memories of a wilderness lost. Wolves disappeared from many parts of the West years ago, but here in isolated country near the San Isabel National Forest, wayward purebreds and hybrids find refuge. They arrive here as washed-up "movie actors" from Hollywood or onetime pets to unsuspecting owners unaware that wolves cannot be domesticated, living out their lives in dignity in acre-sized, fenced enclosures with the dedicated, passionate help of Mission:Wolf.

But for their recent reintroduction in Wyoming's Yellowstone National Park, the fate of the canny canine in the West remains dire. For years now, Kent Weber and his staff have made public education a top priority. Intrepid visitors to the remote Mission: Wolf site find a recently constructed visitors center that provides a good introduction to this wild animal. A full-time caretaker next escorts you around the property, where intimate encounters with the forty-five resident wolves make an indelible impression about their stature, grace, strength and beauty. From piercing eyes and noble countenance to huge, wide paws like snowshoes, it's a rare image of cunning creatures ideally suited to range freely in a landscape today made inhospitable to the wolf by pressures of the modern world.

Mission:Wolf is open to the public from 9 A.M. until sunset year-round. Camping is allowed. No admission fee, but donations are appreciated. From Hwy. 69, it's located north and east of Gardner on dirt roads. For exact directions and other information contact (719) 746-2919; www.indra.com/fallline/mw.

BEST BIRD-WATCHING
Monte Vista National Wildlife Refuge

It's an ancient call that echoes from snow-covered peaks. Still and silent mornings are pierced with the rusty honks of thousands of birds on the wing. The scene evokes images of the great preserves of Africa. But every spring, for millennia, the skies of the San Luis Valley in Colorado are filled with the sleek, gray bodies of the sandhill crane. Wave upon wave arrives from Mexico as their feet droop down for a pterodactyl-like landing in the wetlands of the Monte Vista National Wildlife Refuge. During their two-month stay here along this time-tested flyway, the birds load up on abundant food sources in the valley as they prepare to continue the long flight to summering grounds in Idaho.

From late February until mid-April, Monte Vista is alive with this annual spectacle. The Sandhill Crane Festival on a long weekend in March offers opportunities for naturalist-led tours, seminars and workshops. With markings of red and black, the charcoal-gray cranes stand as high as four feet. A delicate dance can be observed in the fields as they flutter and dip in their unique mating ritual. If you're lucky, you might catch a glimpse of one of the few remaining endangered whooping cranes. It's a rare sight to see this majestic crane with an eight-foot wingspan in flight. The Monte Vista National Wildlife Refuge is located on Hwy. 15 south of Hwy. 160. For information about the spring festival call 1-800-835-7254.

☺ BEST FOSSILIZED BUGS
Florissant Fossil Beds

Long before Pikes Peak rose to dominate the horizon thirty-five million years ago, a volcano towered above this valley, spewing lava. Mudflows covered giant sequoias, cedars and pines. Tons of ash trapped layer after layer of thousands of insects that thrived in a warm, humid climate. Almost like ancient photographs, exquisite forms of delicate bodies and wings are preserved on thin sheets of shale. More than eleven hundred species of butterflies, caterpillars, spiders and other long-gone bugs can be seen along with petrified redwood stumps and a huge variety of cones, leaves, flowers and twigs. All this contributes to this world-renowned snapshot of a onetime Colorado swamp.

Geologists estimate there are probably eighty or ninety petrified tree stumps in the park, most of them still buried underground. The one-mile Petrified Forest Loop Trail takes you past stumps up to seventy-four feet around, and other trails meander through this natural park. In addition to the geologic history of the Florissant Fossil Beds, Adeline Hornbek's cabin, barn, shed and root cellar preserve human history in the valley. This single mother brought her children here in 1878, becoming one of the first women in the West to take advantage of the Homestead Act. Take Hwy. 24 west from Colorado Springs to the small town of Florissant. Follow signs south to the Fossil Beds. **(719) 748-3253; www.nationalparks.org.**

☺ BEST WHEELCHAIR WILDERNESS EXPERIENCE
Wilderness on Wheels (Pike National Forest)

Roger West spent a lifetime in the outdoors with his dad. When he learned that his elderly father had become wheelchair-bound, his heart sank. How would his father ever again enjoy smelling the scents of the forest or landing a rainbow trout? How could any disabled person take part in outdoor activities the rest of us take for granted? Out of his grief, an idea was born. Now, for more than a decade, Wilderness on Wheels has provided the answer.

Built with lots of heart on years of volunteer labor and generous donations from places like lumberyards and hardware stores, an eight-foot-wide board-walk winds over a mile through the Pike National Forest. With a gentle grade and numerous pullouts (sort of like scenic rest stops with picnic tables), people in wheelchairs work their way up the hillside, rolling past a mountain stream, casting a line into a fishing pond or setting up camp in the pine forest. Quite a few tent platforms and two wheelchair-accessible cabins allow anyone to stay several nights in the woods. Wilderness on Wheels has also been discovered by once-active elderly folks who, even if it's with a walker, have a way to reconnect with the outdoors. All ages with every kind of disability find a sense of independence here.

One spur of the boardwalk descends to an outdoor amphitheater with a stage

Roger West takes a walk with a wheelchair-bound friend on a fall day in the Pike National Forest. *Photo by Doug Whitehead.*

for concerts and room for three hundred people to gather for an outside event. With boardwalks becoming increasingly popular, more and more disabled people are gaining access to the outdoors. Wilderness on Wheels hopes to be a model for other efforts around the country and the world. Even though Roger West's father did not live to visit what his son created, the legacy of their bond will live for generations to come. (303) 751-3959; www.wildernessonwheels.org.

☺ BEST DESERT IN THE MOUNTAINS
Great Sand Dunes National Monument (near Alamosa)

It's a scene out of *Lawrence of Arabia*. Strong and steady winds blow over an ever-changing landscape of shimmering dunes of sand. Here, the dunes lie thousands of miles inland surrounded by towering fourteen-thousand-foot, snow-covered peaks.

This footprint in the sand will soon disappear as steady winds constantly shape the landscape at Great Sand Dunes National Monument. *Photo by Doug Whitehead.*

The Great Sand Dunes National Monument lies at the base of the Sangre de Cristo Range at the eastern edge of the San Luis Valley.

Ages ago, the entire valley was a swamp. Today, with the water not very far beneath the surface of the ground, giant mounds of sand are held in place by the moisture. Constant wind currents run up against a wall of mountains, depositing airborne sand particles at this very spot. In the springtime, visitors are quickly engulfed in the landscape as they cross the wide and shallow flow of Medano Creek and approach the hills and dales of dunes that reach up to seven hundred feet high. Winds blow a continual carpet of moving sand over the curves, ridges and slopes of this scene in constant flux. From early morning through late afternoon, a changing palette of light mixes with moving angles of the sun as shadows lengthen and stretch on this unique wilderness canvas.

The visitors center is the best place to start your visit to the sand dunes, with exhibits and explanations about this natural feature. One hundred eighty first-come, first-served campsites sit at the edge of the dunes, where deer, elk and other wildlife also visit. Take Hwy. 160 west from Walsenburg to Hwy. 150. Go sixteen miles north to the entrance of the park and the visitors center. (719) 378-2312; www.nationalparks.org.

☺ BEST OUT-OF-PLACE ANIMALS
Colorado Alligator Farm (north of Alamosa)

Mama, don't let your babies grow up to be . . . alligator wrestlers! Lynne Young didn't follow that advice, but her son Jay doesn't seem to mind. In fact, he's pretty comfortable with the seventy-five gators that live outdoors at the Colorado Alligator Farm. These critters, more likely seen in a Louisiana bayou, may seem a little out of place in the San Luis Valley, but that's precisely why they're such a novelty.

The alligators weren't intended to be the main attraction. The Young family raise tilapia here, a tropical perch consumed by people around the world. Alligators were brought in as garbage disposals to clean up dead fish and waste from processing. The same geothermal waters that make it possible for the fish to survive brutal Colorado winters also act as a kind of gator spa. A well produces water at a constant 87 degrees at this farm seventeen miles north of Alamosa, making it an ideal environment for these otherwise warm-weather creatures.

When locals became fascinated with the presence of alligators in their neighborhood, the Youngs realized they needed to cater to the public. You can feed the nasty-looking things and even get your picture taken holding a real live baby gator. The first alligator hatched in Colorado, Sir Chomps O' Lot, and other hatchlings can be seen here. Since they introduced the gators in 1987, the Young family has added iguanas, turtles, pythons, rattlesnakes and even two sharks to its menagerie.

The annual Gatorfest attracts thousands of visitors every July 4 weekend to see alligator wrestling, shark feeding, turtle racing and other special events. There's a gift shop with all sorts of T-shirts and gator memorabilia. **(719) 589-3032;** www.gatorfarm.com.

☺ BEST HOT SPRINGS
Mount Princeton Hot Springs (Nathrop)

How do you choose the best hot springs when each is unique and wonderful in its own way? Cottonwood, Valley View or Mount Princeton? It's not an easy job, but someone has to make the tough decision. After an exhaustive search for the best place to relax in thermal waters, Mount Princeton gets our nod.

Smooth, mineral-laden waters fill two large swimming pools at these historic hot springs, but that's not what sets Mount Princeton apart. Along the banks of Chalk Creek, which carries melting snow from surrounding fourteen-thousand-foot peaks, springs gurgle to the surface from deep underground. Bathers arrange rocks to create their own custom coves with a mix of earth-hot waters and snow-cold runoff. Soaking in perfect temperatures at creek level in their natural, stone grottos, bodies relax to the soothing sounds of a flowing stream in an awesome alpine setting. With low sulfur content, these waters are devoid of the rotten-egg odors common to some mineral springs.

Mount Princeton Hot Springs is located south of Buena Vista off of Hwy. 285. Follow County Rd. 162 from Nathrop about five miles to the resort. Call **1-888-395-7799** for more information. You'll find the rock masonry pools of Cottonwood Hot Springs five miles west of Buena Vista on the Cottonwood Pass Rd. At Valley View Hot Springs in the San Luis Valley west of the intersection of Hwy. 285 and Hwy. 17, bathing suits are optional and the public is welcome Monday through Friday.

☺ BEST MUSIC FESTIVAL
Jazz in the Sangres (Westcliffe)

It started in a downpour. When a few jazz bands played from a flatbed wagon in 1984, the heavens opened up. Everyone crammed into the Feed & Seed Restaurant to get out of the rain, and the music played on. A few years later, the Big Tent went up in Westcliffe's Town Park, and weather hasn't been an issue since. On lawn chairs and blankets, about eighteen hundred fans gather every summer in the shadow of the Sangre de Cristo Mountains for an intimate weekend of Jazz in the Sangres.

The list of musicians over the years reads like a "Who's Who" of jazz: Spike Robinson, the Wallace Roney Quintet, Herbie Mann, Spyrogyra, "Sweets" Edison, Dotsero, Queen City Jazz Band and Hot Tomatoes Dance Orchestra, just to scratch the surface. Beginning Friday night (with a simultaneous wine-tasting party) and continuing through the weekend, you'll hear every variation of this indigenous American music form—traditional, Dixieland, swing, blues and classical. As a long-standing tradition at the festival, "The Heavenly Echoes" belt out gospel tunes on Sunday morning with a majesty to match the mountains. With a mix of local and regional acts and national headliners, Jazz in the Sangres attracts top-flight talent. Musicians love the nine-foot Steinway piano that graces the stage, and the sound system always seems to carry the music loud and clear. Festivalgoers mingle with musicians in the autograph tent, and artists around the region display their works. With food and drink concessions and a playground for the kids, this is a well-organized family weekend of music.

Join the festivities on the second weekend of August. For ticket information call **(719) 783-3785** in Westcliffe or **(303) 794-4170** in Denver.

BEST SNOWCAT SKIING
Monarch Ski and Snowboard Area

White, fluffy flakes pile up every winter on the Continental Divide at the southern end of the Sawatch Range. Monarch Ski Area has always been known for its abundant snow and small crowds, but now, thanks to snowcats, nine hundred acres of backcountry terrain make deep, untracked powder available to hard-core skiers and boarders in the Waterdog Lakes region of the San Isabel National Forest. Avoiding the chairlifts and groomed trails at this alternative to Colorado's mega-resorts, schussers and shredders drop a thousand feet on runs in this private playground with almost thirty feet of annual snowfall.

With Crested Butte more than an hour to the west and Ski Cooper and the resorts of Summit County well to the north, Monarch sits like an alpine oasis in Colorado's winter paradise. Though the area makes for a good family outing with lower lift prices and uncrowded easy and moderate trails, its reputation for extreme snowboarding and skiing continues to grow. With the addition of snow-cats to the scene, the smooth, soft, steep snow in more remote reaches of the area presents new challenges to hearty downhillers.

A group of twelve skiers can rent a snowcat for $1,500 a day. Reservations are required. The area is located on Hwy. 50 near the top of Monarch Pass, about fifteen miles west of Poncha Springs. **1-888 996-7669; www.skimonarch.com.**

☺ BEST NORDIC SKIING
Fairplay Nordic Center

An eternal wind blows through this Colorado sky, its patterns reflected in contours shaped on fields of driven snow. Sheltered from the prevailing scouring winds, you'll discover some great cross-country ski trails in undiscovered South Park. The snow stays on the ground here, providing a smooth, soft surface for those seeking winter solitude.

Only a ninety-minute drive from a population of millions along the Front Range, the Fairplay Nordic Center has surprisingly few devotees of its fourteen miles of groomed trails. Even when other people are here, it feels as though you're skiing by yourself. As you glide through the aspen at the edge of a high ridge north of Fairplay, the 13,822-foot summit of Mount Silverheels rises into view. The mountain was named by appreciative miners for the legendary Silver Heels, a beautiful dance-hall girl who tended the sick during a smallpox outbreak in the old mining town of Buckskin Joe. Somehow her selfless spirit carries on a zephyr of cool, rarefied air as you whoosh along these tranquil trails. Take Hwy. 285 to Fairplay and follow signs from Fourth St. to the Fairplay Nordic Center. **(719) 836-2658.**

Where to Eat, Drink & Stay

BEST SOUTHWESTERN FARE
Emma's Hacienda (San Luis)

In Colorado's oldest town, the town's oldest restaurant serves the region's best Mexican food. San Luis was founded in 1851, and for more than fifty years of its existence, a small brick building in the center of town has been home to Emma's Hacienda. Because Emma Espinoza, her daughters and granddaughters learned to cook their mouthwatering enchiladas, burritos, tacos, tamales and green chile right here in San Luis, they don't refer to their cuisine as "Mexican." They say they prepare "Food of the Southwest" the way they do at home: from scratch.

So particular is Emma that she's been known to send a whole truckload of chiles back to New Mexico because they weren't quite right. Her daughters, who do most of the cooking today, will tell you that ever since their parents opened the restaurant in 1947, Emma has instilled her unwavering dedication to quality. Roasting their own chiles; mixing fresh tomatoes, herbs and spices in the green and red chiles; and preparing their own special dough for sopaipillas, the dishes at Emma's Hacienda leave a vivid, lingering taste in your mouth without a heavy feeling in your stomach. Spread the homemade honey butter on your sopaipilla to end your meal and you'll leave Emma's with a lasting impression. Nowhere else does food like this taste so good.

Spry and effervescent, well dressed and always in high heels, eighty-something Emma still greets her customers like old friends, and many of them are. Even on your first visit, you'll feel like you're part of the family. **355 Main St.; (719) 672-9902.**

An unassuming exterior offers little hint of the culinary delights inside Emma's Hacienda. *Photo by Doug Whitehead.*

BEST STEAKHOUSE
True Grits (Alamosa)

It doesn't look like much from the outside, but judging from all the parked cars, this is a popular spot to eat. Even inside, with basic decor and tables packed tightly together, you wonder what you're in for. But if you can trust John Wayne, his pictures omnipresent on the restaurant walls testify to the hearty meal you're about to enjoy.

Order from a wide variety of steak and whatever, with shrimp or chicken or catfish as the second choice on your plate. When the salad arrives and the signature soda bread is placed on your table, you might think that's meal enough. The portions could satisfy "the Duke" after a long day in the saddle. But even his eyes would roll at the Texas-size steak and grapefruit-size baked potato that show up for the main meal. Somehow, of course, you find room for this Colorado beef and locally grown spuds. And after you can hardly move anymore, you're pleasantly surprised by the check. Prices are reasonable at this Alamosa institution. True Grits is located on Hwy. 160 on the east edge of town, just past the turnoff to Hwy. 12. Reservations suggested. **(719) 589-9954.**

BEST DINING IN THE BOONDOCKS
Antero Grill (north of Salida)

When we passed the Texas longhorns on Hwy. 285 south of Buena Vista, we should've had a clue. After all, this is cattle country. But still, the Antero Grill was a total surprise. Fourth-generation restaurateurs from Santa Fe call their fare "Modern American cowboy cuisine." No cowboy ever ate like this.

Imagine the chuck wagon out on the range offering as an appetizer "Frontier-Style Wild Game Sausage" or "Gunpowder Rock Shrimp Quesadillas." Well, that's just a spicy taste of things to come at the Antero Grill. Executive Chef David Woolley has created a list of entrees we've never seen in a place like the boondocks of the Upper Arkansas Valley. Braised rabbit, turkey medallions, vegetable torte and beef tenderloin tips, to name a few, come with various combinations of side dishes, including "Roasted Sweet Corn Mashed Potatoes" and apple-cornbread stuffing. The "Open Fire Bone-In Pork Loin" is prepared with "Native American spices." The steaks are aged, and everything, they say, is made from scratch.

The western ambiance includes everything from cowboy paintings to lassos on the wall, "barbed-wire" swizzle sticks and leather napkin rings. With wooden beams on the ceiling and a fireplace on the main floor, it feels like the trail boss's living room.

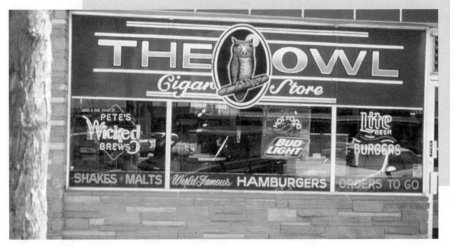

The Owl Cigar Store has graced Canon City's Main Street for decades. *Photo by Doug Whitehead.*

There's a deck out back and alcoves downstairs with private tables. Conjuring up images of the campfire, s'mores are served for dessert with homemade marshmallows, chocolate and graham crackers. The menu changes seasonally. The Antero Grill is located sixteen miles south of Buena Vista on the east side of Hwy. 285. Reservations suggested. Call **(719) 530-0301**, or e-mail them at **anterogrill@bewellnet.com**.

BEST CHEAP BURGERS AND MALTS
The Owl Cigar Store (Cañon City)

Pete Santilli was a pretty good poker player. Stationed in Italy during World War II, he sent his winnings back to his brothers in Colorado. When Pete got home in 1943, they had enough money to buy a Cañon City institution. The Owl Cigar Store has been in the family ever since.

Sitting at the worn marble counter on a red swivel stool, you can play six mostly 1960s tunes on the jukebox for a quarter. At one time you could buy a burger for 10 cents, but today burgers are still a good deal at only a buck. Or get a thick malt for $1.90, the most expensive item on the menu. It's made from hard vanilla ice cream.

Mounted deer, antelope and a bighorn sheep shot by long-gone patrons stare down from the walls. Big fish, historic photos, old advertisements and dated license plates (one is from 1929) finish out the decor. Pete can't remember exactly when the old wooden bar was installed, but he'll tell you this has been a local watering hole since the turn of the century. For a long time, he couldn't sell anything but 3.2 beer, but that has changed. And so has the space. Pete added on to the building to make room for pool tables and burnt-orange vinyl booths. You could find a bigger burger somewhere else, but none come with the nostalgia of The Owl Cigar Store.

Pete's son and nephew run the place now, but you'll see Pete Sr. here most every day of the week. Daughter Susan works behind the counter. And yes, they still sell a few cigars. If you can't find The Owl Cigar Store in downtown Cañon City, just ask somebody. Everyone knows where it is. **626 Main St.; (719) 275-9946.**

BEST CHEAP EATS
Cripple Creek Casinos

What are the odds the food's any good? Well, we can't guarantee the quality, but we bet you won't complain about the price. In an effort to entice gamblers hungry for more than a jackpot, many casinos in Cripple Creek keep your stomach full for cheap while you empty your wallet in the slots. We rolled the dice down Bennett Ave. and came up with quite a serving of deals for meals:

Bronco Billy's—Coming up like snake eyes, two eggs stare back from your breakfast plate, along with bacon, hash browns and toast for only 49 cents.

Palace Hotel and Casino—A full house for breakfast with a full stack of pancakes for $1.99.

Tourists ride in a horse-drawn carriage along Cripple Creek's Bennett Avenue. *Photo by Doug Whitehead.*

Virgin Mule Casino—Dealing a hot hand and hot dogs at 25 cents, tamales for 99 cents and bratwurst with kraut, chips and soda for $2.95.

Gold Rush Hotel and Casino—Mining for gamblers "All Day, Every Day" with the New York Strip Steak Special with fries, vegetables and roll at $2.99.

Creeker's Casino—After all your losses, the "All You Can Eat" Saturday buffet includes prime rib, crab legs, oysters, crawfish, clam chowder and more for $9.95.

☺ BEST DRIVE-IN WITHOUT A CAR
Movie Manor (Monte Vista)

It's your basic Best Western Motel with nice enough rooms and decent rates, but Movie Manor on the outskirts of Monte Vista is unlike any motel in the world. As the sun goes down, you get your popcorn, turn up the volume, settle back and wait for the movie to start. A drive-in? Well, yes, but you're not in your car, you're in your room! With a speaker in each room and the big screen outside the window, guests simply open the curtain, watch the movie and then settle in for a good night's sleep.

George Kelloff remembers pumping a player piano at his mother's silent movie theater when he was a kid, so the movies are in his blood. He built a drive-in theater in 1955 and then got the idea to add the motel nine years later. Each door of all sixty rooms is labeled with the name of a big star like Humphrey Bogart, Marilyn Monroe, John Wayne or Ann-Margret. Posters and paintings of Hollywood's greatest decorate the walls. First-run movies come to Movie Manor from the theater the Kelloff family owns in downtown Monte Vista. Area residents can still come to the drive-in, a vanishing American institution, and visitors to the motel get the most unique moviegoing experience of their lives. Only G-rated and PG-13 movies are shown at the motel. The Foundation of Motion Picture Pioneers has honored Mr. Kelloff with a Golden Movie Pass that gives him free access to any movie theater in America. Well into his eighties, he now lets his son run the business, so he's got more time to watch his favorite movies.

Check out the banquet rooms of Movie Manor's restaurant. More posters and photographs from Hollywood, including some original Mickey Mouse art, hang on the walls. It's located about two miles west of Monte Vista on Hwy. 160. **1-800-771-9468**; **www.coloradovacation/motel/movie.com.**

BEST SMALL-TOWN BED-AND-BREAKFAST
El Convento (San Luis)

You don't have to be Catholic, or even religious, to stay overnight in this refurbished convent. From the 1930s until 1957, the Sisters of Mercy taught grade school and high school in this two-story historic building. In what looks like a class picture, a photograph of the nuns in their black-and-white habits hangs in a hallway. Today, the local parish runs El Convento as an inn, welcoming travelers for a good night's rest. Located next to Sangre de Cristo Catholic Church in San Luis, it's only a block from the trail that leads up to a hill above town following the Stations of the Cross (see Best Religious Shrine on page 132).

Large windows and high ceilings allow light to pour into each of the four spacious rooms on the second floor of this building, built in 1905. With simple, wooden furniture, wood floors and hanging plants, these quiet lodgings feel like home. Two of the rooms include an adobe-style, nonworking fireplace for a little southwest ambiance. You won't find a phone in your room, but you can watch TV. Walking down the steep staircase to the first floor in the morning, you smell the coffee brewing and breakfast cooking. Sit down in the dining room to your choice of juice, fruit, cereal, eggs, sausage and toast. To get there, take I-25 south to Walsenburg. Go west on Hwy. 160 to Fort Garland and then south sixteen miles on Hwy. 159 to San Luis. Contact the rectory of Sangre de Cristo Church for reservations. **(719) 672-3685.**

BEST HISTORIC HOTEL
Imperial Hotel (Cripple Creek)

Back-to-back fires nearly destroyed Cripple Creek in 1896, but just as soon as the wooden buildings burned to the ground, the town was rebuilt brick by brick. With more than twenty-five thousand residents and fifty-six passenger trains arriving daily in the world's richest mining district, a grand hotel rose from the ashes in the heart of this thriving boomtown. For more than a hundred years, the history of Cripple Creek has passed through the doors of the Imperial Hotel.

Around the turn of the century, industrialists, politicians and celebrities enjoyed the opulence of the Imperial, one of the few places in the country to feature the modern convenience of electricity. Little at the hotel has changed since then. With no elevator, crooked staircases today lead to rooms on the second and third floors with some shared bathrooms at the end of the hall and some private ones. Many of the original light fixtures hang from the ceilings; telephones and televisions are about the only contemporary appliances to be added. Antique furniture, claw-footed bathtubs and steam-heat radiators contribute to an atmosphere unchanged since Grover Cleveland was president of the United States and Albert W. McIntire was governor of Colorado. Though the classic rooms are clean and comfortable, the Imperial Hotel appeals to those looking not for the latest amenities but to experience an era gone by.

With a bustling casino, popular Friday and Saturday buffets and a Sunday brunch, the Imperial now caters to gamblers hoping to strike it rich in the town that once produced great fortunes. It's located near the corner of Third St. and Bennett Ave.; 1-800-235-2922.

Ghosts of the past still prowl the halls of the Imperial Hotel in Cripple Creek. *Photo by Doug Whitehead.*

Southwest

Previous page: Columbine, the state flower, thrives near Crested Butte, the Wildflower Capital of Colorado. *Photo by Doug Whitehead.*

Southwest

The world seems tinted blue in truth. Sky, flowers, distant mountains all are stained with it.
—James Grafton Rogers,
from *My Rocky Mountain Valley*

White-capped peaks do glimmer in the rarefied air of the "Shining Mountains." Known by that name for centuries by the native Ute Indians, the San Juan Mountains have enticed people for centuries to their almost incomprehensible dimensions, elevation and grandeur. Raging rivers, high meadows and immeasurable forests provided an abundance of wildlife to the Utes, age-old caretakers of their pristine homeland. During a few short decades in the 1800s, though, the Utes lost everything to white settlers' thirst for gold. Today, the landscape lies riddled with the dramatic accomplishments of an industrial invasion into these sacred hills. With backbreaking labor, mine shafts were sunk and narrow-gauge tracks were laid in seemingly inaccessible mountain locales so steam engines could haul out the ore holding incredible wealth. Those old trails now provide travelers with a way to explore the remote backcountry of the San Juans, marveling at the achievements that fueled the growth of the United States and changed forever the fortunes of the Utes.

The San Juan Skyway, a ribbon of road connecting much of this region's resources, provides a continuous source of amazement as it loops through high mountains and drops through river valleys. You can spend all your time along Hwy. 550 in Ouray, Silverton and Durango, but that would be just scratching the surface! Enjoy a different festival every week during the summer in Telluride, or explore the nation's newest national park, the deep and narrow chasm called the Black Canyon of the Gunnison. Wildflowers burst into brilliant colors in Crested Butte, Colorado's official Wildflower Capital. The list goes on and on.

The burgeoning population of southwest Colorado has never reached the numbers present in antiquity. The extraordinary remains of the Anasazi, ancestors of modern Pueblo tribes, offer testament to a thriving culture. The ruins of Mesa Verde, Hovenweep, Chimney Rock and the Ute Mountain Tribal Park, along with similar sites in adjoining states, reveal a highly organized, flourishing civilization.

The abrupt end to the Anasazi in A.D. 1300 remains a mystery to this day. The cliff dwellings, towers, kivas, potsherds and rock art left behind provide plenty of clues but only guesses for answers. The wealth of nature and history in the San Juan Mountains of southwest Colorado can never be fully explored, not even in a lifetime. But even one visit can spawn a lifetime of interest.

Cultural & Historical

BEST WALK AMONG THE ANCIENTS
Ute Mountain Tribal Park (Towaoc)

What happened to the Anasazi? It's the biggest mystery of Colorado's past. The remains of their once-thriving culture lie scattered across southwest Colorado and the Four Corners region. It's impossible not to wonder about the circumstances that led to these extraordinary communities and why they were abandoned so quickly around A.D. 1300. The most spectacular examples of their cliff dwellings are found at Mesa Verde National Park, but the most intimate experience with the "Ancient Ones" comes at Ute Mountain Tribal Park.

A rugged landscape of flattops, cones and needles stretches miles in every direction on your approach south from Cortez. As you travel a dusty road eastward, a Ute Indian guide points out potsherds that lie strewn across the canyon floor and rock art chipped out of the desert varnish of sandstone and shale. The slender Mancos River snakes its way through bottomlands lined with cottonwood trees. Then, rising to the mesa top, the road carries you through piñon and juniper forest to the brink of narrowing arroyos and canyons. From here, you tread the same paths, toe the same chiseled footholds, climb down the same steep canyon walls and enter the same doorways of shelters once inhabited by the ancestors of modern Pueblo tribes. Fingerprints from builders remain pressed in adobe bricks. From this cliffside perch, you see similar homes in equally improbable locations tucked in shallow caverns up and down the canyon. The forces that bound people together in this unlikely neighborhood may never be fully understood, but without the crowds of visitors at Mesa Verde to the north, your mind's eye is freer here to contemplate those ancient lives.

To get here, take Hwy. 160 west through Durango to Cortez. Go south on Hwy. 160/666 through the small town of Towaoc, which is the tribal headquarters of the Ute Indians. Continue south several miles to the small Ute Tribal Park Museum. You'll get an introduction to the park from the artifacts, photographs and artworks in this one-room museum. Begin your guided tour here. Tours offered daily May through October. To make reservations, call **1-800-847-5485**.

BEST ANASAZI TOUR
Trail of the Ancients
(Durango–Cortez vicinity)

A thousand years ago, more people lived in southwest Colorado than call it home today. Evidence of a flourishing civilization remains in canyons and arroyos, on mesas and mountaintops, along remote stretches of river and on parched plateaus. Tying many of these sites together for the modern motorist, the Trail of the Ancients Scenic Byway reveals the fascinating history of the Anasazi.

Mesa Verde National Park—Perhaps the most spectacular concentration of cliff dwellings in the region, Mesa Verde can overwhelm your senses for the sheer scale and majesty of its architectural achievement. Extensive ruins lie tucked in the steep walls of rugged, isolated canyons. Located south of Hwy. 160 between Durango and Cortez, Mesa Verde makes a good starting point on the Trail of the Ancients. **1-800-253-1616**.

Anasazi Heritage Center—Continue west toward Cortez on Hwy. 160, then head north on Hwy. 145 to the small town of Dolores. Signs will lead you to this museum and research center

The Spruce Tree House ruins in Mesa Verde National Park draw millions of visitors a year.
Photo by Doug Whitehead.

created when the nearby McPhee Reservoir was built. Before sixteen hundred ancient sites were flooded, more than two million artifacts were gathered, cataloged and stored to provide a broad picture of the lives of these ancestors of modern Pueblo and Hopi tribes. A short trail takes you to ruins just above the facility. **(970) 882-4811.**

Lowry Pueblo—From Dolores, take Hwy. 184 west to Hwy. 666. Go north to Pleasant View and follow signs west about nine miles to this National Historic Landmark. Surrounded by wide-open ranchland, you'll see the Great Kiva, one of the largest of circular ceremonial structures to be found in the Four Corners region. Forty rooms sitting three stories high once housed a community here. The unique Painted Kiva survives with several layers of murals preserved on its walls. Call the Anasazi Heritage Center for information (see previous listing).

Hovenweep National Monument—From Lowry Pueblo, Scenic Byway signs will direct you along a pretty good dirt road southwest to ruins that straddle the Utah–Colorado border. Set on the rims, slopes and floor of a gentle arroyo, the remains of buildings of different shapes and sizes lie sprinkled throughout the landscape. From the Square Tower Ruins, trails lead you through private land to several other remote sites in the area. A campground and ranger station with maps and information are located at the main site on the Utah side. For information, call the Natural Bridges National Monument in Utah at **(435) 692-1234.**

Ute Mountain Tribal Park—Follow signs from Hovenweep and follow the paved road back into Colorado through McElmo Canyon to Hwy. 160/666 south of Cortez. See "Best Walk Among the Ancients," in this region, for details.

Crow Canyon Archaeological Center—Just north of Cortez on Hwy. 666, a sign will point you a mile west to this place where daylong and weeklong programs offer amateurs a chance to join ongoing archaeological digs at various Anasazi sites. Accommodations, meals and educational workshops make this a unique adventure into an ancient world. For a catalog of programs and other information, call **1-800-422-8975.**

Chimney Rock Archaeological Area—Though this site is not included on the Trail of the Ancients Scenic Byway, it's worth a mention. The trailhead for ranger-led hikes to these ruins high above the Piedra River lies 3.5 miles south of Hwy. 160 between Pagosa Springs and Durango on Hwy. 151. Tours are offered early May through mid-September. Call **(970) 883-5359.**

BEST MOUNTAIN DRIVE
San Juan Skyway
(Ouray, Durango, Telluride)

This wide loop of paved highways would take about six hours if you drove nonstop, but the trip would be so much better if you gave yourself at least a week. Circling the circumference of the heart of Ute Indian homelands, the San Juan Skyway passes through some of the most rugged and scenic country in Colorado. Victorian mining towns and modern ski resorts, Anasazi ruins and bubbling hot springs, luxury accommodations and backcountry camping and historic mountain passes with steep, winding descents all combine for a breathtaking, inspiring, almost overwhelming journey.

Leaving the hot springs pool of Ouray behind, Hwy. 550 follows a route pioneered by Otto Mears, Colorado's "Pathfinder" who blazed trails in the 1800s. A seemingly endless series of switchbacks climbs past ruins of mines and mills surrounded by towering mountain peaks. The avalanche-prone road crests at 11,018 feet at the summit of Red Mountain Pass and drops down to Silverton, surrounded by the remains of mines and mills from the gold- and silver-mining days. The highway rises again over Molas Pass, passing Trimble Hot Springs and Purgatory Ski Resort. Then you enter Durango, capital of the Four Corners region and southern terminus of the Durango & Silverton Narrow Gauge Railroad (see Best Ride on the Rails on page 168). Hwy. 160 heads west past Mesa Verde (see Best Anasazi Tour on page 165) to Cortez, where Hwy. 145 begins its northward trek over Lizard Head Pass to Telluride, home to a thriving destination ski resort. The trip continues to Placerville, where Hwy. 62 heads back east over Dallas Divide, with its incredible views of Mount Sneffels, to Ridgway, where Orvis Hot Springs lies just ten miles north of your starting point of Ouray.

With miles of hikes, four-wheel-drive roads, museums, mine tours and much, much more, explorations along the San Juan Skyway could even take a lifetime. The route is best taken during the summer and fall months. Portions of the route are sometimes closed during winter. Chambers of Commerce: **Ouray,** 1-800-228-1876; **Silverton,** 1-800-752-4494; **Durango,** 1-800-GO-DURANGO; **Cortez,** 1-800-253-1616; **Telluride,** 1-800-525-3455.

The Durango & Silverton Narrow Gauge Railroad pulls into Silverton after winding through the San Juan Mountains. *Photo by Doug Whitehead.*

☺ BEST RIDE ON THE RAILS
Durango & Silverton Narrow Gauge Railroad

When the whistle blows, you can hear it all over town. Look for its source and you find black smoke belching into the sky. Follow your senses to the hustle and bustle and join passengers as they climb on board the historic railcars of the Durango & Silverton Narrow Gauge Railroad. Steam hisses, the whistle blasts again and the coal-fired locomotive lurches forth to begin the long pull into the San Juan Mountains for one of the world's great scenic railroad adventures.

From downtown Durango, the train snakes north along the Animas River through forested glades. Soon enough, steel wheels on the narrow track hug the ledges of canyon walls high above the roaring river below. Following the same route on which precious ore was once hauled from the abundant mining districts farther north, you begin to sense the incredible manpower and chutzpah it took to construct this marvel of engineering through sixty miles of Colorado's most rugged mountains. With coal cinders flying, passengers in open-air railroad cars gasp at the sheer drop-offs and stunning scenes that greet them around every twist and turn of the track. At times, the canyon is so narrow you can reach out and touch the rock. At other times, you're almost eye to eye with river runners as the train follows alongside the rafts. Finally, after three hours, the train pulls into the depot in the hardrock town of Silverton. Passengers flock to the souvenir shops, candy stores and restaurants of this mountain burg that once hummed with the raucous comings and goings of miners blowing their dollar-a-day wages on a once-a-month furlough.

In the summer months, the round-trip from Durango to Silverton and back takes about seven hours. The train operates in the winter for the two-hour trip from Durango to Cascade Canyon and back. To make reservations on the Durango & Silverton Narrow Gauge Railroad, contact 1-888-TRAIN-07; www.durangotrain.com.

☺ BEST BOAT RIDE
Black Canyon Boat Tours (west of Gunnison)

This adventure begins on a stairway to paradise. Paradise is the majestic Black Canyon. First you descend two hundred wooden steps following Pine Creek as it tumbles down to the Gunnison River. After dropping one thousand feet to the canyon below, a great chasm looms ahead as you walk about a mile along the worn narrow-gauge railroad bed where the "Scenic Line" once carried nineteenth-century tourists. At the end of a leisurely trek, you board a boat, not a train, for this modern-day scenic excursion.

Between the Blue Mesa and Morrow Point dams, the *Curecata II* slices through calm, cold, green waters past steep gray canyon walls. Under an azure Colorado sky, a cool breeze blows on faces turned toward the canyon rim high above. A tour guide describes how, for millennia, the river cut through the Precambrian rock, the world's oldest, on this journey through the basement of geologic time. Camera shutters whir as the open-air pontoon boat passes close to the spray of a waterfall that pours a silver stream from a rocky ledge. Anglers on smaller fishing boats show off their catch to the applause of passengers on this canyon cruise.

Then, rounding a bend in the river, the Curecanti Needle appears. This natural monument of stone, the trademark of the old "Scenic Line," juts into the sky as it dominates a breathtaking panorama already saturated with towering stone. The Needle is easily seen from the canyon rim, but there's no substitute for the view from the river below.

The boat finally turns around and winds its way back to the dock. The hike out and up the wooden stairway leaves plenty of time to contemplate the wonders you have just witnessed. Black Canyon boat tours run from late May through August. For reservations, call the Elk Creek Marina on Blue Mesa Reservoir at (970) 641-0402.

☺ BEST MINE TOUR
Old Hundred Mine (near Silverton)

With the boom days long gone, Colorado's legendary mines have long since shut down. A handful around the state, however, operate today as tourist attractions, offering many visitors their first experience underground. The Bachelor–Syracuse in Ouray and the Lebanon Mine near Georgetown are two good examples. Novices enter cool, dark, subterranean tunnels where miners once toiled long hours doing backbreaking, dangerous work extracting ore from deep inside a mountain. Though most mine tours exhibit the tools of the trade, the Old Hundred Mine just outside Silverton adds one twist the others miss: The tour guides actually operate the mining equipment underground.

Donning hard hats and yellow rain jackets, guests enter the mountain on a small train for the three-minute ride through a narrow bore in the hardrock. Drips of seeping water splash on faces as the train rumbles down a tunnel lit by the headlamp of the group's leader and the occasional dim bulb hung from the ceiling. Arriving in a much wider cavern, the onetime-miner-turned-tour guide leads the crew off the train for a firsthand education about how hardrockers spent their days. At one point, he fires up an air-powered stoper, a long metal drill that burrows into the rock. Hands instinctively cover ears as the din of what sounds like a jackhammer reverberates off the walls in these tight quarters. At another location, the guide runs a mucker. This machine wheels up and down railroad track with a bucket that scoops rock much like a front-end loader, dumping it in an ore cart. Each time machinery is operated down here, the racket lasts less than a minute, but it leaves a lasting impression for those trying to put themselves in the shoes of men who did this work day after day, month after month, year after year. The Old Hundred Mine is located between Silverton and Animas Forks (see Best Ghost Town below). Admission fee. Tours run May through September. 1-800-872-3009.

BEST GHOST TOWN
Animas Forks (north of Silverton)

Like so many other ghost towns from Colorado's past, there should be hardly anything left of Animas Forks. Decades of long winters with heavy snows should have weathered these more-than-century-old buildings into the ground. Rusty nails, maybe a few bricks from a foundation or the wooden planks of a sagging wall might have survived. But here many of the buildings still stand, in various stages of collapse, preserved for a glimpse of a fleeting yet intense moment in Colorado history.

Arriving in Animas Forks, you wonder how this town could exist in such harsh conditions at such a high altitude in such a remote location. Exploring the ruins of mines and mills in surrounding valleys even higher up and yet more remote, you realize that this mountain hamlet was the center of activity for a flourishing mining district in the heart of the unforgiving mountains of the San Juan. At more than eleven thousand feet in elevation, nearly five hundred people, two newspapers, plenty of saloons and rock-solid determination made up this town in the 1870s. A sign of that prosperity stands as a landmark today. The bay window of a two-story house owned by a successful businessman in town overlooks the rushing headwaters of the Animas River below. Because the structure has been shored up and stabilized by the Bureau of Land Management and the San Juan County Historical Society, visitors can stand in the living room and look through the window's three-paneled frame. The jail is still there, and the extensive remains of the mill lie just below town. Ore was delivered to the mill in buckets strung high on a cable that ran between a series of towers reaching far up to surrounding mines.

By the mid-1880s, Animas Forks was already in decline. It died a slow death, as for some the dream of riches persevered for decades. The last full-time resident occupied a house there into the 1940s. As mountain winds carry voices of the past through Animas Forks, this town remains rooted in its hardrock history for generations to come. Take Hwy. 550 south from Montrose through Ouray and over Red Mountain Pass to Silverton. Go through town and look for the dirt road toward Animas Forks. Take your four-wheel-drive vehicle about twenty miles to the ghost town. The route is drivable only in the summer months. For more information call the Silverton Chamber of Commerce, **1-800-752-4494**.

Spectacular views can be seen from the bay window of this house preserved in Animas Forks. *Photo by Doug Whitehead.*

Horses pull the stagecoach on this authentic, Old West ride in a remote corner of Southwest Colorado. *Photo by Doug Whitehead.*

☺ BEST STAGECOACH RIDE
Mancos Valley Stage Line

Steel-rimmed, wooden-spoked wheels spin faster and faster as the coach picks up speed down the rough and steep "Devil's Dive." Dirt and dust kick up from the hooves of four horses in full gallop as they pull your stage along a rutted road. You hold on tight as you bump and rumble inside. The road levels out past a dilapidated barn and old wooden silo, and you realize riding the Mancos Valley Stage Line is just like the real thing.

Operating in a distant corner of southwest Colorado since 1994, Dennis and Carole Bartels make the experience as genuine as possible. They've done a lot of research into the old stage lines. Their thirty-something-year-old son Eric, decked out in cowboy hat, boots and duster, sits up top, driving a team of horses as he regales you with stories from the historic Overland and Butterfield Routes. The coaches are built by Will Stone, a local man from Mancos whose attention to detail produces authentic reproductions of stagecoaches from the 1800s. You can choose two different routes, the first a half-hour ride that whets your appetite. The second follows a county road five miles for a half-day or overnight ride into remote Weber Canyon, where wild turkeys trot through the piñon and juniper forest. You arrive at an old homestead with a chicken coop, stables and other out-buildings. Two bachelor brothers also built tiny cabins where each of them lived in the 1800s. To these weathered structures, the Bartels family added a rustic log cabin with rooms for sleeping and a kitchen for cooking. They'll whip up some steak and potatoes for dinner and a hearty breakfast if you stay for the night.

Nearby, guests explore Anasazi ruins similar to those in adjacent Ute Mountain Tribal Park and Mesa Verde (see Best Walk Among the Ancients and Best Anasazi Tour on page 164).

The Mancos Valley Stage Line operates from May through September. The office is located 4.5 miles south of the town of Mancos. **1-800-365-3530.**

☺ BEST INDIAN MUSEUM
Ute Indian Museum (Montrose)

In 1880 the Utes were officially removed by the U.S. Army from their homelands in the young state of Colorado—despite a federal treaty guaranteeing their ownership of tribal lands. Chief Ouray died earlier that year. He had lived the final year of his life with his wife, Chipeta, on a homestead near the present-day city of Montrose. The Ute Indian Museum occupies that site today.

A monument to Ouray and Chipeta was erected by the State of Colorado in 1926. It sits on the grounds of this museum, which contains one of the most extensive collections in the United States concerning one particular tribe. In recent years, the Ute Indian Museum has undergone a renovation of spirit and space. The building has been expanded and improved, and the museum's mission has new energy from its director, C. J. Brafford, a Lakota Sioux. Brafford's Native American heritage enables her to offer more accurate interpretations of Ute history. Their story is honestly told through exquisite artifacts and thought-provoking exhibits. You'll see ceremonial garb the controversial Ouray wore during negotiations in Washington, D.C. He was empowered by the U.S.

government to represent the Utes, even though the Utes themselves did not recognize his authority to do so. In addition to his story and Chipeta's, you'll learn about traditional life, like the Bear Dance, one of the oldest continuous ceremonies of the Ute people.

The Ute Indian Museum sits on land once homesteaded by Chief Ouray and his wife Chipeta. *Photo by Doug Whitehead.*

The story of the Utes is woven into the fabric of the mountainous terrain of southwest Colorado. For the first time in history, flags of the three Ute tribes— Southern, Ute Mountain and Northern—fly together in unity, carrying the Ute story into the future. The museum is open year-round; hours are shorter in the winter. A regular series of educational programs is offered. The museum is located a few miles south of Montrose on Hwy. 550. **(970) 249-3098.**

BEST NAVAJO WEAVINGS
Toh–Atin Gallery (Durango)

When Jackson Clark went to work for the Durango Pepsi Cola distributor in the mid-1950s, one of his first accounts was the Two Grey Hills Trading Post on the Navajo Indian Reservation in northern New Mexico. He noticed some beautiful weavings in a back room. Trading soft drinks for rugs, he returned home with a carload and, in one night, was able to sell the traditional, handcrafted works to friends. Thus began a relationship that created a gallery that has grown into one of the top dealers in the world for Navajo weavings.

Weaving styles had been identified for years by the trading post from which they came, but the Jackson family started to distinguish the individual artists. As a result, names like Helen Begay and Mae Jim, among others, have become nationally known in the world of Navajo art. The Toh–Atin Gallery eventually branched out to include all kinds of Native American art. The pottery of Maria Martinez rekindled recognition of pottery as an art form. The jewelry of Ben Nighthorse Campbell was represented at Toh–Atin long before he became a U.S. senator from Colorado. In a stunning array of color, texture, form and medium, rugs, baskets, kachinas, jewelry, sculpture, paintings and other fine art now fill the gallery with works by top artists in their fields.

Today the Toh–Atin is run by Jackson Clark Jr. and his sister Antonia. Traveling with their father while they were growing up, they acquired a knowledge and respect for Native American art unsurpassed by any other dealer. The gallery is located at **145 W. Ninth St.** in Durango; **1-800-525-0384.** Just around the corner, Toh–Atin's Art on Main carries prints and posters, greeting cards and even western clothing. It's located at **865 Main Ave.**

Outdoor Activities & Events

BEST WHITE-WATER ADVENTURE
Upper Animas River (Silverton)

When the snow starts melting in the San Juan Mountains, the hearts of river runners begin to pound. Gathering momentum as it flows south from the Victorian mining town of Silverton, the Animas River drops faster and steeper than almost any other river in the state. Adventurers on rafts and kayaks float for two days and twenty-eight miles on almost unending white water through spectacular Colorado scenery.

The roar of the rapids is overpowered only by the wail of the whistle as the Durango & Silverton Narrow Gauge steam locomotive periodically winds its way alongside the river. Fourteen-thousand-foot peaks loom overhead as rafts splash through bellowing waves of water and bounce through seemingly impenetrable gardens of rock. Several stretches of the most difficult white water challenge river guides, who know there is no room for error in these rough waters. The precarious course through "No Name" rapids takes the skill of an expert to negotiate the powerful forces of the river through a narrow drop of giant boulders. At the halfway point, rafters camp for the night in remote surroundings at Needleton. No road exists anywhere near this backcountry. Next day, the big rapids of "Broken Bridge" and "Soda Pop Falls" await any flotilla of river rats bold enough to tackle one of the last undammed rivers of the West. The canyon finally becomes so narrow that rafts can no longer pass through, requiring takeout at Rockwood, almost thirty miles north of Durango. The train stops to let the river runners load their gear in a freight car and then hop on board to ride the rails the rest of the way out.

Several outfitters in Durango have permits to run trips on the Upper Animas River. Try Mountain Waters Rafting in Durango at **1-800-748-2507**.

BEST SINGLE-TRACK MOUNTAIN BIKING
Gunnison National Forest

Step out the door, hop on your mountain bike, and within a few blocks you're riding a section of what some believe is the best nine hundred miles of single-track trails anywhere. Of all the roads that lead to Crested Butte, only one is paved. The other dirt roads over passes and ridges are connected by a web of dirt paths, many developed by mountain-biking pioneers.

A short twenty years ago, hard-core locals started riding their one-speed Schwinn clunkers for thrills downhill. Since those legendary early days of the sport, mountain bike technology has made quantum leaps, enabling riders to venture farther into sometimes challenging and always spectacular terrain.

The Upper Loop trailhead at Crested Butte Ski Area winds down a couple of steep drops through aspen groves, over a creek and into miles of meadow filled with wildflowers and wide-open views. At the west end of Teocalli Ave. in town, the Lower Loop follows an old railroad bed toward the alpine scenery of the Paradise Divide. Check with local bike shops for extensive trail maps of the area.

Crested Butte holds the world's oldest Fat Tire Festival every June. The Mountain Bike Hall of Fame and Museum in town documents the rapid development of this ever-growing sport. Vintage bikes, photographs, memorabilia and high-

lights of historic races and events fill a small room in the Heritage Museum at Second St. and Sopris Ave. The Hall of Fame inducts pioneers of the sport every year. The annual Pearl Pass Tour to Aspen each September is the oldest organized mountain-biking event in the world. For information call the Crested Butte Chamber of Commerce at **1-800-454-4505**.

Paradise Divide looms in the background as mountain bikers return to Crested Butte on a single track trail. *Photo by Doug Whitehead.*

BEST FOUR-WHEEL-DRIVE ADVENTURE
Alpine Loop Scenic Byway
(Lake City, Ouray, Silverton)

If the Colorado gold rush had never occurred, rugged roads through seemingly impassable mountains would not exist today. With the discovery of gold in 1859, seekers of fortune were motivated to find the shortest routes to and from their remote wealth-producing mines. Today, rich scenery and mountain lore await those who dare traverse these bone-jarring alpine passages.

Harrowing four-wheeling stories abound from mountain passes with names like Black Bear, Imogene and Ophir. But Engineer Pass and Cinnamon Pass in the heart of the San Juans cut the widest path. Both roads begin in the old mining town of Lake City. They follow two different routes through the high mountains to form a jolting loop that connects Lake City with the historic mining towns of Ouray and Silverton. The roads ascend past dilapidated ruins of once-thriving mining operations disintegrating from decades of harsh weather. On long, rocky, winding climbs to the tops of Cinnamon and Engineer, the intense blues and whites of the columbine, Colorado's state flower, are reflected in the summer sky and year-round snowfields at elevations reaching over thirteen thousand feet. From the summits, an alpine panorama of jagged peaks blankets the view for 360 degrees. Both roads then descend to the ghost town of Animas Forks (see Best Ghost Town on page 170), where weathered buildings are all that's left of the boom days when five hundred people thrived in the 1870s. From here, where creeks converge at the headwaters of the Animas River, the road continues past still more historic mines and on into Silverton. Above Animas Forks on the west side of Engineer Pass, an even more difficult and treacherous spur of the byway drops down into Ouray.

The Alpine Loop Scenic Byway is passable by four-wheel-drive vehicles for three or four months out of the year, from mid-June through mid-October. For more information contact the Silverton Chamber of Commerce, **1-800-752-4494**.

A four-wheel-drive vehicle descends from Cinnamon Pass toward Animas Forks. *Photo by Doug Whitehead.*

BEST WHITE-KNUCKLE DRIVE
Black Bear Pass (Telluride)

In the San Juan Mountains, where treacherous, four-wheel-drive roads outnumber paved highways by a long shot, Black Bear Pass claims the title "King of the Hills." The beginning of this notorious, one-way passage to Telluride can be deceiving. The dirt road climbs quickly and easily enough from the top of Red Mountain Pass on Hwy. 550 (see Best Mountain Drive on page 167) to incredible vistas in all directions. Cresting the summit and rumbling down the west side past year long snowfields gets a little dicey, but you probably aren't holding the wheel in a death grip quite yet. As the faraway town of Telluride appears like Shangri-la in the valley below, you might still be wondering what gives Black Bear Pass its nasty reputation.

Suddenly and frighteningly, there's no turning back. Dirt road transforms to solid rock. The grade drops severely, following a once-meandering creek as it plunges abruptly in a torrent. Calling this the "Stair Steps," veterans of the drive stay in ultralow gear and tap carefully on the brakes, inching their way down. Tires crunch and slide in a heart-stopping descent as the driver directs the wheels precariously high on the edge, dodging disaster by keeping the transmission from slamming on big boulders in the middle of the road. Finally through the worst, you're immediately met with a series of sharp, steep switchbacks that demand that the driver back up several times to make it safely around each corner. Once again, catastrophe is averted by avoiding sheer drop-offs at every turn.

Approaching the end of this white-knuckle adventure, stop and catch your breath in the cool mist of Colorado's longest waterfall, Bridal Veil Falls. The roar of water plummeting 325 feet somehow soothes the nerves for the final few twists and turns down to Telluride. We recommend you go with a backcountry tour operator first. Then decide if you want to try it yourself. Local chambers of commerce can supply a list of outfits that have been in business for a while: **Silverton,** 1-800-752-4494; **Ouray,** 1-800-228-1876; **Telluride,** 1-800-525-3455.

BEST NATURAL WONDER
Wheeler Geologic Area
(near Creede)

It's no Sunday drive to get here, but the destination inspires the awe of a parishioner. A cathedral of stone is surrounded by the dense pine forest of the La Garita Wilderness near Creede. Tall spires and mosque-shaped domes made from ancient volcanic ash tower in the distance. First recorded in the diaries of Spanish explorers carrying Christianity from Mexico deep into the New World, these monumental rock formations are unlike any others found in Colorado.

After a seven-mile hike, you finally turn a corner to be met with an extraordinary sight. Standing on a wilderness stage, a natural amphitheater created by eons of erosion through the soft volcanic "tuff" fills your view. High above, a jagged outline of rock extends across the horizon; below, deep crevasses widen out to an array of terraces of twisted and tortured conglomerations. As you explore what seems like a lunar surface, fragile rock crunches underfoot. Narrower grooves that carry small rivers of runoff fan out across an open expanse. Twenty-foot-high mounds of cementlike stone lie scattered as if dripped from a volcanic cauldron and frozen in place. A more serene mountain panorama falls away into the distance from this scene so spectacular that Teddy Roosevelt once designated it a national monument.

To get here, take Hwy. 160 to the town of South Fork in the San Luis Valley. Go north toward Creede on Hwy. 149 to Wagon Wheel Gap. Follow the dirt road about twelve miles to Hanson's Mill. From here, hike seven miles into the Wheeler Geologic Natural Area or continue another twelve miles on a rough four-wheel-drive road to the boundary of the La Garita Wilderness. Contact the Creede office of the Divide Ranger District of the Rio Grande National Forest at (719) 658-2559.

BEST CANYON

Black Canyon of the Gunnison National Park

Sheer, narrow, dark and deep. Powerful and grand. Cut by erosion over two million years by the steady forces of the Gunnison River, this gash in the earth's surface is, perhaps, one of the least-known natural wonders of the West. The Black Canyon of the Gunnison dwarfs those who venture to its jagged rims, where human figures shrink to a speck against massive walls that drop, at the highest point, 2,689 feet to the roaring river below. Golden eagles, red-tailed hawks, turkey vultures and peregrine falcons negotiate the air currents of this canyon that has remained, with few exceptions, all but impassable.

The Black Canyon splits open a mesa top in rugged country high above the Uncompahgre Valley. The popular South Rim Road winds to a series of overlooks and nature trails that lead to precipitous walls of the canyon. A hiker can walk through shoulder-high gambel oak unaware of the abrupt drop-off just strides away. Standing as if perched on an aerie, one beholds a scene too large to take in all at once. Peripheral vision competes with the view straight ahead as you strive to perceive unfathomable depths and faraway vistas at the same time. The East Portal Rd. follows a circuitous, 16 percent grade to the river near the park's southeast boundary. Many a car's brakes have burned on the way down, so use your lowest gear. The North Rim Rd. traverses the more remote side of the Black Canyon, leading to equally stunning and fantastic views. Though no marked trails down into the canyon exist, a backcountry permit allows hikers to descend on primitive, winding routes best described by park rangers.

There are two campgrounds available at the Black Canyon, one on each rim. Stop at the visitors center on the South Rim for all the information you need, including maps and books. A half-hour video shown throughout the day reveals the sweep of geologic and human history in the canyon. In fall 1999, the Black Canyon of the Gunnison was granted new status, joining Mesa Verde and Rocky Mountain as Colorado's third national park. The south entrance is fifteen miles east of Montrose from Hwy. 50; the North Rim can be reached from Hwy. 92 on an eighty-mile dirt road from Crawford. **(970) 249-7036; www.nationalparks.org.**

BEST FLOAT FISHING
Gunnison Gorge

This could be the most beautiful, productive fifteen miles of river you'll ever get to fish. Located between the Black Canyon of the Gunnison National Park and the North Fork, this dramatic rock canyon creates isolated beauty and some of the best float fishing around. In addition to mere fishing, enjoy the many bird species and wildlife viewing opportunities.

You can get to various points of this gorge by trail, but nothing compares with floating at the same pace as your fly, just waiting for a large trout to strike. The water flow can vary quite a bit—especially in May and June, thanks to the dams above—but even when running high, the fishing can be good. Unfortunately, with many side canyons and little creeks, a quick rainshower can leave the river murky and the fishing slow going. But when it's raining clean, be on the lookout for deep pools, eddies and riffles to throw your caddies, green drakes or pale morning duns. If you catch the salmon fly hatch in June, nothing compares to the thrashing that occurs when you lay down a properly placed sofa pillow. Large rainbows and browns comprise most of the native trout on this Gold Medal stretch. Consider hiring an outfitter for this trip. Hank Hotze of Gunnison River Expeditions runs the best trips we know; reach him at **1-800-297-4441** or **(970) 249-4441.**

BEST SCENIC RESERVOIR
Taylor Park Reservoir
(northeast of Gunnison)

Okay, so picking "most scenic" is like choosing "best pie" at the Cherry Pie Bake-Off. They're all pretty darn good. Well, we've been to quite a few reservoirs, and it seems none can beat this one. Winters never really go away during summers high up on Cottonwood Pass. Melting snowpack in the alpine basin that stretches all the way over to Taylor Pass provides a constant flow of precious western water to the Taylor River. Where the wide-open park cinches down into a narrow canyon, a small dam creates a large lake. Taylor Park Reservoir glistens under the white peaks of the Sawatch Range.

Sheer cliffs rise out of the water near the dam, reflecting their grandeur on the mirrorlike surface of the lake. Trolling in boats, anglers cast their lines in search of brown and rainbow trout and even kokanee salmon. But some aren't satisfied with anything but the famous Mackinaw trout, which reach sizes upward of twenty-one pounds. On the far side where the river enters the lake, fly fishermen work their way upstream for some more good fishing.

You feel as small as a drop of rain in a downpour in this high-altitude mountain bowl. Within a mile below the dam, Gold Medal waters produce rainbow trout so big that even a five-pounder is considered small by Taylor River standards! Farther downstream, several outfitters float the boulder-strewn river for some challenging white-water rafting.

Take the Cottonwood Pass Rd. west through Buena Vista over into Taylor Park, or take Hwy. 135 north from Gunnison to Almont and follow the Taylor River up to the reservoir. The Taylor Park Marina sits at the edge of the lake and offers bait and lures, boat rentals and snacks. Several National Forest campgrounds dot the area. The marina operates from mid-May through mid-October. **(970) 641-2922.**

☺ BEST ACCESSIBLE STATE PARK
Ridgway State Park (south of Montrose)

Even if it wasn't one of the most accessible parks in the country for wheelchairs, Ridgway State Park would still rank as one of the best anywhere. Spread out in the Uncompahgre River Valley about twenty miles south of Montrose, the park sits between the San Juan Mountains to the south and the Cimmarons to the east. With Ridgway Reservoir as its centerpiece, this park acts as base camp for excursions into southwest Colorado's outdoors.

Spectacular views are available to anyone from this wheelchair-accessible deck at Ridgway State Park. *Photo by Doug Whitehead.*

The modern design of Ridgway State Park encompasses a network of gently sloping paths and a total of more than 260 campsites dispersed in different areas of the park, the majority of them accessible to wheelchairs. Picnic areas, the swim beach and visitors center can all be utilized by disabled visitors. The Dakota Terrace campgrounds are situated within easy walking distance just above the swimming area. An accessible fishing deck is especially designed for people in wheelchairs. From RV hookups and a camper services building with laundry, showers and flush toilets to fishing access on a specially designed trail along the river below the dam, there is very little here that wheelchair-bound campers cannot do.

Heading south on Hwy. 550 from Montrose, look for entrances to three separate areas of the park: Dallas Creek, Dutch Charlie and Pa Co Chu Puk. (970) 626-5822; www.coloradoparks.org. The Ridgway Marina can be reached at (970) 626-5094.

BEST TIME TO SEE WILDFLOWERS
Crested Butte Wildflower Festival

Spring and summer don't last very long in the Colorado high country, so Mother Nature takes full advantage of what little time she has. Wildflowers bloom with a brilliance and intensity that sparkles in scenes already brimming with deep blue sky, lush green foliage and silver-gray mountains. What people in Crested Butte have known for years, the Colorado legislature made official in 1989: Crested Butte was declared the Wildflower Capital of Colorado.

The unmistakable purple and white petals of the columbine, Colorado's state flower, spread throughout the aspen forests and high meadows, reflecting the majesty of surrounding snowcapped peaks. Every flower imaginable sets the hillsides ablaze with color: lemony-yellow mule's ear sunflowers, orange scarlet gilia (hummingbirds love them), pink wild rose, blue lupine and violet flax. For one week each July, the town celebrates its botanical abundance with the Crested Butte Wildflower Festival. Along with daily hikes and tours, experts offer workshops in everything from photography, butterflies, painting and drawing, herbal medicine, natural history and gardening to slide shows, lectures, concerts and the annual Wildflower Art Show and Sale.

With a variety of accommodations and a wealth of local restaurants (see Best Small-Town Dining on page 191), this onetime coal-mining town makes for a stunning week. **Crested Butte Wildflower Festival, P.O. Box 216, Crested Butte, CO 81224; (970) 349-2571.**

BEST SCENIC LINKS
The Cliffs Golf Course at Sheraton Tamarron Resort (Durango)

If the difficulty of the golf doesn't take your breath away, the scenery will. One of the hardest golf courses in Colorado to play, with the toughest greens anywhere, also happens to be one of the most beautiful. Nestled in a narrow valley below Hwy. 550 eighteen miles north of Durango, the Cliffs at Sheraton Tamarron Resort live up to the name. Surrounded by majestic mountain views and set among pine trees and scrub oak, the fairways and greens of this par 72 championship course are rimmed by sheer rock formations, creating an intimacy similar to the feeling of hiking along a canyon floor.

Sloping from north to south, the course, designed by noted architect Arthur Hills, takes advantage of a descending landscape to produce some formidable holes. The seventh hole challenges golfers to hit a small perch in the fairway where the hole makes not a dogleg but a severe left turn as the ground drops away. With the flag now visible way down there, the ball must be hit from this lofty roost over a steep and bramble-filled rough to the manicured green below. On the back nine, cliffs run alongside some holes so close you can almost bounce a ball right off a rock wall and back onto the fairway.

Maybe you'll want to forget your score, but you'll never be able to ignore the setting. *Golf Digest* has rated the Cliffs one of the top fifty resort courses in America. The public is welcome, but guests of the resort have priority for tee times. (**970**) **259-2000**.

BEST COLLECTION OF FESTIVALS
Telluride

Skiing isn't the only reason to head to Telluride. As soon as the snow begins to melt from the slopes, this mountain town fills up almost every summer weekend for one kind of classy celebration or another. For the entire rundown, get in touch with the Telluride Visitor Center at **1-800-525-3455**; **www.telluridemm.com.** Here are some highlights:

Telluride Bluegrass Festival—Toes have been tapping at this four-day festival for more than a quarter century. Offering both traditional and modern music, the event has included Doc Watson, Emmy Lou Harris, Willie Nelson, Tim O'Brien, Bela Fleck and a host of nationally known artists. Held the last part of June. **1-800-624-2422**; **www.bluegrass.com.**

Telluride Jazz Celebration—Since 1976, hot jazz has been heating up cool mountain air with daytime performances outdoors at Town Park and nighttime jams in downtown clubs. Held the first weekend in August. (**970**) **728-7009**; **www.telluridejazz.com.**

Telluride Mushroom Festival—Mycophiles flock here for hikes, lectures and workshops about the versatile and varied mushroom. Whether they be edible or poisonous, psychoactive or benign, you'll learn to identify, cook and appreciate these toadstools in the wild. Last weekend in August. Check out their website at **art_goodtimes@infozone.org.**

Telluride Chamber Music Festival—Another long-standing Telluride tradition, this mid-August classical classic begins with a free sunset concert surrounded by mountain peaks and ends in the historic elegance of the Sheridan Opera House. Tickets are available through the Telluride Visitor Center. 1-800-525-3455; www.telluridemm.com.

Telluride Film Festival—After more than twenty-five years, this has become one of the world's most important film festivals. *The Crying Game*, *Bullets over Broadway* and *The Piano* are just some of the films that have premiered in Telluride. Limited passes go fast, so get yours early. Free films are offered in an outdoor theater. Held Labor Day weekend. (603) 643-1255; www.telluridefilmfestival.com.

☺ BEST AGRICULTURAL FESTIVAL
Olathe Sweet Corn Festival

Sink your teeth into sweet kernels on the cob. Roasted or boiled, upwards of eighty thousand ears of this golden treat get gobbled up at one of the Western Slope's largest events. One day every August, the tiny town of Olathe (population

fifteen hundred) swells to nearly twenty-five thousand people, all of them here to celebrate the community's cash crop. When harvesttime comes, Olathe Sweet becomes the corn of choice for corn lovers far and wide. At the Olathe Sweet Corn Festival, the corn flows freely all day long.

A wacky early-morning parade, with a new theme every year, starts things off. (In 1999, "Corn to Be Wild" brought out some pretty corny floats.) Free shuttle buses carry festivalgoers to Olathe Community Park

Corny costumes liven up the parade that kicks off the day at the Olathe Sweet Corn Festival. *Photo by Doug Whitehead.*

along Hwy. 50 just south of town. Contests like corn eating, cornhusking and kernel spitting challenge adults and kids alike to show their skills. Musical acts and dance teams perform on the Main Stage in between karaoke singers trying to impress the audience. Live music on the Western Slope Ag Center Stage keeps fiddles fiddling and toes tapping.

Almost two hundred vendors peddling food, drink and arts and crafts provide plenty of diversion for adults, and the Corny Kids Club keeps younger ones busy with games and prizes. As the sun sets, a big-name concert rounds out the day. A huge fireworks display sends home the corn-fed crowd.

In 1992, economically depressed local farmers agreed to plant a hybrid corn seed developed by David Galinant, and the rest is history. At the big tent up on the hill at the festival, volunteers hand out free cobs of Olathe Sweet like candy to eager eaters. The Olathe Sweet Corn Festival is held the first part of August. Reasonably priced day passes, evening concert extra. (970) 323-6006.

BEST OUT-OF-THE-WAY CULTURE
Creede Repertory Theater

You wouldn't expect to find much of a general store, much less a nationally known repertory theater, in tiny Creede. But in this out-of-the-way corner of Colorado, with a sheer canyon wall as a backdrop, you can enjoy the talents of young actors who converge here from around the country. The Creede Repertory Theater has been building a stellar reputation each year since 1966.

This former silver-mining boomtown used to attract three hundred newcomers a day, which contributed to the town's reputation for wild nightlife. In 1892 publisher Cy Warman penned a memorable poem to celebrate the town's attractions called "And There Is No Night in Creede." Although this town has quieted down, you can still find memorable nightlife—in the form of energetic musicals, light comedies and historical dramas.

Visitors come from up and down the Rio Grande Valley to enjoy this unlikely slice of culture and the historic and nicely restored Creede Opera House right on the town's main street. Here, you can count on seeing some outstanding performers, because as the company's reputation has grown, so too has the number of auditions—some seven hundred actors compete for only thirty or so summer slots. Many of the plays sell out early, so be sure to reserve tickets soon. In addition to plays, the Creede Opera House hosts several musical events each season. For information call (719) 658-2608.

☺ BEST CELEBRATION OF UTE CULTURE
Council Tree Pow Wow and Cultural Festival (Delta)

Oh, if the Council Tree could talk! In the shade of this 185-year-old cottonwood near the banks of the Gunnison River, tribal elders would meet to discuss affairs of the Ute nation. After the Ute people were removed to reservations in the 1880s, the Council Tree was abandoned as an important meeting place. A farm and ranch community grew up around it, but the eighty-five-foot-tall tree's role in Ute life was never forgotten. Beginning in 1995, the City of Delta invited the Ute tribes back to their ancestral lands to the annual Council Tree Pow Wow and Cultural Festival.

"The tree is happy. We are back home." That sentiment, expressed by a modern Ute elder, captures the spirit of this three-day gathering in late September. Children learn from Ute artisans how to make pottery, dream catchers and other traditional arts and crafts. A colorful dance competition and drum contest enthrall the crowds in the Arbor, a cedar-log, circular outdoor arena. More than sixty vendors offer a wide choice of arts, jewelry, kachinas and, of course, food. The popular Tipi Village contains at least fourteen traditional lodges, some of which can be rented for overnight stays during the festival.

A collection of films and documentaries about the Utes show throughout the event. In addition to the Southern, Ute Mountain and Northern Utes, tribes from fourteen states and three Canadian provinces join with non-Indians in this unique cultural celebration.

During the powwow in 1995, councils of the three Ute tribes met for the first time in over a hundred years. That can only bode well for the future. The Council Tree Pow Wow and Cultural Festival is held the fourth weekend of September at Confluence Park in Delta, located on Hwy. 50 between Montrose and Grand Junction. Call Wilma Erven or Glenna Gieck at **1-800-874-1741**; **www.counciltreepowwow.org**.

BEST FALL-COLORS DRIVE
Kebler Pass (Crested Butte)

Every autumn, for a brief moment in time, nature's brush paints a brilliant Colorado canvas. Mountainsides burst from pine-forest green to every shade of orange and yellow and gold imaginable. Aspen leaves and scrub oak glow intense colors that have only a short time to grab your attention. From early September through mid-October, gold-seekers hit the road to capture that perfect combination of deep blue sky, crisp cool air and fluttering golden leaves. No road approaches perfection like Kebler Pass.

The thousands of trees of an aspen grove are actually shoots from the root system of one giant living organism. For thirty miles on a well-maintained dirt road between the distinctive peak of Crested Butte and the North Fork of the Gunnison River, Kebler Pass traverses one of the largest contiguous aspen forests in the world. Travelers follow a well-worn route as the road rises from the mountain town of Crested Butte toward the old ghost town of Irwin, where five thousand people once mined silver.

Irwin's cemetery sits on top of Kebler Pass. An inscription on the gravestone of seventeen-year-old Mary Bambrough, Irwin's first death in 1881, offers this advice: "My good people, as you pass by, as you are now, so once was I. As I am now you soon shall be. Prepare yourselves to follow me." Instead, follow the road down into a wide-open valley where the changing aspens spread like a carpet of color over the landscape. The West Elk Wilderness falls away to the south, and the Raggeds Wilderness juts up to the north. They act as a rugged border to this broad vista of burning autumn hues.

Reach Kebler Pass by taking Hwy. 50 to Gunnison. Go north on Hwy. 135 to Crested Butte. On the north side of town, follow signs to Kebler Pass. You can also catch the road on the west side near the small town of Paonia. Call the Crested Butte Visitors Center at 1-800-545-4505.

☺ BEST HOT SPRINGS
Pagosa Hot Springs

It's a welcome sight to mountain travelers. Clouds of steam hover in the alpine air as pure hot waters gurgle to the earth's surface. From these soothing and healing waters, aching muscles and weary souls have found relief for centuries. Here along the banks of the San Juan River in the small town of Pagosa Springs, a series of fabricated grottos dots the hillside.

Even on the coldest winter night, bathers clad only in bathing suits meant for the sunniest beach walk narrow, rocky pathways to any of fourteen pools built into the embankment. From the uppermost pool, with water around 99 degrees, you look down on an array of outdoor dens of different sizes and temperatures. The "Lobster Pot" tests your mettle at 112 degrees. Some pools are connected to others by small rivers of thermal waters. With faces turned upward into a warm cascade, visitors revel in one waterfall that pours from the stream above. Couples

Steam rises from the thermal waters of Pagosa Hot Springs along the banks of the San Juan River. *Photo by Doug Whitehead.*

sneak a little privacy in a pool tucked into rocks over on the side. From the lowest pool, hearty swimmers leave their hot-water pocket to ease into the cold and invigorating currents of the San Juan River. A floating boardwalk with heavy ropes as handrails acts as a pathway across a shallow, warm-water pond from one side of the hot springs to the other. After an active day in the mountains, this is the place to stop and rest.

The Pagosa Hot Springs are open twenty-four hours a day. If you stay at the adjacent Spring Inn, access to the waters is included in the price of your room. Call the inn at 1-800-225-0934. Otherwise, there is a charge. To find Pagosa Hot Springs, take Hwy. 160 west over Wolf Creek Pass to the town of Pagosa Springs. Look for steam rising right in the middle of town.

BEST ICE CLIMBING
Ouray Ice Park

As if the town called "The Little Switzerland of America" doesn't get enough snow and ice in the middle of a San Juan Mountains winter, Gary Wild started making *more* ice! He set up a series of sprinklers along the edges of a narrow crevasse known as Box Canyon, spraying water down canyon walls, creating sheets of ice a hundred feet in length that end at the Uncompahgre River below. The result: Ice climbers flock to Ouray the way mountain bikers swarm to Moab, Utah.

Ice climbing was once the province of adventurers seeking remote, backcountry cliffs where the hike in can be at least as difficult as the climb itself. Here at the Ouray Ice Park, climbers spend all of their time on the ice. With each move up the frigid wall, chunks of ice shatter like broken glass from jagged spikes of crampons strapped to their feet and ice axes swung to get a grip. As belayers hold ropes for protection, even beginners dare to tackle the frozen elements, employing seldom-used muscles on the icy ascent.

Even though the ice is manufactured, the setting is hardly artificial. Summer crowds hike deep into this river-cut chasm to its roaring waterfall, but the picturesque town used to go into hibernation when the cold weather set in. These days the ever-growing Ouray Ice Festival highlights the winter season. Every year around the third weekend in January, climbers and spectators bring the town alive with a celebration of ice. The Victorian Inn in Ouray acts as unofficial headquarters to the Ice Park. For information call **(970) 325-7222**; www.ouray-icepark.com.

BEST POWDER SKIING
Wolf Creek Ski Area

When Colorado's other ski areas are busy making artificial snow, Wolf Creek tends to get dumped on by Mother Nature. So reliable are the 465 inches of annual snowfall, this ski area in the southern San Juan Mountains should be the pick for powder hounds, especially those who like to tackle the steep glades and chutes along the Continental Divide.

Extreme skiers and snowboarders get shuttled by snowcat to Knife Ridge, an area of breathtaking vertical exposure at an elevation of over eleven thousand feet. Floating on clouds of dry, light, fluffy powder, adventurers find their rhythm down the deeply blanketed inclines of this high-altitude playground. Strong intermediate skiers may want to try the milder but no less awesome terrain of Water Fall.

Beginners can take advantage of the green runs down by the base. Skiers on the slopes of this small, family-owned and -operated ski area sacrifice nothing in quality while they avoid the long lift lines of Colorado's larger resorts. And with reasonably priced all-day adult lift tickets, Wolf Creek remains one of the best bargains in the state.

Wolf Creek Ski Area is located on Hwy. 160 near the top of Wolf Creek Pass. Lodging is available in South Fork and Pagosa Springs, on either side of the pass. For updated snow conditions, contact 1-800-SKI-WOLF; www.wolfcreekski.com.

BEST STEEP AND DEEP SKIING
Telluride

No place in Colorado compares so favorably to the Alps as the incredible views from the ski mountain at Telluride. A mining boomtown from more than a century ago, Telluride again has boomed and now entices skiers and snowboarders to the long steep front of the mountain and its mellow backside. Contrasts continue between the mountain and the two separate bases. The front of the mountain connects directly to the funky, historic town with its refurbished miners' homes and picturesque main street. The backside, hidden three miles away by road, ties via gondola with Telluride Mountain Village, an upscale development of million-dollar homes, condos and its own golf course. Regardless of where you choose to stay, you will appreciate the variety of skiable terrain that lies in the middle.

With a verticle drop of more than 3,100 hundred feet and a base elevation of 8,725 feet, the snow here often remains some of the best in the state. Weather patterns often favor this high-mountain area, providing ample amounts of light, dry powder. Warning: This area's expert runs truly require expert skills. When you see a black diamond, it means you had better have honed skills for the physically demanding slopes. Those who enjoy steeps will find few places that compare to the front of Telluride, with its ungroomed legends of Spiral Stairs and The Plunge. Massive bumps combined with a steep pitch will make you feel like you somehow got placed atop a slow-moving jackhammer. Take your time, stop to catch your breath and enjoy the sweeping views over the historic town and out to surrounding thirteen- and fourteen-thousand-foot peaks. It may be the only way to get down, other than by toboggan. 1-800-525-3455; www.telski.com.

Where to Eat, Drink & Stay

BEST SMALL-TOWN DINING
Crested Butte

In a business that sees restaurants open and close as often as the hungry mouths they feed, Crested Butte is an aberration. For sheer longevity, the variety of cuisine and high quality of the eateries in this mountain town hold distinction. In Crested Butte, many restaurants have been around for decades. Here's a sampling:

Bacchanale—Northern Italian cuisine has been served at this restaurant since the early 1970s. Veal dishes, cannelloni, specialty desserts and Italian wines. Dinner served nightly. Reservations accepted. **208 Elk Ave.; (970) 349-5257.**

Donita's—Known for its homemade salsa, this Mexican restaurant has long been a Crested Butte tradition. The chile rellenos are especially good, or try the fajitas. Open only for dinner, it's located on the corner of **Fourth St. and Elk Ave.; (970) 349-6674.**

Le Bosquet—This family-owned and -operated restaurant has been serving delicious French cuisine since 1976. Entrees like elk, duck and salmon are presented with delectable sauces. Reservations recommended. Located at **Sixth St. and Belleview Ave.** in the Majestic Plaza; **(970) 349-5808.**

Soupçon—The continental menu changes every day as the chef uses fresh, in-season ingredients. Shrimp, oysters, lamb, salmon, homemade soups and desserts. Located behind the Forest Queen Hotel. Reservations recommended. **(970) 349-5448.**

Paradise Café—For more than fourteen years, the casual atmosphere and good food have drawn diners here for breakfast, lunch and dinner. Located in the Company Store building in the middle of town on Elk Ave; **(970) 349-6233.**

The small mountain town of Crested Butte contains more than its share of high-quality eateries. Photo by *Photo by Doug Whitehead.*

BEST COUNTRY DINING
Glenn Eyrie Restaurant (Montrose)

You can easily miss this 1940s country home in the midst of new development just south of Montrose. Tucked away in a grove of evergreens and fruit trees, Glenn Eyrie offers European flair in simple yet elegant surroundings. Given its Irish name by the original owners in 1974, the restaurant has featured the continental cuisine of Viennese-trained Austrian chef Johannes "Chef Hansl" Schwathe since 1983. He and his wife Barbara have maintained a reputation for consistently high quality over the years.

Even if you've just pulled off the road after a long day's drive, your casual dress is welcome at finely set tables with pewterware and linens. Homemade soup made from mushrooms picked by Barbara on nearby Grand Mesa or preserves made from apricots grown on trees just outside the dining-room window give a strong hint of the culinary delights to come. Chateaubriand, Steak Diane or "Glenn Eyrie Scampi" are served flaming and sizzling at your table. Halibut, salmon or catfish can be ordered lightly blackened with wonderful spices. Many entrees, including a stir-fry vegetable pasta or tender, locally raised elk, are cooked with homegrown herbs and served with fresh vegetables from the garden when available. Try the garlic mashed potatoes to round out your meal, and save room for cheesecake and other scrumptious desserts. A fine wine list is available.

Glenn Eyrie is open all year long Tuesday through Saturday from 5 P.M. to 9 P.M. Reservations are recommended. **2351 S. Townsend Ave.; (970) 249-9263.**

BEST PIZZA
Farquart's (Durango)

January 31, 1998: the day the music died at Farquart's. Luckily for its patrons, though, the pizza is alive and well. Beginning in 1972, owner Toby Peterson presented homemade pizza and live rock music for unbeatable nightlife in downtown Durango. In recent years, instead of his friends, his friends' kids were now coming through the doors. He realized that his musical tastes were not shared by the new generation, so he took out the stage and made more room for people to sit down and enjoy what's been voted "Durango's Best" for years.

The whole-wheat crust at Farquart's is a long-standing tradition. Not too thick or heavy, this pizza holds all the toppings you'd imagine. Looking around this restaurant with a high ceiling and brick walls covered by old posters and photographs, you notice that pizza is not the only popular offering at Farquart's.

Huge meatballs sit atop linguini smothered in marinara sauce and spicy chiles add flavor to big portions of Mexican entrees. Salads are fresh, and there's a bar full of domestic and imported beers. Customers will tell you, though, that first you've just got to try the pizza.

For you rock music aficionados, all is not lost. During the winter, Farquart's runs a restaurant at the Purgatory Ski Area, and the music still blares there loud and long into the evening. The Durango location stays open all year long. **725 Main St.; (970) 247-5440.**

BEST STEAKHOUSE
Ole Miner's Steakhouse
(east of Pagosa Springs)

Weathered lumber makes the building look like an old mine high in the Colorado mountains. Enter the doors and you immediately feel like you're walking down a mine shaft. Wait for your table in a sitting room that seems like the mine boss's home with comfortable couches and chairs, a fireplace and paintings on the wall. Many parties can be seated at once, yet each table feels private. Of course, when you're in a steakhouse, order steak.

Paul Aldridge has been owner and chef at the Ole Miner's Steakhouse since 1982. He cuts every New York strip, top sirloin and filet fresh for each order. Each is as tender a steak as we've found. The menu also includes kabobs, seafood, a variety of chicken entrees, Cornish game hen and quail. The salad bar is well stocked with fresh vegetables and fixings. The only drawback for some diners: The restaurant doesn't have a liquor license. The food is a little pricey, but it's well worth the money. Open for dinner only; closed Sundays. The Ole Miner's Steakhouse is located on Hwy. 160 two miles east of Pagosa Springs. **(970) 264-5981.**

BEST HISTORIC HOTEL
Strater Hotel (Durango)

The four-story, red brick building with white windows on the corner of Seventh and Main Sts. stands like a monument to Durango's past, but it's anything but a relic. Operating continuously since 1887, the Strater Hotel preserves the opulence of a rich history, renovating and updating all along the way. What Henry Strater

The imposing Strater Hotel dominates the corner of Seventh and Main Streets in historic downtown Durango. *Photo by Doug Whitehead.*

built and nurtured, three generations of the Barker family have improved upon since 1927.

Each of the ninety-three rooms at the Strater is individually decorated and furnished. Antique four-poster beds, marble-top dressers, custom-made drapes and everything else in the room create an elegant experience of days gone by. The lobby, staircases and hallways serve as a museum, with displays containing items from the 1800s such as combs, watches, dolls and toys. Even some original, hand-painted photographs by the famed western photographer William Henry Jackson hang on the walls. But history here doesn't just lie still. Ragtime tunes dance from the piano in the raucous Diamond Belle Saloon. Cheers, boos and hisses emanate from the Diamond Circle Theater. Every summer, six nights a week since 1961, professional melodramas and vaudeville revues entertain crowds looking for a slice of Old West entertainment.

Rooms at the Strater Hotel do not come cheap, but they do include a full breakfast buffet heaped with fresh fruit, muffins, pastries, pancakes, waffles, eggs and other fixings. Henry's Restaurant also features a fine dinner menu prepared by a world-class chef. Located in the heart of downtown Durango, the Strater can be used as a headquarters for exploring southwest Colorado. **699 Main St.**; **(800) 247-4431**; www.strater.com.

BEST BED-AND-BREAKFAST
Blue Lake Ranch (near Hesperus)

The Garden of Eden has nothing on Blue Lake Ranch. Fragrant flower gardens, quiet footpaths through the trees, a well-stocked lake and cozy dwellings tucked in secluded, forested nooks combine to make this seventy-acre paradise an elegant retreat for work-weary city dwellers looking for a break.

"This is the place to do nothing," says Shirley Isgar. She and her husband, David Alford, have turned this onetime homestead into a one-of-a-kind country inn. David's got the green thumb at Blue Lake Ranch. Hollyhocks, asters, columbine and a canopy of flowers color and grace the grounds of each of fourteen handicapped-accessible cabins, cottages, "casitas" and rooms. We stayed at the "Cottage in the Woods" with its king-sized bed in a large, light-filled room, small kitchen, bathroom with Jacuzzi and covered patio.

A short walk through the piñon pine leads to trout-filled Blue Lake, where far-away views of the La Plata Mountains stretch over the horizon. Overlooking this scene, the "Cabin on the Lake" with its wraparound deck and stone fireplace in the living room offers enough room to sleep up to eight people comfortably. At the Main Inn, afternoon tea is served in the solarium with fresh fruit, nuts, chicken legs and cookies. During our stay, breakfast included a tasty green chile posole,

A colorful garden of wildflowers surrounds this recently constructed private "casita" at Blue Lake Ranch. *Photo by Doug Whitehead.*

eggs and pastries with homemade preserves. If you plan to do more than "nothing," the staff is well versed on how to best make use of your time touring southwest Colorado. The ranch is located only fifteen miles from the east entrance of the Ute Mountain Tribal Park, where a guide will meet you to explore thought-provoking Anasazi ruins (see Best Walk Among the Ancients, this region).

The cultivated accommodations of Blue Lake Ranch fit in harmony with its natural surroundings. Before you leave, be sure to stock up on the owners' own brand of flower seeds for your garden. The ranch is located eleven miles west of Durango and about six miles south of Hesperus. 1-888-BLUELAKE; bluelakeranch.com.

BEST SMALL-TOWN LODGINGS
Ouray County

For such a small, year-round population, Ouray County sure provides accommodations for a lot of people, and they do it with style. From historic Victorian buildings and chalets to more modern, southwestern architecture, the area is replete with charming and fascinating lodgings. For a complete list, call the Ouray Chamber Resort Association at 1-800-228-1876. Here's a sampling of our favorites:

Wiesbaden Hot Springs and Lodgings—If you don't want to share the waters of Ouray's public hot springs pool, the Wiesbaden features its own enclosed, private outdoor hot tub and geothermal vapor caves accessible right from the lobby. Suites with kitchens available. (970) 325-4347.

Manor B&B—This three-story, renovated house in Ouray has a Georgian/ Victorian mix of architecture and is

The shops of downtown Ouray offer plenty of variety to visitors to this scenic mountain town.
Photo by Doug Whitehead.

on the National Register of Historic Places. Each room is individually decorated. Private baths. **(970) 325-4574.**

Main Street House—Two century-old homes in downtown Ouray have been completely redone with elegant furnishings. In between you'll find a gazebo in a nice little courtyard. A separate cottage sits out back. Open mid-May through early October. **(970) 325-4871.**

Chipeta Sun Lodge—Wrapped with a wall of windows, this imaginative adobe-style building in Ridgway, ten miles north of Ouray, offer's great views of the San Juans. A creative, healthful breakfast is served in the plant-laden solarium. Check out the hot tub in an adobe turret on the third floor. **1-800-633-5868.**

Alphabetical Listing of Places & Activities

ACCOMMODATIONS

Guest Ranches
C-Lazy-U (near Granby), 103
Latigo Ranch (North Park), 75

Historic Hotels
Brown Palace Hotel (Denver), 44
Cliff House (Manitou Springs), 44
Hotel Jerome (Aspen), 72
Imperial Hotel (Cripple Creek), 159
Strater Hotel (Durango), 194
The Broadmoor (Colorado Springs), 45
Trappers Lake Lodge (east of Meeker), 73

Unique Lodgings (including bed-and-breakfasts)
10th Mountain Division Hut System, 64
Abriendo Inn (Pueblo), 43
Blue Lake Ranch (near Hesperus), 196
Chicosa Canyon Bed-and-Breakfast, 127
El Convento (San Luis), 159
Elk Echo Bed-and-Breakfast, 127
Grand Lake Lodge, 99
Hot Sulphur Springs Resort, 100
Hyatt Regency (Beaver Creek), 74
Mount Princeton Hot Springs
  (Nathrop), 151
Movie Manor (Monte Vista), 158
Ouray County Lodgings, 197
Pagosa Hot Springs, 188
RiverSong (Estes Park), 101
Sod Buster Inn Bed-and-Breakfast, 127
The Lodge at Breckenridge, 102

AMUSEMENTS
Colorado Springs, 5
Colorado State Fair (Pueblo), 30
Kit Carson County Carousel (Burlington), 114
Six Flags/Elitch Gardens (Denver), 20

THE ARTS
Arvada Center for the Performing Arts, 13
Camera Obscura Gallery (Denver), 6
City of Loveland Outdoor Art, 118
Creede Repertory Theater, 186
Eppie Archuleta's Studio (Capulin), 141
Foothills Art Center (Golden), 8
Stations of the Cross (San Luis), 132
Toh–Atin Gallery (Durango), 174

BIKING
Colorado Trail/Waterton Canyon
  (Denver), 27
Denver Greenway Trails, 21
Glenwood Canyon Trail, 52
Golden Gate State Park (near Denver), 24
Grand Mesa, 55
Gunnison National Forest, 175
Horsetooth Mountain Park and Lory
  State Park (Fort Collins), 25
Jefferson County Open Space, 24
Lake Pueblo State Park, 27
Lathrop State Park (Walsenburg), 120
Marble, Crystal and Lead King Basin, 59
Monarch Crest Trail, 145
Mount Evans Road, 87

Washington Park (Denver), 19
Winter Park and Fraser, 86

CAMPING
Black Canyon of the Gunnison
  National Park, 179
Colorado State Forest, 57
Golden Gate State Park (near Denver), 24
Grand Mesa, 55
Great Sand Dunes National Monument
  (near Alamosa), 149
Horsetooth Mountain Park and Lory State
  Park (Fort Collins), 25
Jefferson County Open Space, 24
Lake Pueblo State Park, 27
Lathrop State Park (Walsenburg), 120
North Park, 51
Poudre River, 90
Ridgway State Park (south of Montrose), 181
Wilderness on Wheels (Pike National
  Forest), 148

CLIMBING
Eldorado Canyon (near Boulder), 28
Ouray Ice Park, 189
Shelf Road Recreation Area (near Cañon
  City), 145

COLLEGE SCENE
University of Colorado at Boulder, 4
University of Denver Hockey, 14

COMPETITIONS
Bolder Boulder, 29
Colorado State Fair (Pueblo), 30
Kinetic Conveyance Challenge, 30
Meeker Classic Sheepdog Championship
  Trials, 61

CROSS-COUNTRY SKIING
10th Mountain Division Hut System, 64
Ashcroft, 53
Aspen, 65
Colorado State Forest, 57
Fairplay Nordic Center, 153
Grand Mesa, 55

Hyatt Regency (Beaver Creek), 74
Pine Creek Cookhouse (Ashcroft), 68
Sunlight Mountain Resort (near Glenwood
  Springs), 67
The Ski Train from Denver to Winter Park, 81

DINING
Cheap Eats
Bruce's (Severance), 125
Brush Livestock Exchange/Drover's
  Restaurant, 123
Coney Island (Aspen Park), 97
Cripple Creek Casinos, 157
Farquart's (Durango), 198
Fireside Junction Restaurant (Limon), 123
Mustard's Last Stand (Boulder and
  Denver), 37
The Owl Cigar Store (Cañon City), 156
Winona's (Steamboat), 72

Quality Dining
Alpine Café (Breckenridge), 97
Antero Grill (North of Salida), 155
Boulder Dushanbe Teahouse, 40
Castle Café (Castle Rock), 42
Crested Butte Dining, 191
Daily Bread Café (Glenwood Springs), 68
Emma's Hacienda (San Luis), 154
Glenn Eyrie Restaurant (Montrose), 193
Grand Lake Lodge, 99
La Cueva (Denver), 42
Lucille's (Boulder), 38
Old Miner's Steakhouse (east of Pagosa
  Springs), 194
Pine Creek Cookhouse (Ashcroft), 68
Redstone Inn, 68
The Happy Cooker (Georgetown), 98
The Lodge at Breckenridge, 102
True Grits Steakhouse (Alamosa), 155

DISABLED
National Sports Center for the Disabled
  (Winter Park), 91
Ridgway State Park (south of Montrose), 181
Wilderness on Wheels (Pike National
  Forest), 148

DOWNHILL SKIING/BOARDING

Arapahoe Basin, 95
Aspen, 65
Berthoud Pass, 94
Hyatt Regency (Beaver Creek), 74
Mary Jane (Winter Park), 93
Monarch Ski and Snowboard Area, 153
National Sports Center for the Disabled
    (Winter Park), 91
Steamboat Springs, 67
Summit County, 95
Sunlight Mountain Resort (near Glenwood
    Springs), 67
Telluride, 191
The Ski Train from Denver to Winter Park, 81
Vail, 66
Wolf Creek Ski Area, 190

FASCINATING LANDMARKS

Bishop Castle (north of San Isabel), 134
Cañon City Scenic Drives, 136
Dinosaur Ridge (west of Denver), 10
Florissant Fossil Beds, 147
Highway of Legends (southwest of
    Walsenburg), 136
Ludlow Memorial Monument (north of
    Trinidad), 111
Picket Wire Canyonlands (south of
    La Junta), 113
Picture Canyon (near Springfield), 108
Route of the Silver Kings (Leadville), 139
Stations of the Cross (San Luis), 132
Wheeler Geologic Area (near Creede), 178

FESTIVALS AND EVENTS

Arkansas River, 143
Aspen Music Festival, 50
Colorado State Fair (Pueblo), 30
Council Tree Pow Wow and Cultural
    Festival (Delta), 187
Crested Butte Wildflower Festival, 183
Glen Miller Festival (Fort Morgan), 121
Greek Festival (Denver), 13
Jazz in the Sangres (Westcliffe), 152
Kinetic Conveyance Challenge, 30

Meeker Classic Sheepdog Championship
    Trials, 61
Monte Vista National Wildlife
    Refuge, 147
Olathe Sweet Corn Festival, 185
Ouray Ice Park, 189
Picture Canyon (near Springfield), 108
Renaissance Festival (Larkspur), 11
Rocky Grass Festival (Lyons), 89
Telluride Festivals, 184

FISHING

Arkansas River, 143
Black Canyon of the Gunnison National
    Park, 179
C-Lazy-U (near Granby), 103
Colorado State Forest, 57
Colorado Trail/Waterton Canyon
    (Denver), 27
Fryingpan River, 54
Grand Mesa, 55
Gunnison Gorge, 180
Lake Dillon, 13
Lake Pueblo State Park, 27
Lathrop State Park (Walsenburg), 120
Latigo Ranch (North Park), 75
Poudre River, 90
Ridgway State Park (south of Montrose),
    181
Taylor Park Reservoir (northeast of
    Gunnison), 181
Trappers Lake Lodge (east of Meeker), 73
Wilderness on Wheels (Pike National
    Forest), 148
Yampa River (Steamboat Springs), 56

FOUR-WHEEL-DRIVE TRIPS

Alpine Loop Scenic Byway (Lake City,
    Ouray, Silverton), 176
Animas Forks (near Silverton), 170
Black Bear Pass (Telluride), 178
Marble, Crystal and Lead King Basin, 59
Rattlesnake Canyon (west of Grand
    Junction), 60
Wheeler Geologic Area (near Creede), 178

GHOST TOWNS
Alpine Loop Scenic Byway (Lake City, Ouray, Silverton), 176
Animas Forks (near Silverton), 170
Ashcroft, 53
Kebler Pass (Crested Butte), 187
Marble, Crystal and Lead King Basin, 59
North Park, 51
Pine Creek Cookhouse (Ashcroft), 68
South Park City (Fairplay), 138

GOLF
Arrowhead Golf Club (near Denver), 31
Edora Park (Fort Collins), 32
Hugo Golf Club, 120
Lathrop State Park (Walsenburg), 120
Pole Creek (near Fraser), 84
Riverdale Dunes (Brighton), 32
Steamboat Sheraton, 55
The Cliffs Golf Course at Sheraton Tamarron Resort (Durango), 183

HIKING
Black Canyon of the Gunnison National Park, 179
Chautauqua Park (Boulder), 23
Colorado State Forest, 57
Colorado Trail/Waterton Canyon (Denver), 27
Eldorado Artesian Springs (near Boulder), 26
Florissant Fossil Beds, 147
Glenwood Canyon Trail, 52
Golden Gate State Park (near Denver), 24
Grand Mesa, 55
Great Sand Dunes National Monument (near Alamosa), 149
Horsetooth Mountain Park and Lory State Park (Fort Collins), 25
Jefferson County Open Space, 24
Lake Pueblo State Park, 27
Lathrop State Park (Walsenburg), 120
Mount Evans Road, 87
Mounts Democrat, Cameron, Lincoln and Bross, 85

Pawnee National Grassland (north of Greeley), 119
Picket Wire Canyonlands (south of La Junta), 113
Picture Canyon (near Springfield), 108
Rattlesnake Canyon (west of Grand Junction), 60
Ridgway State Park (south of Montrose), 181
Rocky Mountain National Park, 88
Roxborough State Park (near Denver), 22
Trappers Lake Lodge (east of Meeker), 73
Ute Mountain Tribal Park (Towaoc), 164
Wheeler Geologic Area (near Creede), 178
Wilderness on Wheels (Pike National Forest), 148

HOMEGROWN PRODUCTS
Bruce's (Severance), 125
Celestial Seasonings (Boulder), 36
Fort Collins Breweries, 35
Olathe Sweet Corn Festival, 185
Palisade Wine Tasting, 72
Pueblo Chiles, 36
Rocky Ford Cantaloupe, 124
Wynkoop Brewing Company (Denver), 41

HORSEBACK RIDING
C-Lazy-U (near Granby), 103
Grand Mesa, 55
Horsetooth Mountain Park and Lory State Park (Fort Collins), 25
Latigo Ranch (North Park), 75
Trappers Lake Lodge (east of Meeker), 73
Wheeler Geologic Area (near Creede), 178

IN-LINE SKATING
Denver Greenway Trails, 21
Glenwood Canyon Trail, 52
Washington Park (Denver), 19

KID FRIENDLY
Cultural/Historical
Arvada Center for the Performing Arts, 13
Bent's Old Fort National Historic Site (near La Junta), 109

Bishop Castle (north of San Isabel), 134

Black Canyon Boat Tours (west of Gunnison), 169

Buffalo Bill Museum and Grave (near Golden), 81

Butterfly Pavilion and Insect Center (Westminster), 17

Centennial Village (Greeley), 112

City of Loveland Outdoor Art, 118

Colorado Springs, 5

Cumbres and Toltec Scenic Railroad (Antonito to Chama, New Mexico), 139

Dinosaur Ridge (west of Denver), 10

Durango & Silverton Narrow Gauge Railroad, 168

Fort Garland, 143

Genoa Tower and Museum, 117

Georgetown Loop Railroad, 82

Greek Festival (Denver) 13

Koshare Indian Museum (La Junta), 111

Limon Heritage Museum and Railroad Park, 116

Mancos Valley Stage Line, 172

National Center for Atmospheric Research (Boulder), 9

Ocean Journey (Denver), 15

Old Hundred Mine (near Silverton), 170

Picket Wire Canyonlands (south of La Junta), 113

Renaissance Festival (Larkspur), 11

Royal Gorge Route (Cañon City), 140

South Park City (Fairplay), 138

Swetsville Zoo (near Fort Collins), 14

The Ski Train from Denver to Winter Park, 81

Tiny Town (west of Denver), 10

U.S. Mint (Denver), 7

Ute Indian Museum (Montrose), 173

LIVING CREATURES

Brush Livestock Exchange/Drover's Restaurant, 123

Butterfly Pavilion and Insect Center (Westminster), 17

Cheyenne Mountain Zoo (Colorado Springs), 33

Colorado Alligator Farm (near Alamosa), 149

Colorado State Fair (Pueblo), 30

Colorado State Forest, 57

Denver Zoo, 34

Elk Echo Bed-and-Breakfast, 127

Krablooniks (Snowmass), 63

Mission: Wolf (near Gardner), 146

Monte Vista National Wildlife Refuge, 147

Mount Evans Road, 87

North Park, 51

Ocean Journey (Denver), 15

Rocky Mountain National Park, 88

MINING TOURS

Georgetown Loop Railroad, 82

Old Hundred Mine (near Silverton), 170

Route of the Silver Kings (Leadville), 139

MOUNTAINS, CANYONS & PRAIRIES

Alpine Loop Scenic Byway (Lake City, Ouray, Silverton), 176

Animas Forks (near Silverton), 170

Black Bear Pass (Telluride), 178

Colorado State Forest, 57

Colorado Trail/Waterton Canyon (Denver), 27

Dinosaur National Monument, 62

Florissant Fossil Beds, 147

Golden Gate State Park (near Denver), 24

Grand Mesa, 55

Great Sand Dunes National Monument (near Alamosa), 149

Gunnison National Forest, 175

Horsetooth Mountain Park and Lory State Park (Fort Collins), 25

Kebler Pass (Crested Butte), 187

Lake Pueblo State Park, 27

Mancos Valley Stage Line, 172

Marble, Crystal and Lead King Basin, 59

Monarch Crest Trail, 145

Monte Vista National Wildlife Refuge, 147

Mount Evans Road, 87

Mounts Democrat, Cameron, Lincoln and Bross, 85

North Park, 51

Pawnee National Grassland (northeast of
Greeley), 119
Picture Canyon (near Springfield), 108
Rattlesnake Canyon (west of Grand
Junction), 60
Rocky Mountain National Park, 88
Roxborough State Park (near Denver), 22
San Juan Skyway (Ouray, Durango,
Telluride), 167
Ute Mountain Tribal Park (Towaoc), 164
Wilderness on Wheels (Pike National
Forest), 148

MUSEUMS
Bent's Old Fort National Historic Site (near
La Junta), 109
Black Canyon of the Gunnison National
Park, 179
Bloom Mansion (Trinidad), 115
Boggsville (Las Animas), 110
Buffalo Bill Museum and Grave (near
Golden), 81
Fort Garland, 143
Genoa Tower and Museum, 117
Highway of Legends (southwest of
Walsenburg), 136
Jack Dempsey Museum (Manassa), 142
Koshare Indian Museum (La Junta), 111
Limon Heritage Museum and Railroad
Park, 116
National Center for Atmospheric Research
(Boulder) 9
Ridgway State Park (south of
Montrose), 181
South Park City (Fairplay), 138
Taylor Park Reservoir (northeast of
Gunnison), 181
Trail of the Ancients (Durango–Cortez
vicinity), 165
U.S. Mint, 7
Ute Indian Museum (Montrose), 173
Wheeler Geologic Area (near Creede), 178

MUSIC
Arvada Center for the Performing Arts, 13
Aspen Music Festival, 50

Central City Opera, 80
Colorado State Fair (Pueblo), 30
Creede Repertory Theater, 186
Glen Miller Festival (Fort Morgan), 121
Jazz in the Sangres (Westcliffe), 152
Kinetic Conveyance Challenge, 30
Red Rocks Amphitheater (near Denver), 18
Rocky Grass Festival (Lyons), 89

NATIVE AMERICAN
Council Tree Pow Wow and Cultural
Festival (Delta), 187
Fort Garland, 143
Koshare Indian Museum (La Junta), 111
Sand Creek Massacre Memorial, 114
Toh–Atin Gallery (Durango), 174
Trail of the Ancients (Durango–Cortez
vicinity), 165
Ute Indian Museum (Montrose), 173
Ute Mountain Tribal Park (Towaoc), 164

NIGHTLIFE
Aspen, 70
LoDo (Denver), 38
Wynkoop Brewing Company (Denver), 41

OUTDOOR ACTIVITIES & EVENTS
Chautauqua Park (Boulder), 23
Cheyenne Mountain Zoo (Colorado
Springs), 33
Colorado Alligator Farm (near Alamosa), 149
Colorado State Fair (Pueblo), 30
Colorado State Forest, 57
Colorado Trail/Waterton Canyon
(Denver), 27
Denver Greenway Trails, 21
Denver Zoo, 34
Edora Park (Fort Collins), 32
Eldorado Artesian Springs (near Boulder), 26
Evergreen Lake Skating, 93
Fairplay Nordic Center, 153
Golden Gate State Park (near Denver), 24
Great Sand Dunes National Monument
(near Alamosa), 149
Horsetooth Mountain Park and Lory State
Park (Fort Collins), 25

Jazz in the Sangres (Westcliffe), 152
Jefferson County Open Space, 24
Kinetic Conveyance Challenge, 30
Lake Pueblo State Park, 27
Lathrop State Park (Walsenburg), 120
Mount Evans Road, 87
Mount Princeton Hot Springs (Nathrop), 151
National Sports Center for the Disabled
    (Winter Park), 91
Olathe Sweet Corn Festival, 185
Pagosa Hot Springs, 188
Pearl Street Mall (Boulder), 18
Rocky Grass Festival (Lyons), 89
Rocky Mountain National Park, 88
Roxborough State Park (near Denver), 22
Six Flags/Elitch Gardens (Denver), 20
Strawberry Park Hot Springs (Steamboat
    Springs), 60
Sunlight Mountain Resort (near Glenwood
    Springs), 67
Washington Park (Denver), 19
Wilderness on Wheels (Pike National
    Forest), 148
Winter Park and Fraser Sledding, 92
Yampa River (Steamboat Springs), 56

ROMANCE
Abriendo Inn (Pueblo), 43
Alpine Café (Breckenridge), 97
Blue Lake Ranch (near Hesperus), 196
Boulder Dushanbe Tea House, 40
Brown Palace Hotel (Denver), 44
Cliff House (Manitou Springs), 44
Crested Butte Dining, 191
Glen Miller Festival (Fort Morgan), 121
Hotel Jerome (Aspen), 72
Hyatt Regency (Beaver Creek), 74
Ouray County Lodgings, 197
Palisade Wine Tasting, 72
Pine Creek Cookhouse (Ashcroft), 68
Redstone Inn, 68
RiverSong (Estes Park), 101
Strater Hotel (Durango), 94
The Broadmoor (Colorado Springs), 45
The Lodge at Breckenridge, 102
The Ski Train from Denver to Winter Park, 81

SCENIC DRIVES
Cañon City Scenic Drives, 136
Colorado State Forest, 57
Eldorado Canyon (near Boulder), 28
Glenwood Canyon Trail, 52
Grand Mesa, 55
Highway of Legends (southwest of
    Walsenburg), 136
Kebler Pass (Crested Butte), 187
Mount Evans Road, 87
North Park, 51
Poudre River, 90
Rocky Mountain National Park, 88
Route of the Silver Kings (Leadville), 139
San Juan Skyway (Ouray, Durango,
    Telluride), 167
Shelf Road Recreation Area (near Cañon
    City), 145
Trail of the Ancients (Durango–Cortez
    vicinity), 165

SHOPPING
Camera Obscura (Denver), 5
Foothills Art Center (Golden), 8
McGuckins (Boulder), 15
Pearl Street Mall (Boulder), 18
Tattered Cover (Denver), 11

SOAKING & SWIMMING
Eldorado Artesian Springs (near Boulder),
    26
Hot Sulphur Springs Resort, 100
Lake Pueblo State Park, 27
Mount Princeton Hot Springs (Nathrop), 151
Pagosa Hot Springs, 188
Strawberry Park Hot Springs (Steamboat
    Springs), 60
Yampa River (Steamboat Springs), 56

SPIRITUAL DESTINATION
Crestone, 133
Stations of the Cross (San Luis), 132

TRAINS
Cumbres and Toltec Scenic Railroad
    (Antonito to Chama, New Mexico), 139

Durango & Silverton Narrow Gauge
  Railroad, 168
Georgetown Loop Railroad, 82
Limon Heritage Museum and Railroad
  Park, 116
Royal Gorge Route (Cañon City), 140
The Ski Train from Denver to Winter
  Park, 81

URBAN PARKS
  Chautauqua Park (Boulder), 23
  Denver Greenway Trails, 21
  Jefferson County Open Space, 24
  Washington Park (Denver), 19

WATER CRAFTS/RAFTING
  Arkansas River, 143
  Black Canyon Boat Tours (west of
    Gunnison), 169

Dinosaur National Monument, 62
Glenwood Canyon Trail, 52
Gunnison Gorge, 180
Lake Dillon, 13
Lake Pueblo State Park, 27
Poudre River, 90
Taylor Park Reservoir (northeast of
  Gunnison), 181
Trappers Lake Lodge (east of Meeker), 73
Upper Animas River (Silverton), 175
Yampa River (Steamboat Springs), 56

WINTER ACTIVITIES
  Evergreen Lake Skating, 93
  Ouray Ice Park, 189
  The Ski Train from Denver to Winter Park, 81
  Winter Park and Fraser Sledding, 92

Index

Note: *Page numbers in boldface indicate photographs.*

Abriendo Inn, 43–44
Agriculture, 110, 124, 185–186
Aldridge, Paul, 194
Alferd Packer Grille, 4
Alligators, **129**, 151
Alma, 85
Alpine Café, 97–98, **98**
Alpine Loop Scenic Byway, 176–177, **177**
American Red Cross, 86
Anasazi, xvii, 163, 164–167
    ruins at Manitou Springs, 5
Anasazi Heritage Center, 165–166
Anders, Kim, 84, **84**
Anheuser-Bush Brewery, 35
Animas Forks, 170–171, **171**, 177
Animas River, 168, 171
    rafting, 175
Antero Grill, 155–156
Antonito, 139
Apache, 109
Arapaho, 24, 114
Arapaho National Wildlife Refuge, 51
Arapahoe Basin, 95
Archuleta, Eppie, 141, **141**
Arkansas Headwaters Recreation Area, 144
Arkansas River, 28, 107, 109, 113, 124, 131, 137
    headwaters, 131
    rafting, 143–144, **144**
Arkansas River Outfitters Association, 144
Arkansas Valley Fair, 124
Arrowhead Golf Club, 31–32
Art. *See* Cherry Creek Arts Festival, Colorado Art
    Open, Denver Art Museum, Foothills Art
    Center, Loveland outdoor art, North
    American Sculpture Exhibition, Rock art
Arvada Center for the Performing Arts, 13
Ashcraft, T. E., 53

Ashcroft, 53–54
Ashcroft Ski Touring Center, 69
Aspen, 49, 53, 70. *See also* Ute City
    clubs and bars, 70
    skiing, 65–66, **65**
Aspen Historical Society, 54
Aspen Music Festival and School, 50, **51**
Aspen Park, 97

Baca, Felipe, 115
Bacchanale, 192, **192**
Bachelor–Syracuse mine, 170
Bambrough, Mary, 188
Bandar, Prince, 70
Bartels, Dennis and Carole, 172
Bartels, Eric, 172
Basalt, 54
"The Bastille," 28
Battle of Glorieta Pass, 143
Battle of the Little Bighorn, 114
Bear Creek State Park, 22
Bear Dance, 173
The Beatles, 18, 45
Beaver Lake, 59
Begay, Helen, 174
Benson, Maxine, 3
Benson Park, 118
Bent, William, 109
Bent's Fort on the Santa Fe Trail, 107
Bent's Old Fort National Historic Site, 109
Benton, Barbi, 70
Berthoud Pass, 92
    skiing, 94
Bishop, Jim, 134–135
Bishop Castle, 134–135, **135**
Black Bear Pass, 177, 178
Black Canyon Boat Tours, 169

Black Canyon of the Gunnison, 163, 169, 179
Black Canyon of the Gunnison National
     Park, 179–180
Black Kettle, 107, 114
Blackfeet, 111
Blackhawk, 25
Bloom, Frank, 115
Bloom Mansion, 105, 115–116
Blue Lake Ranch, 196–197, **196**
Blue Mesa Reservoir, 169
Bluebell Shelter, 23
Boggs, Thomas, 110
Boggsville, 110, **110**
Bolder Boulder, 29–30
Bon Appetit, 72
Boomerang amusement ride, 20, 20
Booth, Bob, 142
Boreas Pass Road, 102
Boulder County Open Space, 9, 23
Boulder Dushanbe Tea House, 40–41, **40**
Boulder Reservoir, 30–31
Box Canyon, 189
Boy Scout Troop 232, 111
Brafford, C. J., 173
Breckenridge Ski Area, 95, 96, **96.** *See* also
     Lodge at Breckenridge
Breweries and brewpubs, 35
Bridal Veil Falls, 178
The Broadmoor, 45–46
Bronco Billy's, 157
Brown, James J., 139
Brown, Molly, 131, 139
Brown Palace, 44–45
Bruce's, 125
Brush Livestock Exchange, 122–123
Brush Sale Barn, 122
Buckskin Joe, 153
Buffalo, 107, 125–126
Buffalo Bill Museum and Grave, 81
Bureau of Land Management, 6
Burley, Roy, 83–84
Burshears, Buck, 110–111
Butterfield Route, 172
Butterfly Pavilion and Insect Center, xv, 17,
     17
Byer's Peak, 99

C-Lazy-U, 103
Cache la Poudre River Canyon, 79, 90
Cache la Poudre Wilderness Area, 90
Camera Obscura Gallery, 6–7, **7**
Campbell, Ben Nighthorse, 174
Cañon City area scenic drives, 136–137
Cantaloupe, 124, **124**
Carhart, Arthur, 73
Caribou Club, 70
Carlson Vineyards, 72
Carpenter, Mary Chapin, 30
Carson, Kit, 107, 110, 126, 136, 143. *See* also
     Kit Carson County Carousel
Cascade Canyon, 169
Cascade Creek, 139–140
Castle Café, 42
Castle Creek, 53
Cathedral of the Assumption (Greek
     Orthodox), 13
Cave of the Winds, 6
Cedaredge, 56
Celestial Café, 36
Celestial Seasonings Tour of Tea, 36–37
Celts, 108
Centennial Village, 112
Central City, 25, 79
     gold discovery, 79
Central City Opera, 79, 80
Chama, New Mexico, 139, 140
Charles Court, 46
Chatfield State Park, 22
Chautauqua Park and Dining Hall, 23
Cheesman Canyon, 27
Cherry Creek, 21, 22
Cherry Creek Arts Festival, 8
Cherry Creek State Park, 22
Cherry Pie Bake-Off, 181
Cheyenne Mountain, 45
Cheyenne Mountain Zoo, 33
Cheyenne, 24, 109, 114
     Dog Soldiers, 114
Chicosa Canyon Bed-and-Breakfast, 126–127,
     127
Children's Hospital, 91
Children's Museum, 16, 21
Chiles, 36, 107

Chimney Rock, 163
Chimney Rock Archaeological Area, 166–167
Chipeta, 173
Chipeta Sun Lodge, 198
Chippewa, 111
Chivington, John, 107, 114–115
Chubbuck, Jerry, 116–117
Cimmaron Mountains, 181
Cinnamon Pass, 177
Cinnamon rolls, 72
Civil War, 131, 143
Clark, Jackson, 174
Clark, Jackson Jr., 174
Clarke-Gruber Company, 7
Clear Creek, 82
Cleveland, Grover, 160
Cliff House, 44
The Cliffs Golf Course at Sheraton Tamarron
   Resort, 183–184
Climbing
   City of Boulder climbing instruction, 29
   Eldorado Canyon, 28–29
   Shelf Road Recreation Area, 145–146
Clinton, Bill, 141
Cody, William Frederick (Buffalo Bill), 81
Cokedale, 136
Collegiate Peaks, 144, 153
Colorado
   highlights, xvi–xvii
   history, xvii
   map, **xviii**
   peaks, xvi
   public land, 6
   rivers and streams, **xvii**
   Theodore Roosevelt on, 49
   Walt Whitman on, xv
Colorado, University of, at Boulder, 4–5, 18
   Macky Auditorium, **5**
   Museum, 5
Colorado Alligator Farm, 151
Colorado Art Open, 9
Colorado Clay Exhibition, 9
Colorado Coalfield War, 111
Colorado College hockey team, 14
Colorado Historical Society, 83, 115–116
A Colorado History, 3

Colorado History Museum, 4
Colorado Mountain Club, 29
Colorado Mountain Winefest, 72
Colorado National Monument, 60
Colorado River, 16
Colorado Rockies, 38–39
Colorado Springs, 5–6
Colorado State Fair, 30
Colorado State Forest, 57–58
Colorado Trail, xvi-xvii, 22, 27
Colorado Vacations, 79
Colorado's Fourteeners, 86
Columbines, **161**, 183
Comanche, 109
Comanche National Grasslands, 107, 109, 113
Coney Island, 97
Confluence Park, 21
Coopersmith's Pub and Brewing Company, 35
Copper Mountain Resort, 95, 96
Corn, 185–186
Cottonwood Hot Springs, 151, 152
Cottonwood Pass, 181
Council Tree Pow Wow and Cultural
   Festival, 187
Crack Cave, 108
Creede Opera House, 186
Creede Repertory Theater, 186
Creeker's Casino, 158
Crested Butte, 153, **161**, 163, 188
   dining, 191–192
Crested Butte Ski Area, 176
Crested Butte Wildflower Festival, 183
Crestone Mountain Zen Center, 134
Crestone spiritual centers, 133–134
Cripple Creek, 137
Cripple Creek Casinos, 157–158, **157**
Crow Canyon Archaeological Center, 166
Crow Valley, 119
Cruise Room at the Oxford Hotel, 40
Crystal, 59
Crystal River, 59, 69
CU Heritage Center, 5
Cuchara, 136
Cuchara Pass, 136
Cuchara Valley, 131
Cultural Trolley, 16

Cumbres & Toltec Scenic Railroad, 139–140
Cumbres Pass, 140
Curecanti Needle, 169

Daily Bread Café, 68
Dakota Terrace campgrounds, 182
Dallas Divide, 167
Daniel L. Ritchie Center, 14
Deckers, 27
Dempsey, Jack, 142
Denver
    attractions, 4
    as economic engine, 3
    marble in downtown buildings, 59
    origins, 3, 21
    skyline, 1
Denver, University of, hockey team, 14
Denver & Rio Grande railroad, 53
Denver Art Museum, 4, 8
Denver Chop House and Brewery, 39
Denver Greenway Trails, 21–22, 21
Denver International Airport, 19
Denver South Park & Pacific railroad, 27
Denver Zoo, 34, 34
Devil's Gate, 82
DU Pioneers, 14
DIA. See Denver International Airport
Diamond Belle Saloon, 195
Diamond Circle Theater, 195
Dickinson, Carol, 8
Dillon Marina, 83, 84
Dinosaur National Monument, 49, 62–63
Dinosaur Quarry, 63
Dinosaur Ridge, 10
Dinosaurs, xvii, 107
    Dinosaur Ridge, 10
    Garden Park Fossil Area, 137
    Picket Wire Canyonlands, 113, 113
    Swetsville Zoo, 14–15
Divine Mother, Temple, 133
Donita's, 192
Dot's Diner, 38
Dotsero, 152
Double Diamond Stables, 25
Drover's Restaurant, 122–123
Durango, 163, 167

Durango & Silverton Narrow Gauge Railroad,
    167, 168–169, 168, 175
Dushanbe Tea House, 40–41, 40
Dye, Perry, 32
Dye, Peter, 32
Dylan, Bob, 30

Easter sunrise service, 18
Eastern Plains, 107–108
Echo Lake, 87
Edbrooke, Frank, 44
Edison, "Sweets," 152
Edora Park, 32-33
Eisenhower, Dwight D., 26, 45
El Convento, 159
El-Chapultepec, 39
Eldorado Artesian Springs, 26–27
Eldorado Canyon, 26, 28–29
Eldorado Canyon State Park, 26
Elitch Gardens Amusement Park, 20, 114. See
    also Six Flags/Elitch Gardens Amusement Park
Elk, 125–126, 126
Elk Creek Marina, 169
Elk Echo Ranch Bed-and-Breakfast, 125–126
Ellyngton's, 45
Emma's Hacienda, 154, 154
Engineer Pass, 177
Espinoza, Emma, 154
Estes Park, 79, 88
Evans, Bob, 83
Evergreen Lake, 93

Fairplay, 131
Fairplay Nordic Center, 153
Farquart's, 193–194
Fat Tire Classic, 86
Fat Tire Festival, 176
Fiery Foods, 36
Fireside Junction Restaurant, 123
First Baptist Church (Limon), 116
Fish Creek, 55
Flagstaff Mountain, 23
Flat Tops Wilderness, 73
Flatirons, 23
Fleck, Bela, 184
Florissant Fossil Beds, 147–148